Why Businessmen Need Philosophy

The Capitalist's Guide to the Ideas Behind
Ayn Rand's Atlas Shrugged

Revised and Expanded Edition

Edited by Debi Ghate and Richard E. Ralston

with articles by
Ayn Rand

additional articles by
Leonard Peikoff
and

Harry Binswanger, Yaron Brook, Alex Epstein, Debi Ghate, Onkar Ghate,
Keith Lockitch, John B. Ridpath and Peter Schwartz

 NEW AMERICAN LIBRARY

NEW AMERICAN LIBRARY
Published by New American Library, a division of
Penguin Group (USA) Inc., 375 Hudson Street,
New York, New York 10014, USA
Penguin Group (Canada), 90 Eglinton Avenue East, Suite 700, Toronto,
Ontario M4P 2Y3, Canada (a division of Pearson Penguin Canada Inc.)
Penguin Books Ltd., 80 Strand, London WC2R 0RL, England
Penguin Ireland, 25 St. Stephen's Green, Dublin 2,
Ireland (a division of Penguin Books Ltd.)
Penguin Group (Australia), 250 Camberwell Road, Camberwell, Victoria 3124,
Australia (a division of Pearson Australia Group Pty. Ltd.)
Penguin Books India Pvt. Ltd., 11 Community Centre, Panchsheel Park,
New Delhi - 110 017, India
Penguin Group (NZ), 67 Apollo Drive, Rosedale, North Shore 0632,
New Zealand (a division of Pearson New Zealand Ltd.)
Penguin Books (South Africa) (Pty.) Ltd., 24 Sturdee Avenue,
Rosebank, Johannesburg 2196, South Africa

Penguin Books Ltd., Registered Offices: 80 Strand, London WC2R 0RL, England

Published by New American Library, a division of Penguin Group (USA) Inc.

First Printing, April 2011
10 9 8 7 6 5 4 3 2 1

 REGISTERED TRADEMARK—MARCA REGISTRADA

LIBRARY OF CONGRESS CATALOGING-IN-PUBLICATION DATA:

Why Businessmen Need Philosophy: The Capitalist's Guide to the Ideas Behind Ayn Rand's Atlas Shrugged/
edited by Debi Ghate and Richard E. Ralston.—Rev. and expanded ed.
  p. cm.
 ISBN 978-0-451-23269-4
 1. Business ethics. 2. Capitalism—Moral and ethical aspects. 3. Rand, Ayn. *Atlas Shrugged.* 4. Rand, Ayn.
Why Businessmen Need Philosophy. I. Ghate, Debi. II. Ralston, Richard E.
 HF5387.R36 2011
 174'.4—dc22   2010043881

Printed in the United States of America

PUBLISHER'S NOTE
While the author has made every effort to provide accurate telephone numbers and Internet addresses at the time of publication, neither the publisher nor the author assumes any responsibility for errors, or for changes that occur after publication. Further, publisher does not have any control over and does not assume any responsibility for author or third-party Web sites or their content.

Contents

Part 4: A Defense for Businessmen

Afterword

Part 5: Additional Resources

Part 6: About the Contributors

Preface

"Ideas are the greatest and most crucially practical power on earth."
—Ayn Rand

The publication of the second edition of *Why Businessmen Need Philosophy* comes at a time when the world faces a serious economic crisis. Under the guise of protecting the "public," the government evades its fundamental role in the crisis (e.g., the interest rate manipulations of the Federal Reserve), scapegoats Wall Street, and rapidly expands its already sizeable control over American businesses and the economy. The justification for these attacks usually goes something like this: "We let big businesses get away with too much and look at the mess we're in. But, we can't live without their production. Therefore, we need to force them to stay afloat and maintain output, but under stricter terms, for the sake of the 'public.'" Should businessmen surrender in response to these attacks, or should they fight?

The viewpoint of the essays in this collection is that businessmen can and should respond to the ideological attacks against them. To do so, they need to be armed with the right philosophy. In Part One, several essays examine why philosophy is not an ivory tower escape but a practical necessity at all levels of business, influencing everything from day-to-day decisions to the broadest issues of politics and economics. In Part Two, the philosophical ideas underlying the attacks against businessmen are discussed: to effectively oppose these ideas, one has to understand them. In Part Three, two essays counter the common notion that success in life and in business requires the art of compromise rather than standing on principle. Finally, Part Four offers intellectual ammunition to those businessmen ready to defend themselves against the injustices hurled at them.

The editors wish to thank Ayn Rand's heir, Dr. Leonard Peikoff, with whom the idea for this project originated and who prepared the title essay as a talk to the New York chapter of the Young Presidents' Organization in 1995.

The second edition of *Why Businessmen Need Philosophy* is published in tribute to those businessmen who understand the need to proudly defend the moral stature of their profession—and to the future businessmen who will carry on in their tradition.

Debi Ghate and Richard E. Ralston
Editors

Acknowledgments

We wish to acknowledge and thank the Ayn Rand Institute's staff (in particular, Simon Federman, Donna Montrezza and Jeff Scialabba) for their research and production support for this project. We also wish to thank Dr. Onkar Ghate for his expert guidance for all of ARI's intellectual projects and Dr. Yaron Brook for his tireless efforts in advancing Ayn Rand's ideas in the culture. A special thank-you is owed to ARI's donors whose support over the years has made projects such as this book possible. Finally, we thank Mr. John Allison for providing us with great inspiration as a man who has lived, taught and advocated for what he believes in, and who has shown us that the pursuit of business is both moral and practical.

Introduction

As a long-time CEO, I have had the opportunity to observe many business successes and failures. Sometimes organizations are successful because of fortunate timing. Sometimes organizations fail due to economic factors beyond their control. However, the most common cause of organizational success or failure is the fundamental principles on which the leader of the business acts. Businesses largely succeed or fail based on basic ideas—i.e., their philosophy—not complex strategies or esoteric activities. Sometimes these concepts are held implicitly rather than explicitly, but the leader's actions are driven by his beliefs.

During my almost twenty-year tenure as chairman and CEO of BB&T, the organization grew from $4.5 billion to $152 billion in assets, becoming the tenth largest financial institution headquartered in the United States. BB&T weathered the recent financial storm better than almost any other large financial institution. Why was BB&T able to grow both rapidly and soundly in a very challenging environment?

In one context, the answer is that we had outstanding people who developed successful strategies. At a deeper level, BB&T has been able to attract and retain these outstanding people due to our core beliefs: BB&T is a principle-driven organization and our values are non-negotiable. This commitment to the philosophy we've adopted has been the crucial foundation of BB&T's success.

What are the essential philosophical components that a successful business leader needs?

The most important characteristic of successful leaders is their fundamental commitment to making logical decisions based on the facts, and that what is, is. In other words, these leaders are committed to reality. A commitment to rational thinking as a conscious value is a significant competitive advantage. Conversely, one of the most common causes of business failure is evasion by the leader. When faced with information he does not want to hear, he closes off his thinking process and refuses to hear the facts. Being detached from reality ultimately results in disaster. Most truly destructive business decisions are irrational at the time they are made.

It is true that successful business leaders can sometimes make "gut-level" decisions. However, to be consistently effective these "gut-level" decisions are based on rigorous thinking through disciplined mental focus over a period of time. The leader has been able to subconsciously integrate facts and concepts through his past thinking. Every once in a while, a business leader makes "gut-level" decisions without past thinking and gets lucky. However, if he continues this pattern, he will surely make a killer mistake. This is why the most important value a business leader can hold is an uncompromising commitment to rationality. (By the way, the cliché that you cannot be both rational and passionate is absurd. The best business leaders are both rational and passionate about their work. In addition, rationality demands honesty, integrity, independent thinking, productivity, and justice. It further demands a long-term perspective. You cannot be rational without all of these virtues.)

Why is it difficult for business leaders to be consistently rational in their decision-making? There is a major philosophical trap based on the most common cultural beliefs in our society that undermines many business leaders. This trap is the combination of altruism and pragmatism. Let's look at each of these sets of ideas.

Altruism demands that our primary goal in life is to serve others. You cannot seriously be an altruist and run a successful business in a competitive market. Altruism demands that any time you develop a market advantage, you have to turn over the advantage to your competitors. One would soon be out of business if one were to take this approach seriously. Business leaders often pay lip service to altruism, but they know they cannot be an altruist in practice and still stay in business. However, because they believe they should be altruistic, business leaders experience guilt and conflict, sometimes leading them to make poor decisions and often depriving them of much earned happiness.

This contradiction that businessmen find themselves trying to uphold is an illusion. Business is noble work. The noblest act of a businessman is creating better products and services and earning the wealth which comes from this process. It is very easy to give money away (especially if it isn't yours), but earning it is hard. Think of the irony and injustice that occurs whenever a business leader is told to "give back to the community" or face moral scorn—that business leader has already created a better standard of living for his customers and provided jobs for employees.

Since businessmen cannot be truly altruistic (and should not be, as I will discuss later), they typically become pragmatist, which is the "back-up" philosophy in our culture. Pragmatists "do what works." Since altruism cannot work, the business leader abandons principle and tries to make daily decisions without integrating them into a long-term approach. Unfortunately, many things that work in the short-term are disastrous in the long-term. A clear example is subprime mortgage lending, which caused the failure of a number of major financial institutions. Subprime lending was successful (on the surface) for years before it created huge economic losses. Because pragmatism is short-term focused, it makes rationality and integrity impossible, both of which are long-term concepts. In the end, this combination of altruism and pragmatism, this philosophical trap, destroys many businesses.

The proper foundation for long-term success is a conscious commitment that you (and the fellow members of your team) should act in your long-term, rational self-interest, properly understood. This view, however, is widely rejected because it is misconceived and misunderstood. The proponents of altruism in business have created a selfish "straw man" to attack, and in the process undermined the confidence, self-esteem and success of business leaders. They claim that one cannot justifiably be self-interested in business and offer a set of false alternatives instead.

Conventionally, businessmen are presented with the following choice: take advantage of other people or sacrifice yourself to others. However, neither of these alternatives is rational. Taking advantage of other people is not selfish, it is self-defeating. In the first place, people will not trust you. You might fool Fred and Suzie, but they will tell Tom, Dick and Harry and no one will trust you. Being untrustworthy will put you out of business—not to mention that scheming to manipulate other people's minds is psychologically self-destructive. Of course, one does want to legitimately influence other people's thinking—to convince them—in business. However, when you let go of reality in an attempt to fool others, you only fool yourself and your own psychology will be damaged. Taking advantage of others is self-destructive, not selfish.

The second alternative—that self-sacrifice is a moral ideal for our times—is also self-destructive. An incredibly important question to ask yourself: Do you have as much right to your life as anyone else has to their life? Of course, you do. Why would you believe anything different!

Altruism carried to its logical conclusion is self-sacrifice. Altruism is not only impractical in business but it is also a philosophically self-defeating concept. Why? Because it demands that human action be brought down to the level of the least productive person. If I have anything more than Judy, I am obligated to give it to Judy. However, even though Judy is poor, if she has more than Robert, she is obligated to give it to Robert. Even though Robert is very poor, if he has more than Jane, he is obligated to give it to Jane. Unfortunately, there are always people in the process of dying. The only way to be equal to someone that is dying is to die yourself.

What would consistent altruists look like? Take the monks of the Middle Ages as an example—they were good altruists. In order to be equal to the poorest people, they drank dirty dishwater, slept on stones, and beat themselves with whips. Not a great way to live, and certainly not the road to prosperity and happiness. Taking advantage of other people and self-sacrifice are not proper moral codes. So what is?

The proper moral code is expressed in the trader principle. Life is about trading value for value; getting better together. In our business, we help our clients achieve economic success and financial security. They voluntarily pay us for this service, allowing us to make a profit. Both BB&T and our customers are better off from this win-win relationship. In fact, there are only two stable relationship conditions: win-win and lose-lose. Business is about creating win-win relationships by figuring out ways to benefit your clients while making a profit doing so. (Taking advantage of other people and self-sacrifice are lose-lose.) The trader principle is the only moral code that makes truly free markets beneficial to human well-being.

Of course, it is in your self-interest to help your family, friends, and the people you work with because you care about them—they are valuable to you for identifiable, rational reasons and they enhance your life. Healthy relationships with people who share your values are important to you. It is necessary to hold the complete context about the life you would like to live as you pursue your personal happiness. In addition to rationality in business, this implies participating in activities that will create the kind of world where you want to live—a world that you personally would enjoy helping to create. This may include volunteering your time or supporting charities that advance your carefully chosen values and therefore your life, but not as a sacrifice, rather as a means of creating your kind of world. The trader principle applies to your personal life just as much as in business: creating win-win relationships allows you and those around you to live more happily.

In spite of the conventional views of business and morality, the problem is not that people are too selfish, but rather that they do not consistently act in their rational, long-term self-interest. Doing things that are bad for you (drugs, crime, fraud, etc.) is not selfish. These acts are self-destructive. Taking advantage of other people is self-destructive. Whim-seeking, hedonism, short-sightedness, fraudulent manipulation—these are not acts of a person pursuing long-term happiness. They are acts of a person with low self-esteem. Acting in your long-term, rational self-interest requires a lot of thought, but is the most important thinking you can do. You should also encourage those around you to act in their long-term self-interest. It is in your own self-interest to do so.

The ideas which I have just outlined are very practical, as evidenced by BB&T's story. I believe these ideas are fundamental to business success and to personal happiness. The rest of this book explores these ideas at a much deeper level. It is well worth both your time to read and your mental focus to understand.

—John Allison

Why Businessmen Need Philosophy

The Capitalist's Guide to the Ideas Behind
Ayn Rand's Atlas Shrugged

Part 1

Do Businessmen Really Need Philosophy?

"You might claim—as most people do—that you have never been influenced by philosophy. I will ask you to check that claim."

—Ayn Rand, "Philosophy: Who Needs It," 1974

Why Businessmen Need Philosophy

Leonard Peikoff

The title article of this collection was originally delivered as a talk to the Young Presidents' Organization on January 12, 1995. The essay, which retains the flavor of an oral presentation, explores why businessmen are viewed so negatively in our culture. Dr. Leonard Peikoff explains that in order to effectively defend unjust attacks, businessmen need to understand the range of the philosophic issues that affect them and be armed with the right foundational ideas.

Why Businessmen Need Philosophy

Leonard Peikoff

"Three seconds remain, the ball is on the one-yard line, here it is—the final play—a touchdown for Dallas! The Cowboys defeat the Jets 24–23!" The crowd roars, the cheering swells. Suddenly, silence.

Everyone remembers that today is the start of a new policy: morality in sports. The policy was conceived at Harvard, championed by the *New York Times*, and enacted into law by a bipartisan majority in Washington.

The announcer's voice booms out again: "Today's game is a big win for New York! Yes, you heard me. It's wrong for athletes to be obsessed with competition, money, personal gratification. No more dog-eat-dog on the field, no more materialism—no more selfishness! The new law of the game is self-sacrifice: place the other team above yourself, it is better to give than to receive! Dallas therefore loses. As a condition of playing today it had to agree to surrender its victory to the Jets. As we all know, the Jets need a victory badly, and so do their fans. Need is what counts now. Need, not quarterbacking skill; weakness, not strength; help to the unfortunate, not rewards to the already powerful."

Nobody boos—it certainly sounds like what you hear in church—but nobody cheers, either. "Football will never be the same," mutters a man to his son. The two look down at the ground and shrug. "What's wrong with the world?" the boy asks.

The basic idea of this fantasy, the idea that self-sacrifice is the essence of virtue, is no fantasy. It is all around us, though not yet in football. Nobody defends selfishness any more: not conservatives, not liberals; not religious people, not atheists; not Republicans, not Democrats.

White males, for instance, should not be so "greedy," we hear regularly; they should sacrifice more for women and the minorities. Both employers and employees are callous, we hear; they spend their energy worrying about their own futures, trying to become even richer, when they should be concerned with serving their customers. Americans are far too affluent, we hear; they should be transferring some of their abundance to the poor, both at home and abroad.

If a poor man finds a job and rises to the level of buying his own health insurance, for instance, that is not a moral achievement, we are told; he is being selfish, merely looking out for his own or his family's welfare. But if the same man receives his health care free from Washington, using a credit card or a law made by Bill Clinton, that is idealistic and noble. Why? Because sacrifice is involved: sacrifice extorted from employers, by the employers' mandate, and from doctors through a noose of new regulations around their necks.

If America fights a war in which we have a national interest, such as oil in the Persian Gulf, we hear that the war is wrong because it is selfish. But if we invade some foreign pesthole for no selfish reason, with no national interest involved, as in Bosnia, Somalia or Haiti, we hear praise from the intellectuals. Why? Because we are being selfless.

The Declaration of Independence states that all men have an inalienable right to "life, liberty, and the pursuit of happiness." What does the "pursuit of happiness" mean? Jefferson does not say that you have a duty to pursue your neighbor's pleasure or the collective American well-being, let alone the aspirations of the Bosnians. He upholds a selfish principle: each man has the right to live for his own sake, his own personal interests, his own happiness. He does not say: run roughshod over others, or: violate their rights. But he does say: pursue your own goals independently, by your own work, and respect every other individual's right to do the same for himself.

In essence, America was conceived by egoists. The Founding Fathers envisioned a land of selfishness and profit-seeking—a nation of the self-made man, the individual, the ego, the "I." Today, however, we hear the opposite ideas everywhere.

Who are the greatest victims of today's attitude? Who are the most denounced and vilified men in the country? *You* are—you, the businessmen. And the bigger and better you are, the worse you are morally, according to today's consensus. You are denounced for one sin: you are the epitome of selfishness.

In fact, you really are selfish. You are selfish in the noblest sense, which is inherent in the very nature of business: you seek to make a profit, the greatest profit possible—by selling at the highest price the market will bear while buying at the lowest price. You seek to make money—gigantic amounts of it, the more the better—in small part to spend on personal luxury, but largely to put back into your business, so that it will grow still further and make even greater profits.

As a businessman, you make your profit by being the best you can be in your work, i.e., by creating goods or services that your customers want. You profit not by fraud or robbery, but by producing wealth and trading with others. You do benefit other people, or the so-called "community," but this is a secondary consequence of your action. It is not and cannot be your primary focus or motive.

The great businessman is like a great musician, or a great man in any field. The composer focuses on creating his music; his goal is to express his ideas in musical form, the particular form which most gratifies and fulfills him himself.

If the audience enjoys his concerto, of course he is happy—there is no clash between him and his listeners—but his listeners are not his primary concern. His life is the exercise of his creative power to achieve his own selfish satisfaction. He could not function or compose otherwise. If he were not moved by a powerful, personal, selfish passion, he could not wring out of himself the necessary energy, effort, time and labor; he could not endure the daily frustrations of the creative process. This is true of every creative man. It is also true of you in business, to the extent that you are great, i.e., to the extent that you are creative in organization, management, long-range planning, and their result: production.

Business to a creative man *is* his life. His life is not the social results of the work, but the work itself, the actual job—the thought, the blueprints, the decisions, the deals, the action. Creativity is inherently selfish; productivity is inherently selfish.

The opposite of selfishness is altruism. Altruism does not mean kindness to others, nor respect for their rights, both of which are perfectly possible to selfish men, and indeed widespread among them. Altruism is a term coined by the nineteenth-century French philosopher Auguste Comte, who based it on the Latin "alter," meaning "other." Literally, the term means: "other-ism." By Comte's definition and ever since, it means: "placing others above oneself as the basic rule of life." This means not helping another out occasionally, if he deserves it and you can afford it, but *living* for others unconditionally—living and, above all, sacrificing for them; sacrificing your own interests, your own pleasures, your own values.

What would happen to a business if it were actually run by an altruist? Such a person knows nothing about creativity or its requirements. What *his* creed tells him is only: "Give up. Give up and give away; give away to and for others." What should he give away? Whatever is there; whatever he has access to; whatever somebody else has created.

Either a man cares about the process of production, or he does not. If he cares about the process, it must be his primary concern; not the beneficiaries of the process, but the personal fulfillment inherent in his own productive activity. If he does not care about it, then he cannot produce.

If the welfare of others were your primary aim, then you would have to dismantle your business. For instance, you would have to hire needy workers, regardless of their competence—whether or not they lead you to a profit. Why do you care about profit, anyway? As an altruist, you seek to sacrifice yourself and your business, and these workers need the jobs. Further, why charge customers the highest price you can get—isn't that selfish? What if your customers need the product desperately? Why not simply give away goods and services as they are needed? An altruist running a business like a social work project would be a destroyer—but not for long, since he would soon go broke. Do you see Albert Schweitzer running General Motors? Would you have prospered with Mother Teresa as the CEO of your company?

Many businessmen recognize that they are selfish, but feel guilty about it and try to appease their critics. These businessmen, in their speeches and advertisements, regularly proclaim that they are really selfless, that their only concern is the welfare of their workers, their customers, and their stockholders, especially the widows and orphans among them. Their own profit, they say, is really not very big, and next year, they promise, they will give even more of it away. No one believes any of this, and these businessmen look like nothing but what they are: hypocrites. One way or another, everyone knows that these men are denying the essence and purpose of their work. This kind of PR destroys any positive image of business in the public mind. If you yourselves, by your own appeasement, damn your real motives and activity, why should anyone else evaluate you differently?

Some of you may reply: "But I really am an altruist. I do live for a higher purpose. I don't care excessively about myself or even my family. I really want primarily to serve the needy." This is a possible human motive—it is a shameful motive, but a possible one. If it *is* your motive, however, you will not be a successful businessman, not for long. Why is it shameful? Let me answer by asking the altruists among you: Why do you have such low self-esteem? Why don't you and those you love deserve to be the beneficiaries of *your* efforts? Are you excluded from the Declaration of Independence merely because you are a businessman? Does a producer have no right to happiness? Does success turn you into a slave?

You do not expect your workers to say, "We don't care about ourselves; we're only servants of the public and of our bosses." In fact, labor says the exact opposite. Your workers stand up proudly and say, "We work hard for a living. We deserve a reward, and we damn well expect to get it!" Observe that the country respects such workers and their attitude. Why then are businessmen supposed to be serfs? Aren't you as good as the rest of mankind? Why should you alone spend your precious time sweating selflessly for a reward that is to be given to someone else?

The best among you do not believe the altruist mumbo-jumbo. You have, however, long been disarmed by it. Because you are the victim of a crucial power, against which you are helpless. That power is philosophy.

This brings us to the question of why businessmen need philosophy.

The issue with which we began—selfishness vs. altruism—is a philosophic issue; specifically, it is a moral or ethical issue. One of the important questions of ethics is: should a man live for himself, or should he sacrifice for something beyond himself? In the medieval era, for example, philosophers held that selfishness was wicked, that men must sacrifice themselves for God. In such an era, there was no possibility of an institutionalized system of profit-seeking companies. To the medievals, business would represent sheer wickedness.

This philosophy gradually changed, across centuries, culminating in the view of Jefferson, who championed the selfish pursuit of one's own happiness. He took this idea from John Locke, who got it, ultimately, from Aristotle, the real father of selfishness in ethics. Jefferson's defense of the right to happiness made possible the founding of America and of a capitalist system. Since the eighteenth century, however, the philosophic pendulum has swung all the way back to the medieval period. Today, once again, self-sacrifice is extolled as the moral ideal.

Why should you care about this philosophic history? As a practical man, you must care; because it is an issue of life and death. It is a simple syllogism. Premise one: Businessmen are selfish; which everyone knows, whatever denials or protestations they hear. Premise two: Selfishness is wicked; which almost everyone today, including the appeasers among you, thinks is self-evident. The inescapable conclusion: Businessmen are wicked. If so, you are the perfect scapegoats for intellectuals of every kind to blame for every evil or injustice that occurs, whether real or trumped up.

If you think that this is merely theory, look at reality—at today's culture—and observe what the country thinks of business these days. Popular movies provide a good indication. Do not bother with such obviously left-wing movies as *Wall Street*, the product of avowed radicals and business-haters. Consider rather the highly popular Tim Allen movie, *The Santa Clause*. It was a simple children's fantasy about Santa delivering gifts; it was seasonal family trivia that upheld no abstract ideas or philosophy, the kind of movie which expressed only safe, non-controversial, self-evident sentiments. In the middle of the movie, with no plot purpose of any kind, the story leaves Santa to show two "real businessmen": toy manufacturers scheming gleefully to swindle the country's children with inferior products (allegedly, to make greater profits thereby). After which, the characters vanish, never to be seen again. It was a sheer throwaway—and the audience snickers along with it approvingly, as though there is no controversy here. "Everybody knows that's the way businessmen are."

Imagine the national outcry if any other minority—and you are a very small minority—were treated like this. If a "quickie" scene were inserted into a movie to show that females are swindlers, or gays, or blacks—the movie would be denounced, reedited, sanitized, apologized for and pulled from the theaters. But businessmen? Money-makers and profit-seekers? In regard to them, anything goes, because they are wicked, i.e., selfish. They are "pigs," "robbers," "villains"—everyone knows that! Incidentally, to my knowledge, not one businessman or group of them protested against this movie.

There are hundreds of such movies, and many more books, TV shows, sermons and college lectures, all expressing the same ideas. Are such ideas merely talk, with no practical consequences for you and your balance sheets? The principal consequence is this: once you are deprived of moral standing, you are fair game. No matter what you do or how properly you act, you will be accused of the most outrageous evils. Whether the charges are true or false is irrelevant. If you are fundamentally evil, as the public has been taught to think, then any accusation against you is plausible—you are, people think, capable of anything.

If so, the politicians can then step in. They can blame you for anything, and pass laws to hogtie and expropriate you. After all, everyone feels, you must have obtained your money dishonestly; you are in business! The antitrust laws are an eloquent illustration of this process at work. If some official in Washington decides that your prices are "too high," for instance, it must be due to your being a "monopolist": your business, therefore, must be broken up, and you should be fined or jailed. Or, if the official feels that your prices are "too low," you are probably an example of "cutthroat competition," and deserve to be punished. Or, if you try to avoid both these paths by setting a common price with your competitors—neither too high or too low, but just right—*that* is "conspiracy." Whatever you do, you are guilty.

Whatever happens anywhere today is your fault and guilt. Some critics point to the homeless and blame their poverty on greedy private businessmen who exploit the public. Others, such as John Kenneth Galbraith, say that Americans are too affluent and too materialistic, and blame greedy private businessmen, who corrupt the masses by showering them with ads and goods. Ecologists claim that our resources are vanishing and blame it on businessmen, who squander natural resources for selfish profit. If a broker dares to take any financial advantage from a lifetime of study and contacts in his field, he is guilty of "insider trading." If racial discrimination is a problem, businessmen must pay for it by hiring minority workers, whether qualified or not. If sexual harassment is a problem, businessmen are the villains; they must be fondling their downtrodden filing clerks, as they leave for the bank to swindle the poor widows and orphans. The litany is unmistakable: if anybody has any trouble of any kind, blame the businessman—even if a customer spills a cup of her coffee miles away from the seller's establishment. By definition, businessmen have unlimited liability. They are guilty of every conceivable crime because they are guilty of the worst, lowest crime: selfishness.

The result is an endless stream of political repercussions: laws, more controls, more regulations, more alleged crimes, more fines, more lawsuits, more bureaus, more taxes, more need to bow down on your knees before Washington, Albany or Giuliani, begging for favors, merely to survive. All of this means: the methodical and progressive enslavement of business.

No other group in the world would stand for or put up with such injustice—not plumbers or philosophers, not even Bosnians or Chechens. Any other group, in outrage, would assert its rights—real or alleged—and demand justice. Businessmen, however, do not. They are disarmed because they know that the charge of selfishness is true.

Instead of taking pride in your selfish motives and fighting back, you are ashamed, undercut and silent. This is what philosophy—bad philosophy—and specifically a bad code of morality has done to you. Just as such a code would destroy football, so now it is destroying the United States.

Today, there is a vicious double-standard in the American justice system. Compare the treatment of accused criminals with that of accused businessmen. For example: if a man (like O.J. Simpson) commits a heinous double-murder, mobs everywhere chant that he is innocent until proven guilty. Millions rush to his defense, he buys half the legal profession and is acquitted of his crimes. Whereas, if a businessman invents a brilliant method of financing business ventures through so-called junk bonds, thereby becoming a meteoric success while violating not one man's rights, he is guilty—guilty by definition, guilty of being a businessman—and he must pay multi-million-dollar fines, perform years of community service, stop working in his chosen profession, and even spend many years in jail.

If, in the course of pursuing your selfish profits, you really did injure the public, then the attacks on you would have some justification. But the opposite is true. You make your profits by production and you trade freely with your customers, thereby showering wealth and benefits on everyone. (I refer here to businessmen who stand on their own and actually produce in a free market, not those who feed at the public trough for subsidies, bailouts, tariffs and government-dispensed monopolies.)

Now consider the essential nature of running a business and the qualities of character it requires.

There is an important division of labor not taught in our colleges. Scientists discover the laws of nature. Engineers and inventors apply those laws to develop ideas for new products. Laborers will work to produce these goods if they are given a salary and a prescribed task, i.e., a plan of action and a productive purpose to guide their work. These people and professions are crucial to an economy. But they are not enough. If all we had was scientific knowledge, untried ideas for new products, and directionless physical labor, we would starve.

The indispensable element here—the crucial "spark plug," which ignites the best of every other group, transforming merely potential wealth into the abundance of a modern industrial society—is business.

Businessmen accumulate capital through production and savings. They decide in which future products to invest their savings. They have the crucial task of integrating natural resources, human discoveries and physical labor. They must organize, finance and manage the productive process, or choose, train and oversee the men competent to do it. These are the demanding, risk-laden decisions and actions on which abundance and prosperity depend. Profit represents success in regard to these decisions and actions. Loss represents failure. Philosophically, therefore, profit is a payment earned by moral virtue—by the highest moral virtue. It is payment for the thought, the initiative, the long-range vision, the courage and the efficacy of the economy's prime movers: the businessmen.

Your virtue confers blessings on every part of society. By creating mass markets, you make new products available to every income level. By organizing productive enterprises, you create employment for men in countless fields. By using machines, you increase the productivity of labor, thus raising the working-man's pay and rewards. The businessman, to quote Ayn Rand,

> is the great liberator who, in the short span of a century and a half, has released men from bondage to their physical needs, has released them from the terrible drudgery of an eighteen-hour workday of manual labor for their barest subsistence, has released them from famines, from pestilences, from the stagnant hopelessness and terror in which most of mankind had lived in all the pre-capitalist centuries—and in which most of it still lives, in non-capitalist countries.[1]

If businessmen are such great liberators, you can be sure that those who denounce you know this fact. The truth is that you are denounced partly because you *are* mankind's great providers and liberators, which raises another critical topic.

Selfishness is not the only virtue for which you are damned by today's intellectuals. They invoke two other philosophical issues as a club to condemn you with: reality and reason.

By "reality," I mean the universe around us; the material world in which we live and which we observe with our senses: the earth, the planets, the galaxies. As businessmen you are committed to this world, not to any other dimension alleged to transcend it. You are not in business to secure or offer supernatural rewards, other-worldly bliss or the welfare of an ecological rose garden in the twenty-fifth century. You pursue real, this-worldly values, here and now. You produce physical goods and tangible services. You seek monetary profit, which you intend to invest or spend now. You do not offer your customers out-of-body experiences, UFO rides or reincarnation as Shirley MacLaine. You offer real, earthly pleasures; you make possible physical products, rational services and the actual enjoyment of this life.

This completely contradicts many major philosophical schools. It puts you into conflict with every type of supernaturalist, from the medieval-style theists on through today's "New Age" spiritualists and mystics. All these people like to demean this life and this world in favor of another, undefined existence in the beyond: to be found in heaven, in nirvana or on LSD. Whatever they call it, this other realm is beyond the reach of science and logic.

If these supernaturalists are right, then your priorities as businessmen—your philosophic priorities—are dead wrong. If the material world is, as they claim, "low, vulgar, crude, unreal," then so are you who cater to it. You are materialistic animals devoted to inferior physical concerns. By showering men with material values, you are corrupting and debasing them, as Galbraith says, rather than truly liberating them.

A businessman *must* be worldly and concerned with the physical. From the physical laws ruling your assembly line, to the cold, hard facts of your financial accounts, business is a materialistic enterprise. This is another reason why there could be no such thing as business in the medieval era: not only selfishness, but *worldliness*, was considered a major sin. This same combination of charges—selfishness and materialism—is unleashed against you today by the modern equivalent of the medieval mentality. The conclusion they reach is the same: "Down with business!"

The third philosophic issue is the validity of reason. Reason is the human faculty which forms concepts by a process of logic based on the evidence of the senses; reason is our means of gaining knowledge of this world and guiding our actions in it. By the nature of their field, businessmen must be committed to reason, at least in their professional lives. You do not make business decisions by consulting tea leaves, the "Psychic Friends Network," the Book of Genesis, or any other kind of mystic revelation. If you tried to do it, then like all gamblers who bet on blind intuition, you would be ruined.

Successful businessmen have to be men of the intellect. Many people believe that wealth is a product of purely physical factors, such as natural resources and physical labor. But both of these have been abundant throughout history and are in poverty-stricken nations still today, such as India, Russia and throughout Africa.

Wealth is primarily a product not of physical factors, but of the human mind—of the intellectual faculty—of the rational, thinking faculty. I mean here the mind not only of scientists and engineers, but also the mind of those men and women—the businessmen—who organize knowledge and resources into industrial enterprises.

Primarily, it is the reason and intelligence of great industrialists that make possible electric generators, computers, coronary-bypass surgical instruments and spaceships.

If you are to succeed in business, you must make decisions using logic. You must deal with objective realities—like them or not. Your life is filled with numbers, balance sheets, cold efficiency and rational organization. You have to make sense—to your employees, to your customers, and to yourself. You cannot run a business as a gambler plays the horses, or as a cipher wailing, "Who am I to know? My mind is helpless. I need a message from God, Nancy Reagan's astrologer or Eleanor Roosevelt's soul." You have to *think*.

The advocates of a supernatural realm never try to prove its existence by reason. They claim that they have a means of knowledge superior to reason, such as intuition, hunch, faith, subjective feeling or the "seat of their pants." Reason is their enemy, because it is the tool that will expose their racket: so they condemn it and its advocates as cold, analytic, unfeeling, straight-jacketed, narrow, limited. By their standard, anyone devoted to reason and logic is a low mentality, fit only to be ruled by those with superior mystic insight. This argument originated with Plato in the ancient world, and it is still going strong today. It is another crucial element in the anti-business philosophy.

To summarize, there are three fundamental questions central to any philosophy, which every person has to answer in some way: What is there? How do you know it? And, what should you do?

The Founding Fathers had answers to these questions. What is there? "This world," they answered, "nature." (Although they believed in God, it was a pale deist shadow of the medieval period. For the Founding Fathers, God was a mere bystander, who had set the world in motion but no longer interfered.) How did they know? Reason was "the only oracle of man," they said. What should you do? "Pursue your own happiness," said Jefferson. The result of these answers— i.e., of their total philosophy—was capitalism, freedom and individual rights. This brought about a century of international peace, and the rise of the business mentality, leading to the magnificent growth of industry and of prosperity.

For two centuries since, the enemies of the Founding Fathers have given the exact opposite answers to these three questions. What is there? "Another reality," they say. How do they know? "On faith." What should you do? "Sacrifice yourself for society." This is the basic philosophy of our culture, and it is responsible for the accelerating collapse of capitalism, and all of its symptoms: runaway government trampling on individual rights, growing economic dislocations, worldwide tribal warfare and international terrorism—with business under constant, systematic attack.

Such is the philosophic choice you have to make. Such are the issues on which you will ultimately succeed or fail. If the anti-business philosophy with its three central ideas continues to dominate this country and to spread, then businessmen as such will become extinct, as they were in the Middle Ages and in Soviet Russia. They will be replaced by church authorities or government commissars. Your only hope for survival is to fight this philosophy by embracing a rational, worldly, selfish alternative.

We are all trained by today's colleges never to take a firm stand on any subject: to be pragmatists, ready to compromise with anyone on anything. Philosophy and morality, however, do not work by compromise. Just as a healthy body cannot compromise with poison, so too a good man cannot compromise with evil ideas. In such a set up, an evil philosophy, like poison, always wins. The good can win only by being consistent. If it is not, then the evil is given the means to win every time.

For example, if a burglar breaks into your house and demands your silverware, you have two possible courses of action. You might take a militant attitude: shoot him or at least call the police. That is certainly uncompromising. You have taken the view, "What's mine is mine, and there is no bargaining about it." Or, you might "negotiate" with him, try to be conciliatory, and persuade him to take only half your silverware. Whereupon you relax, pleased with your seemingly successful compromise, until he returns next week demanding the rest of your silverware—and your money, your car and your wife. Because you have agreed that his arbitrary, unjust demand gives him a right to *some* of your property, the only negotiable question thereafter is: how much? Sooner or later he will take everything. You compromised; he won.

The same principle applies if the government seeks to expropriate you or regulate your property. If the government floats a trial balloon to the effect that it will confiscate or control all industrial property over $10 million in the name of the public good, you have two possible methods of fighting back. You might stand on principle—in this case, the principle of private property and individual rights—and refuse to compromise; you might resolve to fight to the end for your rights and actually do so in your advertisements, speeches and press releases. Given the better elements in the American people, it is possible for you by this means to win substantial support and defeat such a measure. The alternative course, and the one that business has unfortunately taken throughout the decades, is to compromise—for example, by making a deal conceding that the government can take over in New Jersey, but not in New York. This amounts to saying: "Washington, D.C., has no right to all our property, only some of it." As with the burglar, the government will soon take over everything. You have lost all you have as soon as you say the fatal words, "I compromise."

I do not advise you to break any law, but I do advise you to fight an *intellectual* battle against big government, as many medical doctors did, with real success, against Clinton's health plan. You may be surprised at how much a good philosophical fight will accomplish for your public image, and also for your pocketbook. For instance, an open public fight for a flat tax, for the end of the capital gains and estate taxes, and for the privatizing of welfare and the gradual phasing out of all government entitlements is urgent. More important than standing for these policies, however, is doing so righteously, not guiltily and timidly. If you understand the philosophic issues involved, you will have a chance to speak up in such a way that you can be heard.

This kind of fight is not easy, but it can be fought and won. Years ago, a well-known political writer, Isabel Paterson, was talking to a businessman outraged by some government action. She urged him to speak up for his principles. "I agree with you totally," he said, "but I'm not in a position right now to do it."

"The only position required," she replied, "is vertical."

Notes

1. Ayn Rand, *For the New Intellectual* (New York: New American Library, 1961), p. 27.

Philosophy: The Ultimate CEO

Harry Binswanger

If businessmen need philosophy to understand their environment, what *is* philosophy? What is its role in one's life, in business and in the culture? What does it mean to say that philosophy is inescapable and there can be a right philosophy? In this February 10, 1999, talk to the Young Presidents' Organization, Dr. Harry Binswanger answers these questions. (Note: This essay retains the character of an oral presentation.)

Philosophy: The Ultimate CEO

Harry Binswanger

Good evening ladies and gentlemen:

Karl Marx had an interesting concept of what it is that you do for a living.

Admittedly, this is a strange way to begin a talk to business leaders. But follow me for a moment, and you'll soon see where I'm going.

Marx thought that you are all useless. Or worse than useless. He regarded you all as parasites, sucking the lifeblood of the actual producers in the society: the workers.

According to Marxists, all that you CEOs do is sit in your fancy offices, with your feet up on the desk, smoking expensive cigars. You have idle chats on the phone, to no good purpose, maybe accompanied by certain lurid Clintonesque activities with your secretaries.

You contribute nothing to the business, Marxists claim. All the real production is done down on the factory floor by the physical laborers. The workers actually make the product, but somehow you have contrived to rake off a share of the proceeds from selling the product they produce. That's why Marx calls you "exploiters." You get money rewards—profit—in exchange for nothing.

That's Marx. What's the truth?

I don't have to tell *you*, but the world has to be told. The truth is that you do everything. Not directly, not by physical labor. But by supplying the overall guiding intelligence. The mind, not muscles, is the source of wealth.

What do you do? You manage. Meaning what? You make the basic decisions and integrate all the operations of the company. You decide what to produce, how it is to be produced, what to charge for it, how to market it, and more.

But your productive contribution is intellectual, not physical. You supply "the vision thing," the overall vision of what to do and how to do it.

As CEOs, you already know that, firsthand. But here's my point. You may have the equivalent of a Marxist view outside of business, in the wider realm of human existence. You may think that *abstract ideas* are as useless as Marxists think CEOs are. If you do think that, I am here to correct you, just as you would correct any Marxist college professor who didn't grasp what it is you do as CEO of your business.

My theme in this talk is that philosophy is the CEO of human life. Philosophy has the same relation to real-life, concrete, daily decisions and actions that you, as

CEOs, have in relation to the real-life, concrete daily decisions and actions of business. And philosophy's role is as unrecognized and unappreciated as your role is.

Philosophy is the CEO of the spirit. Philosophy is the ultimate integrator and manager of everything about man's existence.

Let me define the term "philosophy." Philosophy is the science that studies the fundamental principles of existence and man.

The key concept in this definition is "fundamental." Philosophy determines the fundamentals—the fundamentals of life—just as the CEO determines the fundamentals of a business. And the leadership role of philosophy is just as crucial, just as indispensable, as your leadership role is in your business.

You would indignantly reject the Marxist view of your role in business; I hope you will just as indignantly reject the popular view of philosophy's role in human life—the view that philosophy is a useless game or word play unrelated to and distracting from real life. I want to convince you of the opposite: philosophy rules life, real life, daily life.

Everyone has a philosophy, whether implicit or explicit, true or false, consistent or contradictory. And one's philosophy directs the course of his life. The philosophy that is dominant in the culture at large directs the course of the culture, governing what the laws are, what regulations are imposed on your business, whether the world admires or sneers at what you are doing.

And here Marxism itself, as a philosophy, and a very evil one, is an instructive example. Marx's philosophy produced Soviet Russia, Red China, the Eastern European communist nations, Castro's Cuba, and the socialist or semi-socialist states around the world. That's quite an impressive result for a philosophy, however disastrous and blood-soaked a result it has been.

The history of the twentieth century has been shaped by the collision of two systems of philosophy: *collectivism*, of either the Marxist or the fascist variety, and *individualism*, the philosophy of America's Founding Fathers. America's individualism has been badly damaged by the collectivist philosophy, so that the capitalist system with which we started has been replaced by our present welfare state.

Philosophy rules life whether people accept or deny the power of philosophic ideas. Philosophy operates whether or not anyone recognizes its influence.

Marxism, ironically, holds that philosophy is hot air. What directs societies and human history, Marx taught, is not ideas but economic conditions. But his *philosophy*, not economic conditions, is what put whole nations under the thumb of communist dictatorship. Russia was poor and semi-feudal, but it went communist; Britain was relatively rich and fairly capitalist, but it went socialist for a period, as did Sweden and many other countries. America in 1776 was far poorer than Russia was in 1917, but we went capitalist. Why? Because of a philosophy, the individualist philosophy America inherited from the English philosopher John Locke.

Marx was an economic determinist. He thought money creates ideas. In fact, ideas create money. Or at least rational ideas do. And I'm not referring here to concrete ideas, but to fundamental ones. I don't mean that an idea for a better mousetrap will cause the world to beat a path to your door. Rather, I'm saying that those who accept the irrational philosophic idea of animal "rights" will not even try to build a better mousetrap. They will spend their time trying to protect mice from man's traps. It's your philosophic ideas about the nature of mice and men, and the purpose of your life, that govern your goals and set your values.

The point is that philosophy is so powerful because it sets the fundamentals of a man's life and of a society's institutions.

And let me disabuse you of a thought that may have occurred to you. I don't claim philosophy has this importance because I am a philosopher. It's the other way around: I decided to become a philosopher because I realized that philosophy has this importance. Philosophy has its power to shape human existence because philosophy deals in fundamentals.

What I want to do in this talk is to convince you of the role of philosophy in your life, in your business, and in the culture. The implication, then, is you need to examine your philosophy consciously to make sure it is rational, consistent, and true. (At the end of my talk, I will briefly outline to you the philosophy I have concluded is rational, consistent, and true.)

Philosophy deals with fundamentals. What is it to be a fundamental? Let's look at fundamentals in areas other than philosophy, where it will be easier to grasp their role.

In a business firm, the CEO is the prime mover. He controls what the firm does—not by doing everything himself, but by managing those who do it, and by giving them general guidelines.

The CEO has indirect control, via managing and setting the general goals of the firm. He decides upon the general result, but not every detail.

For example, let's say Bill Gates did not create or even approve the design of the various "wallpaper" background patterns for the Windows "desktop." But he decided, let's say, that the user should have a choice of a range of patterns for the background. Maybe he even said, "the various designs should appeal to different personality types." But he didn't have to approve all the final choices in particular.

Someone under him, some department head, perhaps, approved the patterns, after they'd been created lower down the chain.

So the CEO exerts *general control*. This can mean setting the goals, and it can mean picking the people who implement them. He is the first cause in a series of causes.

Consider now the *scope* of the CEO's job. The CEO has authority over everything, not just over some department or activity. His job description has the widest scope, wider than everyone else's.

The CEO is the *fundamental* officer of the firm in that he has the *widest general control*. The position of the CEO is at the base of everything; he is the fundamental. The term "fundamental" comes from "foundation."

So "fundamental" means: widest overall cause. Something is fundamental if it is the ultimate cause, the ultimate controlling factor, and exerts this control over everything. A tree has many branches and sub-branches growing out of one trunk. The trunk is like the fundamental.

A fundamental is wide and deep. It's wide because it covers everything; it's deep because there are levels of structure, a chain of command, and the fundamental controls the things that control the things that control the most concrete level.

Another example of fundamentality would be in regard to military rank. The commander in chief is the fundamental. He doesn't even go to the battle scene, but he controls everything about the war: he picks the top personnel—the Secretary of Defense and the top Pentagon officers. And obviously the people directly under him, those he commands, command their subordinates, etc., right down to the lowest buck private.

Again: the CIC is the fundamental of the military in that he has completely general control or authority. He has the widest and deepest control over the military.

Now, note that the two examples, the CEO and the CIC, are of positions which are fundamental in a relative sense, not absolutely. There are people above the CEO and the CIC.

Above the CEO is the board of directors, and above them are the owners: the stockholders. The owners are the absolutely fundamental thing here. Only the owners can make the ultimate decisions: whether the company continues to exist, or is sold off, or liquidated, or simply shut down.

The CIC has the widest and deepest control in the military, but he answers to Congress, which has sole power to declare war, and Congress answers to the voters.

But the fundamental of a given domain is the widest and deepest factor in that domain.

Now we turn to consider fundamentality in regard not to people or their positions but to fundamentality in regard to "ideas."

Take economics. Everything in economics rests on certain basic ideas: the law of supply and demand, the idea that money is a medium of exchange, the idea that money is a value.

These ideas are causally controlling factors in regard to other ideas in economics, and consequently in business practice. If one rejects these basic ideas, all the other ideas are changed. For example, if one rejects supply and demand, one cannot understand price. That would mean, in business practice, one would not expect raising the price of one's product to result in fewer units sold. Why does one reward good employees with a raise in pay? Only because one knows that money is a value. Why does one rate a dollar earned in New Jersey as equivalent to a dollar earned in New York? Only because one knows that a dollar is a unit of exchange, so that every dollar is worth the same as every other dollar.

All concrete business decisions depend, explicitly or implicitly, on general laws of economics.

Or, take the ideas in the field of physics. There are basic laws and derivative laws. For example, Newton's laws of motion and gravitation are *basic*, and the laws of planetary motions are *derivative*. Newton used his basic laws to *explain* Kepler's earlier law of planetary motions. And Newton used these same laws to explain the ocean tides, and many other things.

Newton's laws are fundamental, in their domain, because they are wide and deep.

So the lesson is: ideas depend upon deeper and more general ideas. There is a chain of command in the realm of ideas too.

But again fundamentality is relative to the domain in question. Newton's laws are not absolutely fundamental: his laws depend upon more basic principles, such as those regarding the nature of space and time and the nature of matter.

What then is the field that deals with absolutely fundamental ideas, ideas that cover everything? That is what we call "philosophy." Again: Philosophy is the science that studies the fundamental principles of existence and man.

Let me now proceed to explain in a little more detail what philosophy is, by breaking it up into its branches, with an illustration of the kind of topics each branch considers.

1. Metaphysics: What is there? Is reality real—or is it an illusion? Is the world we see around us the only reality, or is there more than one—as in the religious idea of heaven and earth? Is the world governed by cause and effect, or is it the scene of miracles that defy causality? Are there events that occur by sheer chance, without causes? Metaphysics also is concerned with the fundamental nature of man. What is man? Is he a natural, biological organism, or a creature who straddles two realities, with one foot in this world and one in a higher, spiritual world? Does man have free will? Is he in charge of his destiny or is he the plaything of forces beyond his control, whether the force is fate, the genes he inherited, or the "conditioning" of his environment?

2. Epistemology: How do you know? What is knowledge and how does one acquire it? What is proof? Can we be objective or only subjective? Is faith valid? How, if ever, can we attain certainty about our ideas? What is the role of the senses in the acquisition of knowledge? of abstraction? of logic? The goal of epistemology is to provide a methodology for cognition—to tell you the steps to apply to gain and verify your knowledge, knowledge of anything.

3. Ethics: So what? What's life for? What is the meaning or purpose of life? What is good and evil? What is value, and what is the standard of judging value? How in principle do we gain the good?—i.e., what works to achieve that which is worth having? This means: what are the virtues one has to follow and the vices one has to avoid in order to achieve the good? Does honesty, for instance, really pay? Is justice something that benefits our lives or is it something we should try to get around, if possible? What is man's proper relationship to other men? Are others merely a means to one's own ends, or is each man an end in himself? Is one obligated to sacrifice to others or to live independently? The pursuit of wealth—is it right or wrong?

4. Politics: What kind of society and government should we have? Politics is the theory of the good society, it is ethics applied to society and the state. Here the big issue is: individual rights. Does the individual have inalienable rights to his life? Does he have the right to liberty? to property? What kind of government is moral? dictatorship? an anarchic hippie commune? Iran's religious tyranny? Athenian Democracy? the American Republic? Is man to be free and independent, or a slave of his neighbors, society, God, the state?

These are the kinds of question that philosophy deals with. I hasten to add that in the history of philosophy, for every right answer, one hundred wrong answers have been given. Tragically, most philosophers in history have been villains. Most did not even try to find out what is true; they were, instead, trying to rationalize their neurotic feelings.

Nevertheless, the answers provided by philosophy govern everything, because they are absolutely fundamental.

Let me illustrate philosophy's role by showing its relation to physics and to business. I said that Newton's laws were fundamental to physics. But beneath them, controlling them, are philosophical principles.

Newton was able to succeed because of his philosophy: especially, his metaphysics and epistemology. In metaphysics, he held that the material universe is fully real and obeys the law of causality. If he didn't think that, if he had agreed with medieval thinkers that the world is just God's testing-place for man, he would not have been able to be a physicist at all. The medievals didn't produce any physicists. Ethically, the medievals regarded the study of "this low, debased world" as evil. The good man, the medievals thought, turns his soul towards God and doesn't engage in study of the physical world. In fact, they considered such study a sin— the "lust of the eyes," they called it, following Augustine's philosophy.

Epistemologically, Newton based his research on sensory evidence and logical-mathematical reasoning from sensory evidence. He measured things. He defined his terms. He sought to be strictly rational. The medievals thought knowledge came from faith, revelation, and authority. Newton held that knowledge comes from observation, logically interpreted. His epistemology controlled his thinking, as the medievals' epistemology controlled theirs.

Now take business. In metaphysics, business is based on the acceptance of reality and causality. If sales drop, you don't regard it as a punishment inflicted by God, but as due to real causes. Something made sales drop, and if you can find the problem, you can fix it. In regard to man's nature, business is premised on the fundamental of man as a natural, biological organism endowed with free will. In fact, business is the process of conquering nature to make it serve the needs of man's life. And as to free will, the premise of business success is: "I can take charge of my life. I can set my own goals and do what's necessary to achieve them."

You know all the motivational seminars and "how to succeed in business" guides that stress that one should not just submit to the status quo, but actively take charge and change what needs to be changed, including one's own character, if necessary. That's the premise of free will. Consider the kind of employee who thinks he is trapped by conditions, and can't "buck the system," the kind of employee, that is, who has no initiative and feels he has no free will. Such an employee is of little value to anyone, including himself. You are on the lookout, are you not, for "self-starters," people who set challenging goals and then make sure they achieve them, then set even higher goals? That "I can do it" attitude, that sense of ambition, is the conviction of free will.

That's all just on metaphysics. The epistemology, ethics, and politics presupposed by business success are almost too obvious to mention. I will just refer to such issues as: the need to think, to place one's rational judgment above one's momentary feelings—epistemology. The confidence that one can create value, that productivity is a moral pursuit—ethics. The system of capitalism, with its respect for private property rights, its protection of individual freedom of action, as opposed to the plethora of government regulations that tie your hands—those are political issues that you confront on a daily basis.

(Incidentally, I have to confess that I, personally, was shocked to learn a few years ago that larger businesses have to have a whole department of "compliance." That is due to the anticapitalist philosophy that is so prevalent today. In my view, you shouldn't have to "comply" with regulations that violate individual rights. The whole concept of compliance here is disgraceful and un-American.)

Now I want to turn to a different, more personal issue: the fundamental role of philosophy in each individual's own life. Everyone has a philosophy, whether he knows it or not. Few people today hold an explicit philosophy, a philosophy formulated in words, but everyone has an implicit philosophy.

People don't recognize the power of philosophy because they take their own for granted. Their philosophy of life is a constant, it's always there in the background, and it never occurs to them to consider any alternative to it. It's the same way that nobody thinks he speaks with an accent—"I just speak regular, straight; it's only people from other regions who have an accent." But everyone does have his own way of speaking, and everyone does have his own way of thinking and his own assumptions about the way the world is. Everyone has his implicit philosophy.

Every adult, by the time he is an adult, has developed his own answers to the kind of questions I outlined above. It's impossible not to. Why not?

Because the brain is an integrating organ. As you grow up, whatever concrete choices you make tend to set up mental habits, habits that amount to personal, implicit answers to philosophical questions.

For instance, a young child of about three is stacking up blocks. The stack reaches a certain height, then falls down. This is painful and frustrating. How does he deal with it? Does he calm himself, try again, look more closely at what he is doing and try to build a more stable stack next time? Or does he dissolve in tears and run to Mommy for consolation? The choice is his. But as he responds to this and countless other similar choices day by day, he builds up attitudes which amount to a philosophical position on the world, himself, and his mind.

One child sticks to the task, works to solve his problem, and gradually, through hundreds of thousands of such choices, establishes in his character the corresponding values of perseverance, goal-directedness, placing thought above emotions, and many other implicit conclusions. He develops an implicit philosophy that amounts to: the world is stable, knowable, and a source of satisfaction, provided I do the required work, provided I follow reason instead of momentary feelings.

Another child gives in, time and time again, and grows up with the implicit philosophical premise that the world is the scene of causeless, chance catastrophes, that something will block his success, that he is helpless, that emotions are irresistible forces. That's the pattern.

Then, fifteen years later, each child is in a college philosophy class. The professor announces that the world is unintelligible, that life is a mystery, that nothing means anything, that reason has been refuted, and everything is subjective. What do you think are the two students' reactions? The unthinking, passive, emotion-driven child feels emotionally in tune with the professor. "Yes," he leaps to agree. It feels right to him, and he has always treated his feelings as the ultimate authority. "No," the better child reacts. And, being accustomed to thinking, he starts to question the professor's ideas. "How can reason have been refuted? Isn't refutation a use of reason? Life is not a mystery to me, and I don't feel helpless—why does he say that? What examples does he have to support his view, because my experience is the opposite."

Now it's understandable if the better student is somewhat cowed by his professor. His professor is the (supposed) expert, who can summon up all kinds of incredibly tricky arguments to seemingly support his malevolent philosophy. He can raise many questions the student can't answer.

Students are not equipped to answer the attacks on reality, reason, and success that have been put forward in the history of philosophy. Thus they fall victim to the destructive kind of philosophy that is taught in our universities today. The better students in college dismiss philosophy as nonsense. Given what they are taught, I don't blame them.

And in this attitude that philosophy is just hot air, the students are encouraged by the philosophers themselves. Philosophers themselves say that. The anti-philosophy attitude is itself the product of today's philosophy.

But this contempt for philosophy is a tragic mistake, one that is destroying the world. It is not *philosophy* that is nonsense, it is *wrong* philosophy. Right philosophy is the clearest, cleanest framework for successful living. I will indicate what I think is the right philosophy at the end of this talk, but I think I have already given you some idea of where I'm coming from.

Now you might ask: but what about all the people who never took a philosophy course? What about all the people who never even went to college? How do they come to be affected by philosophy?

Well, I have given you part of my answer: through the inescapable generalizing they have done from their own life experiences, as produced by their own choices. But there is another input to the equation. Everyone is bombarded with philosophy every day, outside the classroom. Growing up, he hears his parents' ideas, teachers' ideas, ministers' ideas. As he matures, he reads newspapers, he watches television, reads books, goes to movies, looks at art.

In other words, we are immersed in a culture. All of that culture is the transmission belt that takes the ideas of the academic philosophers and applies them in ways that reach the man on the street, even if he never went to college. The newspaper editors, radio talk-show hosts, ministers, artists, novelists, motivational speakers, etc.—*they* went to college, and there they absorbed the fundamental ideas on which our culture is based.

The man on the street gets his explicit philosophy from the opinion-makers, who got it from their professors of history, literature, political science, women's studies, etc.—all of which professors got their ideas, directly or indirectly, from philosophers.

You ask how the man who never met a philosopher gets his explicit ideas on philosophy? You might as well ask how the boy in the mailroom gets his duties from the CEO, since he never met the CEO. There's a chain of command, in both cases: a chain of business command and a chain of command in the realm of ideas. In both realms, the fundamental is the widest controlling factor, and it sets the framework for and manages everything that goes on.

Most people's implicit philosophy is not consistent. Most people hold contradictions. Sometimes they feel and act as though the universe was open to success, and sometimes they feel and act as though the universe were rigged against them.

There are two reasons for these switches or inconsistencies. First, such people live compartmentalized lives. They live by one set of rules in their work and a different set in their personal lives. They are rational in their business lives but emotionalist in their romantic lives. They work hard to produce during the week, then go to church on Sunday and nod when the preacher says, "Be like the lilies of the field which neither sow nor reap." They struggle to make money during the week but agree when they hear: "It is easier for a camel to go through the eye of a needle than for a rich man to get into heaven."

The second reason for people's inconsistency on their principles is that the philosophy of contemporary American culture is pragmatism. Pragmatism, a philosophy devised by William James, John Dewey, and others, is anti-principle. Pragmatism says that principles are snares and delusions. Pragmatists teach explicitly that contradictions are inevitable and that it is folly to try to define a consistent set of principles. Reality, the pragmatists teach, is an ever-shifting flux; what was true tomorrow may not be true today; it's all relative, and truth is just whatever works *now*. Or, to quote a well-known pragmatist: it all depends on what the meaning of the word "is" is.

Having a philosophy is unavoidable. Your philosophy may suffer from inconsistency—there may be two or more CEO's clashing within you—but no one can face each issue from scratch, without having habits, precedents, and generalizations—all of which, over time, add up to a set of basic principles, a personal philosophy of life.

In summary, let me read you what Ayn Rand had to say about the inescapability of philosophy.

> You have no choice about the necessity to integrate your observations, your experiences, your knowledge into abstract ideas, i.e., into principles. Your only choice is whether these principles are true or false, whether they represent your conscious, rational convictions—or a grab-bag of notions snatched at random, whose sources, validity, context and consequences you do not know, notions which, more often than not, you would drop like a hot potato if you knew.
>
> But the principles you accept (consciously or subconsciously) may clash with or contradict one another; they, too, have to be integrated. What integrates them? Philosophy. A philosophic system is an integrated view of existence. As a human being, you have no choice about the fact that you need a philosophy. Your only choice is whether you define your philosophy by a conscious, rational, disciplined process of thought and scrupulously logical deliberation—or let your subconscious accumulate a junk heap of unwarranted conclusions, false generalizations, undefined contradictions, undigested slogans, unidentified wishes, doubts and fears, thrown together by chance, but integrated by your subconscious into a kind of mongrel philosophy and fused into a single, solid weight: *self-doubt*, like a ball and chain in the place where your mind's wings should have grown.[1]

You know the saying: a house built on weak foundations cannot stand. And in regard to philosophical foundations, a life or a society built on weak foundations cannot stand. Weak or mistaken philosophical foundations lead to disaster, personally and socially. Personally, look at the mess most people make of their lives. That mess is due to the errors and contradictions in their philosophies. Socially, look at history. The societies with the most rational philosophies, such as ancient Greece and the Age of Reason, were the most successful. The societies with the most irrational philosophies, such as the Dark Ages or Soviet Russia and Nazi Germany, left a blood-stained record of failure and destruction.

In conclusion, let me briefly outline the philosophy that will stand, the philosophy of the future, if mankind is to have a future, the philosophy of Ayn Rand.

Metaphysics

Existence exists; there is only one reality—the world we perceive through our senses, and it is fully real. It is what it is; facts are facts; A is A. The universe is governed by the law of cause and effect; what a thing is, determines what it will do. Man exists as a natural living organism of a specific kind with specific needs. His distinction from the rest of the world is that he has a thinking mind. His mind has free will, which is the choice to think or not to think. Man can choose either to put forth the effort of thinking or to lapse into a semiconscious daze, run by his feelings. And his feelings in such cases will be programmed by the ideas he absorbs unknowingly from others. But a rational, thinking individual is independent and is truly a self-made man.

Epistemology

Reason is man's only means of knowledge. Reason is the faculty that identifies and integrates the material provided by man's senses. Reason is the application of logic to sensory observation. Objectivity is possible if a man follows a logical method. Going by what one can prove is the basis of rational certainty. Reason is one's only means of knowing truth and the only proper guide to action. One must choose his values by as rational a process as he uses to reach his factual conclusions.

Ethics

Man faces the alternative of life or death, and this is the basis of the need to act, and hence of ethics. Man's life *qua* man is the standard of moral value. Reason is man's basic means of survival. All that which is proper to the life of man as a rational being is the good, all that which destroys it is the evil. A man is the moral owner of his own life; he exists for his own sake, with the achievement of his own happiness as his highest moral responsibility. Man is not a sacrificial animal. A moral man neither sacrifices himself to others nor others to himself. He lives as an independent being, pursuing his own values, never seeking or granting the unearned. His three cardinal values are: Reason, Purpose, and Self-Esteem. Each value dictates a corresponding virtue: Rationality, Productiveness, and Pride.

> If I were to speak your kind of language, I would say that man's only moral commandment is: Thou shalt think. But a "moral commandment" is a contradiction in terms. The moral is the chosen, not the forced; the understood, not the obeyed. The moral is the rational, and reason accepts no commandments.[2]

This is a morality of rational selfishness. Not mindless whim-worship, not predation upon others, but the rational, independent pursuit of one's own self-interest, without anyone's sacrifice.

Politics

Each man has inalienable rights, the basic one being the right to his own life. Rights are conditions of social existence required by the nature of man in order for him to survive and prosper. Since man survives by the use of his reasoning mind, and since reason cannot function under physical force, man has the right to be free from the physical force that others would initiate against him. There is also an individual right to private property, because man survives by creating material values, for his own use or trade with others. Government is established solely to protect man's individual rights against their violation by physical force. The government's proper functions are only three: the police, the army, and the law courts. The social system that follows from this, the system based upon individual rights, is *laissez-faire* capitalism. Under capitalism, the government may not act as a criminal to violate your rights nor may it act paternalistically to deprive you of the freedom to make your own, peaceful decisions regarding what is in your self-interest. Capitalism is the system of selfishness, rational selfishness, and that is why it is moral.

This is the rushed, merest outline of an integrated system of philosophy based on the absolutism of reality and the needs of man's life in reality. I will close with Ayn Rand's one-sentence summary:

> My philosophy, in essence, is the concept of man as a heroic being, with his own happiness as the moral purpose of his life, with productive achievement as his noblest activity, and reason as his only absolute.[3]

Whether or not you adopt that philosophy and make it your own guide is up to you, of course. My job tonight was simply to sell you on the power and importance of philosophy as such. But if you are interested in Ayn Rand's philosophy—she named it Objectivism—then the first thing you should do is read her novel *Atlas Shrugged*.

Notes

1. Ayn Rand, "Philosophy: Who Needs It," *Philosophy: Who Needs It* (New York: Signet, 1984), pp. 6–7.

2. Ayn Rand, *Atlas Shrugged* (New York: Penguin USA, 1992), p.1018.

3. Ibid., About the Author, pp. 1170–71.

"Wealth is the product of man's capacity to think."

Ayn Rand

In Ayn Rand's *Atlas Shrugged,* she presents the view that money is *made* and *earned* as a result of one's virtues, production and thought. The following excerpt, the "Meaning of Money Speech," from the 1957 novel, outlines the relationship between the mind and the dollar, and exposes the motivations and goals of those who seek to undermine it by slandering money as being "the root of all evil."

"Wealth is the product of man's capacity to think."

Ayn Rand

"So you think that money is the root of all evil?" said Francisco d'Anconia. "Have you ever asked what is the root of money? Money is a tool of exchange, which can't exist unless there are goods produced and men able to produce them. Money is the material shape of the principle that men who wish to deal with one another must deal by trade and give value for value. Money is not the tool of the moochers, who claim your product by tears, or of the looters, who take it from you by force. Money is made possible only by the men who produce. Is this what you consider evil?

"When you accept money in payment for your effort, you do so only on the conviction that you will exchange it for the product of the effort of others. It is not the moochers or the looters who give value to money. Not an ocean of tears nor all the guns in the world can transform those pieces of paper in your wallet into the bread you will need to survive tomorrow. Those pieces of paper, which should have been gold, are a token of honor—your claim upon the energy of the men who produce. Your wallet is your statement of hope that somewhere in the world around you there are men who will not default on that moral principle which is the root of money. Is this what you consider evil?

"Have you ever looked for the root of production? Take a look at an electric generator and dare tell yourself that it was created by the muscular effort of unthinking brutes. Try to grow a seed of wheat without the knowledge left to you by men who had to discover it for the first time. Try to obtain your food by means of nothing but physical motions—and you'll learn that man's mind is the root of all the goods produced and of all the wealth that has ever existed on earth.

"But you say that money is made by the strong at the expense of the weak? What strength do you mean? It is not the strength of guns or muscles. Wealth is the product of man's capacity to think. Then is money made by the man who invents a motor at the expense of those who did not invent it? Is money made by the intelligent at the expense of the fools? By the able at the expense of the incompetent? By the ambitious at the expense of the lazy? Money is *made*— before it can be looted or mooched—made by the effort of every honest man, each to the extent of his ability. An honest man is one who knows that he can't consume more than he has produced.

"To trade by means of money is the code of the men of good will. Money rests on the axiom that every man is the owner of his mind and his effort. Money allows no power to prescribe the value of your effort except the voluntary choice of the man who is willing to trade you his effort in return. Money permits you to obtain for your goods and your labor that which they are worth to the men who buy them, but no more. Money permits no deals except those to mutual benefit by the unforced judgment of the traders. Money demands of you the recognition that men must work for their own benefit, not for their own injury, for their gain, not their loss—the recognition that they are not beasts of burden, born to carry the weight of your misery—that you must offer them values, not wounds—that the common bond among men is not the exchange of suffering, but the exchange of *goods*. Money demands that you sell, not your weakness to men's stupidity, but your talent to their reason; it demands that you buy, not the shoddiest they offer, but the best that your money can find. And when men live by trade—with reason, not force, as their final arbiter—it is the best product that wins, the best performance, the man of best judgment and highest ability—and the degree of a man's productiveness is the degree of his reward. This is the code of existence whose tool and symbol is money. Is this what you consider evil?

"But money is only a tool. It will take you wherever you wish, but it will not replace you as the driver. It will give you the means for the satisfaction of your desires, but it will not provide you with desires. Money is the scourge of the men who attempt to reverse the law of causality—the men who seek to replace the mind by seizing the products of the mind.

"Money will not purchase happiness for the man who has no concept of what he wants: money will not give him a code of values, if he's evaded the knowledge of what to value, and it will not provide him with a purpose, if he's evaded the choice of what to seek. Money will not buy intelligence for the fool, or admiration for the coward, or respect for the incompetent. The man who attempts to purchase the brains of his superiors to serve him, with his money replacing his judgment, ends up by becoming the victim of his inferiors. The men of intelligence desert him, but the cheats and the frauds come flocking to him, drawn by a law which he has not discovered: that no man may be smaller than his money. Is this the reason why you call it evil?

"Only the man who does not need it, is fit to inherit wealth—the man who would make his own fortune no matter where he started. If an heir is equal to his money, it serves him; if not, it destroys him. But you look on and you cry that money corrupted him. Did it? Or did he corrupt his money? Do not envy a worthless heir; his wealth is not yours and you would have done no better with it. Do not think that it should have been distributed among you; loading the world with fifty parasites instead of one, would not bring back the dead virtue which was the fortune. Money is a living power that dies without its root. Money will not serve the mind that cannot match it. Is this the reason why you call it evil?

"Money is your means of survival. The verdict you pronounce upon the source of your livelihood is the verdict you pronounce upon your life. If the source is corrupt, you have damned your own existence. Did you get your money by fraud? By pandering to men's vices or men's stupidity? By catering to fools, in the hope of getting more than your ability deserves? By lowering your standards? By doing work you despise for purchasers you scorn? If so, then your money will not give you a moment's or a penny's worth of joy. Then all the things you buy will become, not a tribute to you, but a reproach; not an achievement, but a reminder of shame. Then you'll scream that money is evil. Evil, because it would not pinch-hit for your self-respect? Evil, because it would not let you enjoy your depravity? Is this the root of your hatred of money?

"Money will always remain an effect and refuse to replace you as the cause. Money is the product of virtue, but it will not give you virtue and it will not redeem your vices. Money will not give you the unearned, neither in matter nor in spirit. Is this the root of your hatred of money?

"Or did you say it's the *love* of money that's the root of all evil? To love a thing is to know and love its nature. To love money is to know and love the fact that money is the creation of the best power within you, and your pass-key to trade your effort for the effort of the best among men. It's the person who would sell his soul for a nickel, who is loudest in proclaiming his hatred of money—and he has good reason to hate it. The lovers of money are willing to work for it. They know they are able to deserve it.

"Let me give you a tip on a clue to men's characters: the man who damns money has obtained it dishonorably; the man who respects it has earned it.

"Run for your life from any man who tells you that money is evil. That sentence is the leper's bell of an approaching looter. So long as men live together on earth and need means to deal with one another—their only substitute, if they abandon money, is the muzzle of a gun.

"But money demands of you the highest virtues, if you wish to make it or to keep it. Men who have no courage, pride or self-esteem, men who have no moral sense of their right to their money and are not willing to defend it as they defend their life, men who apologize for being rich—will not remain rich for long. They are the natural bait for the swarms of looters that stay under rocks for centuries, but come crawling out at the first smell of a man who begs to be forgiven for the guilt of owning wealth. They will hasten to relieve him of the guilt—and of his life, as he deserves.

"Then you will see the rise of the men of the double standard—the men who live by force, yet count on those who live by trade to create the value of their looted money—the men who are the hitchhikers of virtue. In a moral society, these are the criminals, and the statutes are written to protect you against them. But when a society establishes criminals-by-right and looters-by-law—men who use force to seize the wealth of *disarmed* victims—then money becomes its creators' avenger. Such looters believe it safe to rob defenseless men, once they've passed a law to disarm them. But their loot becomes the magnet for other looters, who get it from them as they got it. Then the race goes, not to the ablest at production, but to those most ruthless at brutality. When force is the standard, the murderer wins over the pickpocket. And then that society vanishes, in a spread of ruins and slaughter.

"Do you wish to know whether that day is coming? Watch money. Money is the barometer of a society's virtue. When you see that trading is done, not by consent, but by compulsion—when you see that in order to produce, you need to obtain permission from men who produce nothing—when you see that money is flowing to those who deal, not in goods, but in favors—when you see that men get richer by graft and by pull than by work, and your laws don't protect you against them, but protect them against you—when you see corruption being rewarded and honesty becoming a self-sacrifice—you may know that your society is doomed. Money is so noble a medium that it does not compete with guns and it does not make terms with brutality. It will not permit a country to survive as half-property, half-loot.

"Whenever destroyers appear among men, they start by destroying money, for money is men's protection and the base of a moral existence. Destroyers seize gold and leave to its owners a counterfeit pile of paper. This kills all objective standards and delivers men into the arbitrary power of an arbitrary setter of values. Gold was an objective value, an equivalent of wealth produced. Paper is a mortgage on wealth that does not exist, backed by a gun aimed at those who are expected to produce it. Paper is a check drawn by legal looters upon an account which is not theirs: upon the virtue of the victims. Watch for the day when it bounces, marked: 'Account overdrawn.'

"When you have made evil the means of survival, do not expect men to remain good. Do not expect them to stay moral and lose their lives for the purpose of becoming the fodder of the immoral. Do not expect them to produce, when production is punished and looting rewarded. Do not ask, 'Who is destroying the world?' You are.

"You stand in the midst of the greatest achievements of the greatest productive civilization and you wonder why it's crumbling around you, while you're damning its life-blood—money. You look upon money as the savages did before you, and you wonder why the jungle is creeping back to the edge of your cities. Throughout men's history, money was always seized by looters of one brand or another, whose names changed, but whose method remained the same; to seize wealth by force and to keep the producers bound, demeaned, defamed, deprived of honor. That phrase about the evil of money, which you mouth with such righteous recklessness, comes from a time when wealth was produced by the labor of slaves—slaves who repeated the motions once discovered by somebody's mind and left unimproved for centuries. So long as production was ruled by force and wealth was obtained by conquest, there was little to conquer. Yet through all the centuries of stagnation and starvation, men exalted the looters, as aristocrats of the sword, as aristocrats of birth, as aristocrats of the bureau, and despised the producers, as slaves, as traders, as shopkeepers—as industrialists.

"To the glory of mankind, there was, for the first and only time in history, a *country of money*—and I have no higher, more reverent tribute to pay to America, for this means: a country of reason, justice, freedom, production, achievement. For the first time, man's mind and money were set free, and there were no fortunes-by-conquest, but only fortunes-by-work, and instead of swordsmen and slaves, there appeared the real maker of wealth, the greatest worker, the highest type of human being—the self-made man—the American industrialist.

"If you ask me to name the proudest distinction of Americans, I would choose—because it contains all the others—the fact that they were the people who created the phrase 'to *make* money.' No other language or nation had ever used these words before; men had always thought of wealth as a static quantity—to be seized, begged, inherited, shared, looted or obtained as a favor. Americans were the first to understand that wealth has to be created. The words 'to make money' hold the essence of human morality.

"Yet these were the words for which Americans were denounced by the rotted cultures of the looters' continents. Now the looters' credo has brought you to regard your proudest achievements as a hallmark of shame, your prosperity as guilt, your greatest men, the industrialists, as blackguards, and your magnificent factories as the product and property of muscular labor, the labor of whip-driven slaves, like the pyramids of Egypt. The rotter who simpers that he sees no difference between the power of the dollar and the power of the whip, ought to learn the difference on his own hide—as, I think, he will.

"Until and unless you discover that money is the root of all good, you ask for your own destruction. When money ceases to be the tool by which men deal with one another, then men become the tools of men. Blood, whips and guns—or dollars. Take your choice—there is no other—and your time is running out."

The Businessmen's Crucial Role: Material Men of the Mind

Debi Ghate

This essay, first published in 2009, assumes that the reader is familiar with Ayn Rand's 1957 novel, *Atlas Shrugged*. In her article, Ms. Debi Ghate argues that Rand's story about a strike by the "men of the mind" required businessmen as its central heroes. Because of the material and spiritual nature of business, because of what it requires and produces, it is the industrialists that in essence keep the motor of the world running. And it is only they who can bring that motor to a stop.

Note: Page references to Atlas Shrugged *refer to the Penguin USA 1992 hardcover edition.*

The Businessmen's Crucial Role:
Material Men of the Mind

Debi Ghate

INTRODUCTION

In describing *Atlas Shrugged*, Ayn Rand wrote, "its theme is: the role of the mind in man's existence."[1] This is a very broad theme, one that Rand could have illustrated via countless different story lines. Among the many possibilities, she chose a specific plot-theme. As she explained:

> The link between the theme and the events of the novel is an element which I call the plot-theme. . . . A "plot-theme" is the central conflict or "situation" of a story—a conflict in terms of action, corresponding to the theme and complex enough to create a purposeful progression of events. . . . The plot-theme of *Atlas Shrugged* is "The men of the mind going on strike against an altruist-collectivist society."[2]

In other words, to show the role of the mind in man's existence, she chose as the central action a most unusual kind of strike: what would happen if a certain group of men—the men of intellect—were to withdraw from the world? Among Rand's heroes in *Atlas Shrugged*, we find several businessmen: Hank Rearden, Dagny Taggart, Francisco d'Anconia, and others. This is intriguing; it is rare to find businessmen portrayed as the protagonists in modern literature and movies, and even rarer if the story involves men of the intellect. Businessmen are generally treated with suspicion—they are considered greedy, soulless money-grubbers, out to take advantage of anyone in the name of making a profit. Even when we have no solid reason to doubt their motives, the strong message delivered to the businessman who rises above the crowd is: Don't stand out or we'll relevel the playing field; don't earn too much through your chosen profession, or we'll find a way to redistribute your wealth. We expect caped crusaders to save the day, not suited businessmen.

Yet Ayn Rand cast businessmen as *heroes* in the novel. Was this an optional selection on her part? Could she have written her novel with scientists, philosophers, engineers, lawyers, or doctors as her central heroes? John Galt, the leader of the strike, says that the strikers will return to the world only when the lights of New York City are extinguished. What will it take to extinguish those lights? Who keeps those lights on?

I argue that *Atlas Shrugged*, because of its chosen plot-theme, had to have businessmen such as Hank Rearden and Dagny Taggart as its heroes *by necessity*.

THE POPULAR CONCEPTION OF THE BUSINESSMAN AS MATERIALIST

While I was writing this essay, the United States was facing tremendous economic uncertainty caused by a "credit crisis." During the frenzy, the typical cries against businessmen were once again heard. Presidential candidate John McCain vowed that his administration, if elected, would "put an end to the reckless conduct, corruption and unbridled greed that have caused the crisis on Wall Street."[3] Profit-seeking businessmen are society's downfall: they are the source of our economic woes, and the public suffers for their vice of pursuing wealth. They are certainly not described as "men of the mind," the type of man that *Atlas Shrugged*'s strike removes from society. Instead they are considered men of corruption and sin.

In the novel's setting, what is the response to the businessman? As in today's media accounts, the wealthy businessman in *Atlas Shrugged* is deemed evil and blamed for the current economic crisis facing the country:

> The newspapers had snarled that the cause of the country's troubles . . . was the selfish greed of rich industrialists; that it was men like Hank Rearden who were to blame for the shrinking diet, the falling temperature and the cracking roofs in the homes of the nation; . . . that a man like Hank Rearden was prompted by nothing but the profit motive. . . . as if the words "profit motive" were the self-evident brand of ultimate evil. (476)

Far from being considered a candidate for a strike by men of the mind, a businessman like Hank Rearden is denounced as a "predatory savage" who is nothing but an "ex-ore-digger" (404). Business is dismissed as a trivial activity that any greedy brute can undertake to make a quick buck. When Dagny speaks with Dr. Stadler, a brilliant but corrupt scientist, about an abandoned motor that she believes could revolutionize industry, he spurns the businessman's role, stating: "You'd think any greedy fool of an industrialist would have grabbed it in order to make a fortune. No intelligence was needed to see its commercial value" (356). When a member of the "intellectual class" attempts to flatter Jim Taggart, the businessman with a "social conscience," he says "the best compliment I can pay you is that you're *not* a real businessman." In response, Jim preaches the mantra of the looters: "We are breaking up the vicious tyranny of economic power. We will set men free of the rule of the dollar. We will release our spiritual aims from dependence on the owners of material means. We will liberate our culture from the stranglehold of the profit-chasers" (404).

The contempt for the businessman and the corresponding attitude that he is a force of destruction and chaos, rests on the view that he is an emotion-driven thug who mows down the intellectual as he lustily pursues profit, nurturing greed in others. What is behind this view?

"We will release our spiritual aims from dependence on the owners of material means," says Jim Taggart (404). A well-known author who frequented many parties concurs: "Our culture has sunk into a bog of materialism. Men have lost all spiritual values in their pursuit of material production and technological trickery. . . . They will return to a nobler life if we teach them to bear privations. So we ought to place a limit on their material greed" (133). "Intellectual pursuits are not learned in the marketplace," said the hostess (144). The dominant view is that business is corrupt *because* it is material, and therefore by necessity is nonspiritual.

What is praised as spiritual by those who find the material distasteful? It is the abstract, indefinable, intangible, and impractical realm, the subject matter of highbrow discussion amongst the popular intellectuals in the novel. "No," says an author at a gathering of socialites, "you cannot expect people to understand the higher reaches of philosophy. Culture should be taken out of the hands of the dollar-chasers. We need a national subsidy for literature. It is disgraceful that artists are treated like peddlers and that art works have to be sold like soap" (141). The art works and books that no one wants to buy are spiritual. The ideas that are beyond the grasp of the rational individual are spiritual. "You must learn to see beyond the static definitions of old-fashioned thinking. Nothing is static in the universe. Everything is fluid," said the professor of philosophy at the same party (132). The common view is that it is the *unknowable* and *otherworldly* that constitutes the spiritual.

Because what the businessman does is definable, tangible, concrete, and of-this-world, his work is disdained as material, and therefore not of the intellect or spirit.

BUSINESS AS AN INTELLECTUAL AND SPIRITUAL PURSUIT

Ayn Rand completely rejected the conventional view of the businessman, the view that he is nothing more than a "used car salesman" with a bigger dealership. Rather, Ayn Rand celebrated the businessman and his pursuit of material wealth as *virtuous*. As Francisco d'Anconia states:

> To the glory of mankind, there was, for the first and only time in history,
> a *country of money*—and I have no higher, more reverent tribute to pay
> to America, for this means: a country of reason, justice, freedom, pro-
> duction, achievement. For the first time, man's mind and money were
> set free, and there were no fortunes-by-conquest, but only fortunes-by-
> work, and instead of swordsmen and slaves, there appeared the real
> maker of wealth, the greatest worker, the highest type of human be-
> ing—the self-made man—the American industrialist. (414)

Why did Rand hold the businessman as the "highest type of human being"? To judge whether business requires intellect or not, one must examine
what it consists of. What does a businessman do on a daily basis and over the
span of his career?

Much of the novel concentrates on the lives of two businessmen whom the
strikers consider their greatest enemies, and their greatest potential conquests:
Hank Rearden and Dagny Taggart. Through them, we are exposed to the role
of the mind in business and the full range of activities it involves—when it is
pursued actively and purposefully as a productive venture. Does business require men of intellect?

Hank Rearden

Hank Rearden is an industrialist whose chosen purpose was to invent a new Metal
that would outlast, outperform, and outsell any other material known to man. He
had worked since the age of fourteen in mines, foundries, and mills, learning the
industry from the mine shafts up. By thirty, he owned the mine. He eventually owned Rearden Ore, Rearden Coal, and Rearden Limestone before opening
Rearden Steel. Every stage of his career was an advancement over the last; every advancement brought him closer to his goal: Rearden Metal. As Rearden says
to Francisco d'Anconia, "To me there's only one form of human depravity—the
man without a purpose" (148).

On the night that he finally pours the first heat of Rearden Metal, he reflects on what it took to reach this day. It took him ten years to develop the
metal and "every inch of its course, every pound of its pressure and every
molecule within it, were controlled and made by a conscious intention that
had worked upon it" (28). Rearden envisioned a world built and shaped by
his Metal. He foresaw what multitudes of applications would result if he succeeded in his quest—from kitchen knives to communication wire to airplanes.

With his purpose firmly in mind, Rearden spent years in research laboratories in front of scorching ovens, poring over formulas on paper, testing material, learning from each failed attempt—reformulating, recalculating, reinventing, and always reasoning, reasoning, reasoning—until the solution was found, until the day he could hold the cool metal in his hands. Consider what this required: an integrated understanding of chemistry, physics, mathematics, engineering, metallurgy, among other fields. It required the ability to conceptualize beyond previously identified and readily accessible metals, and to reconfigure existing materials into combinations not previously thought of. It required an ability to persist in the face of failure. On the day his Metal is poured for the first time, Rearden finds that his mind is still sharply focused on what had been his ten-year goal: "The sight of the running metal was still burned into his mind, filling his consciousness, leaving no room for anything else" (34).

Yet, during that ten-year period, as the owner of the most efficient and productive steel mills in the country, Rearden undertakes this inventive effort while expertly overseeing all other aspects of his business. In order to garner the greatest profit and reward from his mills, Rearden must continually identify or create new or larger markets for his Metal. He must envision new, industry-advancing solutions for his customers' manufacturing and engineering needs. For instance, when Taggart Transcontinental wants to build a new bridge using his Metal, Rearden sketches a design that leads to a new method of construction, at a fraction of the previously estimated cost—construction that takes into account the superior quality of Rearden Metal. He has just created a new market segment of unlimited potential, with colossal profits as his just reward. And his customers are now able to pursue new industrial endeavors more efficiently, leading them to increase their own production and wealth—leading them to place larger and more frequent orders for his Metal. Rearden's attitude is summed up in his reply to Dagny, when she tells him a story she once heard in school about the sun losing energy and growing colder and colder each year: "I never believed that story. I thought by the time the sun was exhausted, men would find a substitute" (171).

As an industrialist, Rearden must oversee the design, construction, and any expansion of the physical mills. What methods and efficiencies can he introduce to maximize production and continuously increase the output of his mills? Has he hired the right employees to carry out the work? What directions should he give his superintendent in the face of a crisis? The more the mills produce, the more he produces; the more he produces, the more he sells; the more he sells, the more he earns. How can he produce 600 tons of metal a day on fewer furnaces compared to Orren Boyle's 100 tons using many more furnaces? Rearden is ruthlessly focused on squeezing the most production out of Rearden Steel, leading to larger and larger profits.

But he does not take a short-term, pragmatic view in generating those profits. He recognizes that he must earn the loyalty of the kind of customers he wants to deal with—those who will pay for his Metal and put it to the uses he had envisioned. He must determine at what price to sell his Metal so that his customers can afford it and will return. He must hire and fire employees with varying skills, from researchers to floor sweepers—the right decisions advance his long-term goal to maximize his profits. He must put out a fire at his mills and shovel coal if necessary in an emergency rather than watch and direct the action from afar. And, unfortunately, he must also deal with the Floyd Ferrises, the Wesley Mouches, the Paul Larkins, and their collaborators, who not only distract him from his purpose but actively try to undermine it. Rearden, the industrialist, must personally and simultaneously respond to multiple demands and pressures calmly, with focus, all the while engaged in the creative process of making Rearden Metal. Hank Rearden *is* Rearden Steel.

It was not easy; he experienced fatigue, frustration, and anger. He experienced occasional failure. But Rearden succeeded nevertheless. He was committed to a well-defined purpose, a purpose that he knew *had to be possible to achieve* given his hard-acquired knowledge. He knew that the goal he set—a new, revolutionary metal—would require a high level of sustained effort to attain. He recognized that his mind and spirit were the only sparks he needed to keep himself going (30).

In offering us Hank Rearden, Ayn Rand presents us with a business hero who proudly relies on his mind in the relentless pursuit of his business—for the express purpose of making as much money as possible. She presents us with a man who, through his confident dedication to his purpose, offers the world a product, Rearden Metal, that has the potential to revolutionize industry, providing a wide range of new products at a cheaper price. Through Hank Rearden, we see what intellectual and physical effort must be invested to achieve this, and the overwhelming range of intermediary decisions that rest on his judgment. When combined together in a man like Rearden, a business giant is born, the kind of man who changes the world product by product. Jim Taggart protests: "Rearden. He didn't invent smelting and chemistry and air compression. He couldn't have invented his Metal but for thousands and thousands of other people. *His* Metal! Why does he think it's his? Why does he think it's his invention?" His future wife, Cherryl, asks, puzzled, "But the iron ore and all those other things were there all the time. Why didn't anybody else make that Metal, but Mr. Rearden did?" (262) Without him, there is no revolution in manufacturing. He knows it, as does John Galt and his fellow strikers, as do the looters who try to deny that a man like Rearden is a man of the mind.

Dagny Taggart

Dagny Taggart decided as a child that she would one day run Taggart Transcontinental—"From Ocean to Ocean, forever"—better and faster than anyone, including her legendary grandfather, Nat Taggart. She knows all other industries depend on motive power to gather manufacturing components and transport their finished goods to market. The work she does moves the country—the better and faster she does that the more her company earns, and the more she earns as a stockholder and employee. And that profit is earned from other businesses that are also actively creating wealth from products they make. The more those businesses manufacture, the more her railroad earns by providing them with transportation.

Dagny started as a night station operator and worked her way up to Vice-President in Charge of Operation. In her, we find a competent, energetic professional who is always ready to act on her judgment in a swift and decisive way. Consider this exchange between Dagny and her mealy-mouthed brother and boss, Jim, when she announces her decision to replace the Rio Norte Line using track made of Rearden Metal, something no one has dared to attempt before:

"The consensus of the best metallurgical authorities," he said, "seems to be highly skeptical about Rearden Metal, contending—"

"Drop it, Jim."

"Well, whose opinion did you take?"

"I don't ask for opinions."

"What do you go by?"

"[My] Judgment." . . .

"Then what on earth do you know about Rearden Metal?"

"That it's the greatest thing ever put on the market . . . because it's tougher than steel, cheaper than steel and will outlast any hunk of metal in existence."

"But who says so?"

"Jim, I studied engineering in college. When I see things, I see them."

"What did you see?"

"Rearden's formula and the tests he showed me."

"Well, if it were any good, somebody would have used it, and nobody has." He saw the flash of anger, and went on nervously: "How can you *know* it's good? How can you be sure? How can you decide?"

"Somebody decides such things, Jim. Who?" (21)

Dagny Taggart, Taggart Transcontinental's Vice-President in Charge of Operation, decides these things.

Dagny always seems to know what to do and why. She has a seemingly pure clarity in her thinking. This clarity comes from knowing with certainty that she can make the right decision. This certainty is not without basis, it does not come from arrogance but from an earned confidence. What is the source of that confidence? Dagny knows every aspect of the company's business from the lonely station post to the powerful boardroom. She has invested in learning every key aspect of Taggart Transcontinental's business. She can read every map, operate any signal, construct a complex train schedule, hire expert contractors, and build a new railroad line. Before making her business decisions, Dagny personally examines the evidence, gains a firsthand understanding of the data in front of her, and evaluates all of the known facts. Because she has done so, she has no hesitation in issuing the necessary directions. On whose judgment? Her own. On whose authority? Her own. At whose risk? Her own. Dagny repeatedly and consistently tells employees, government officials, Jim, and the Taggart board of directors, that she personally assumes responsibility for her decisions when no one else dares to act. Her confidence is such that she decides to personally assume the risk of building the John Galt Line, entering into an agreement with Taggart Transcontinental that has it garnering all of the benefit if she succeeds.

What does building the John Galt Line require of Dagny? Her constant goal is: the best, fastest, safest, railroad the world has ever seen. Her constant motivation is: to make as much money as possible for herself and the railroad, boosting the other industries that depend on rail transport along the way so that her own company has long-term customers. Dagny knows that the fate of Colorado's industries, such as Wyatt Oil, Nielsen Motors, Hammond Cars and Stockton Foundry, depends on whether the Line is built or not. She knows that if Colorado's industries vanish, so does the entire country's economy.

Dagny has relied on her own judgment to identify that Rearden Metal is the best material to use for her endeavor even if it has never been used to build a railroad track. Because she is ultimately responsible for making the Line as profitable as possible, she must ensure that it is built to last and to transport as much traffic as possible while doing no harm to Taggart Transcontinental's passengers, or to the cargo entrusted it. To construct a railroad made of a new, untried material, she must resolve numerous engineering, manufacturing, and personnel issues. The consequences of an error are potentially costly to her given her agreement to bear all the risk—passengers could be killed if the rail is unsafe, the shareholders' investment may not pay off, Taggart Transcontinental's profits could crumble, or the commerce of Colorado could wither away, leaving the country's economy in jeopardy. What Dagny's business activities provide is a lifeline—a mechanism for people to move their goods and themselves—a way for them to carry out their own businesses, and therefore earn their livelihoods.

Because she has fully evaluated every component of the Line (human, mechanical, or otherwise), because she has planned for its construction, taking into account all known facts, because she has carefully calculated, designed, tested, and verified her vision, she succeeds—with nothing but her judgment to stand on. As she proudly rides in the engine car on the day the Line opens,

> She wondered why she felt safer than she had ever felt in a car behind the engine, safer here, where it seemed as if, should an obstacle rise, her breast and the glass shield would be the first to smash against it. She smiled, grasping the answer: it was the security of being first, with full sight and full knowledge of one's course—not the blind sense of being pulled into the unknown by some unknown power ahead. It was the greatest sensation of existence: not to trust, but to know. (240)

Because of her dedication to fully understand every aspect of the railroad business, Dagny is able to quickly identify obstacles and, at a rapid-fire pace, direct the necessary actions to remove them. She uses the results of her mind's effort to *act*. When the John Galt Line is built, and she has claimed victory over the naysayers, she decides to lay a track made of Rearden Metal across the country—"From Ocean to Ocean, forever." She is in a position to immediately conclude that this is the best course of action for the success of the railroad.

However, Dagny is not able to pursue that goal. Instead, she must respond to calamity after calamity in an attempt to save Taggart Transcontinental. When the tunnel disaster occurs in Colorado, Dagny's focus immediately turns to solving the problem of how to provide ongoing transportation with the least amount of disruption. She pulls maps from the railroad's early days and issues work orders to begin rerouting tracks in order to resume cross-country operations as soon as possible. When the Comet stalls on the tracks and is abandoned, she personally walks down the track to contact help. Her guiding principle is that "so long as she was still in existence she would know that action is man's foremost obligation, regardless of anything he feels" (334). Her mind is in constant drive and she acts on its output to continuously reach for her goal: a faster and better railroad than has ever been offered to the country before.

But, like Rearden, she must excel at overseeing the details of the business while pursuing her long-term, visionary goal. She must have the kind of intellect and dedication to purpose it takes to revolutionize the transportation industry of an entire nation. It is Dagny that recognizes the value of Rearden Metal in spite of the doubts cast upon it by the country's leading metallurgists. *She* conceives of the Rearden Metal bridge and track, recognizing the durability and speed it would provide. And she recognizes the value of the abandoned motor at the Twentieth Century Motor Company's ghost town factory. It is she who pursues the answer to the motor's riddle, knowing what it would mean for her railroad and for the entire economy.

What is it about the motor that convinces Dagny she must do everything in her power to resurrect it? Dagny understands the potential wealth that the motor could bring, not only to its inventor but to anyone who has the ability to harness its power. The motor is *self-generating*, requiring no outside source to continually replenish it. This means that any motorized process could be significantly accelerated, making more time and materials available for other use. As Rearden responds to her query as to whether he recognizes the value of the motor, if built: "I'd say: about ten years added to the life of every person in this country. . . . That motor could have set the whole country in motion and on fire" (290). And it is Dagny who extracts that invisible potential from an unidentifiable junk heap in the corner of an abandoned factory.

Taggart Transcontinental could not continue to exist but for Dagny's purpose, knowledge, and capacity for action. John Galt and his fellow strikers know this. Dagny senses it. And so do Jim, his board of directors, and the other looters who want to use her mind's products while cursing her existence.

Other Businessmen

There are other businessmen in the novel through whom we learn more about the intellectual power required to properly engage in business. Midas Mulligan, the financier, only makes loans to customers who he judges will pay them back with sufficient interest; he does not run a bank built on hopes, dreams, and pity, but on reality. What does that require? Mulligan must understand enough about the intended activities of his loan applicants to evaluate whether to incur the risk of supporting them (whether they be in mining, car manufacturing, or any other productive venture). In order to decide whether an investment is worth his gold, Mulligan must be in a position to *judge* whether his injection of capital will make that business grow. Ellis Wyatt, the man with no time to waste, works on drawing oil out of shale—previously considered an impossible task. What does that require? Wyatt must first conceive of the possibility, and then sufficiently understand the science and technology involved to lead the effort and hire the right specialists to convert the possibility into fact. He must then work on methods that will allow him to refine more of the oil he draws out of that shale, at a faster rate, in order to fulfill increasing demand from his customers. Ken Danagger, who owns a coal mine, judges that Rearden is a man worth dealing with under any circumstances, including the threat of legal sanction. What does that require? Danagger must be able to exercise independence in the face of popular opinion and evaluate Rearden as a business associate upon whom to stake the future of his coal mines. Danagger must be able to judge the material—and spiritual—benefits of such a business decision. Through these characters, Rand continues to show that business requires a thoroughly engaged and active mind, a mind capable of simultaneously asking a broad range of industry-redefining questions while yielding innovative answers that generate significant wealth for its owner and those he trades with.

What Business Is

Business, when pursued as Rearden, Dagny, and other businessmen in *Atlas Shrugged* pursue it, is indisputably a material endeavor that is equally intellectual and spiritual. Ayn Rand describes the businessman as follows:

> The businessman carries scientific discoveries from the laboratory of the inventor to industrial plants, and transforms them into material products that fill men's physical needs and expand the comfort of men's existence. By creating a mass market, he makes these products available to every income level in society. By using machines, he increases the productivity of human labor, thus raising labor's economic rewards. By organizing human effort into productive enterprises, he creates employment for men of countless professions.[4]

In other words, the industrialist channels the inventions and discoveries of highly specialized professions through carefully designed processes that result in goods and services, elevating our standard of living and making our lives more enjoyable, efficient, and effortless. The businessman converts the raw output of the researcher into a viable product that he can sell as widely and as profitably as possible. Along the way, he hires and therefore sustains many others of varying skill and ability, at all levels of society. That is, at the broadest level, what a businessman does.

This type of businessman is not a work of fiction created by Ayn Rand. Consider one of the earliest industrialists, James Watt (1736 to 1819). Watt is credited with commercializing a key piece of technology that brought about the Industrial Revolution, and thus our modern civilization: the steam engine. While he did not invent the steam engine, it was Watt who recognized its potential value. He began working on existing steam engines in 1764 to increase their output over longer periods of time. In 1765, Watt finally gained the critical insight of separating an engine's condenser from its piston, allowing it to maintain the requisite temperature. He then created a test engine and raised capital to mass produce the improved engine. By 1775, he had gone into business with fellow industrialist Matthew Boulton, and what followed was rapid progress in creating a commercial version of the test engine. Over the next few years, he worked to overcome other major design challenges involving the piston and beam. The result was the birth of the first steam engine of commercial value. Watt continued to work to improve the engine and adapt it for use in more specialized markets. By developing a rotary-motion steam engine in 1781 (replacing the earlier up-and-down pumping model) and introducing other mechanical improvements, Watt made available a steam engine for use in paper, flour, cotton, and iron mills, as well as distilleries, canals, and waterworks. He continued to improve and sell engines, generating significant profits. By the time he retired in 1800, he had patented the steam locomotive and was very wealthy, having reaped the rewards for his intellectual efforts. Watt's commercialization of the steam engine is credited as supplying the foremost source of energy, which made possible the Industrial Revolution.[5]

An industrialist's mind must therefore be such that he can take the scientist's creation, recognize its potential value, adapt it for commercialization and sell it to larger and larger markets. He expects to reap significant financial rewards for his efforts. But as Francisco points out to Rearden, there are easier ways to make money (452). Ultimately, what is it that motivates the businessman to engage in the demanding intellectual work required to successfully achieve his purpose?

It is precisely because the material pursuit of business is *spiritual* that the industrialist is dedicated to it. The businessman's ultimate goal is to create *values*. When Francisco asks Rearden why he spent ten years making his Metal and what he had hoped to achieve by giving his life to this activity, Rearden responds that he is proud of his achievement. He is proud of the John Galt Line because it is the best rail ever made and he wishes to make money by exchanging his best efforts for the best efforts of others. Rearden wants to see his Metal used by the best among men—those whom it will help reach greater and greater achievements—those who understand and appreciate the greatness of his own achievement (452).

Business is an activity that offers the mind challenges of a tremendous scale (on the order of how to create a new metal, how to revolutionize the transportation industry, or how to bring oil out of shale), the successful completion of which leads to the attainment of values. The night that Rearden pours the first heat of his Metal, he thinks: "Whatever it was . . . whatever the strain and the agony, they were worth it, because they had made him reach this day" (31). As Dagny rides in the engine car on the first run of the John Galt Line, she goes to look at the generators, exhilarated:

> She stood in a swaying, sealed chamber of metal, looking at the giant generators. She had wanted to see them, because the sense of triumph within her was bound to them, to her love for them, to the reason for the life-work she had chosen . . . . "The John Galt Line!" she shouted, for the amusement of feeling her voice swept away from

her lips. . . . They *are* alive, she thought, but their soul operates them by remote control. Their soul is in every man who has the capacity to equal this achievement. (245–46)

The pride and immense satisfaction of having created an industry—having accomplished what no one else could with the iron ore, the railroad system, or the shale—and the pleasure and happiness one derives from seeing one's product put to the uses one envisioned, is the spiritual reward the businessman receives for his intellectual effort.

The financial reward that the businessman expects to earn as a result of creating these values is the objective measure of his success. But it also adds to his spiritual reward. It is his means of pursuing and maintaining other values: the friends, ideas, art, projects, and hobbies that he has chosen because they bring him fulfillment and happiness. As Francisco puts it:

Money . . . will take you wherever you wish to go but it will not replace you as the driver. It will give you the means for the satisfaction of your desires, but it will not provide you with desires. . . . Money will not pursue happiness for the man who has no concept of what he wants: money will not give him a code of values. (411)

The pursuit of business so that it generates as much profit as possible therefore supplements the spiritual rewards that the work itself provides: it supplies the means for the businessman to enjoy a full life.

Finally, business is spiritual precisely because it involves material products—the definable, tangible, concrete products created by it. Francisco explains this relationship between material goods and man's spirit:

Dagny, we who've been called "materialists" by the killers of the human spirit, we're the only ones who know how little value or meaning there is in material objects as such, because we're the ones who create their value and meaning. . . . *You* do not have to depend on any material possessions, they depend on you, you create them, you own the one and only tool of production. Wherever you are, you will always be able to produce. (620)

The one and only tool of her production is her mind. Absent her mind, there is no tangible product for her to sell, and there is no resulting wealth for her to pursue her values with or no spiritual satisfaction to derive out of the creative process.

Without the material objects generated by business, the industrialist is unable to derive the spiritual wealth he gets from creating values out of his work. Without the spiritual investment of the industrialist's soul into his business, there is no material wealth possible to him. The two are indivisible. Business is a material *and* spiritual pursuit, demanding the best of one's mind.

As the composer Richard Halley comments in the valley:

> Miss Taggart, do you see why I'd give three dozen modern artists for one real businessman? . . . Whether it's a symphony or a coal mine, all work is an act of creating and comes from the same source: from an inviolate capacity to see through one's own eyes. . . . That shining vision which they talk about as belonging to authors of symphonies and novels—what do they think is the driving faculty of men who discover how to use oil, how to run a mine, how to build an electric motor? That sacred fire which is said to burn within musicians and poets—what do they suppose moves an industrialist to defy the whole world for the sake of his new metal . . . ? . . . [I]f there is more tragic a fool than the businessman who doesn't know that he's an exponent of man's highest creative spirit—it's the artist who thinks that the businessman is his enemy. (782–84)

What Business Isn't

Not all of the characters who claim the title of businessman in *Atlas Shrugged* illustrate the proper role of the mind in man's existence. Jim Taggart, Orren Boyle, Paul Larkin, Horace Bussby Mowen claim to be "businessmen." And why not? After all, they work *at* businesses, claim lofty titles such as president or owner, have big offices and staff scurrying about them, and take high-level meetings with the "who's-who" of Washington and Hollywood. These men are engaged in the full-time activity of trying to steal the income of hard-working people, using as minimal a level of effort as possible. They are corrupt, greedy thieves. *These* are the "predatory savages" that populate the prevailing notion of businessmen and what they do.

Recall Rand's description of the businessman and his role. Do the pseudo-businessmen transform inventions into new products, creating mass markets for them? No, they think of ways to steal the products of others and beg loans from Washington. Do they organize people into effective teams creating productive output? No, they look for ways to have the most number of people do as little productive work as possible. These characters spend their time currying favors, evading facts, avoiding decision-making, trading pull with other pull-peddlers, attending parties to see and be seen, and speaking in half-truths and code. They do everything in their power to remain in a hazy fog and avoid the necessity of action, preferring instead to rely on the Reardens and the Dagnys to do their thinking for them. A day's work for a man like Jim Taggart is to wake up cursing the dawn, to think of who he needs to avoid that day in order not to have a favor called in, and more important, who he needs to entertain and play the sycophant to in order to gain a favor. A man like Orren Boyle spends his days lobbying for increased regulations to throttle his competitors so that he can avoid the difficult task of figuring out how to produce steel. These are not businessmen, they are thugs. Rather than produce, they contrive new mechanisms by which to force others to do their thinking for them. They serve as a stark contrast to Rearden, Dagny, and the other heroic businessmen in the novel. They illustrate the role of the *mindless*.

The Spiritual Field that Sustains Other Fields

But men of the mind exist in every field requiring specialized knowledge and skill. Obviously one must think rationally, have a purpose, and act on one's judgment if one is a physicist designing a self-generating motor, a composer who writes uplifting music, or a philosophy professor who teaches future generations of thinkers. What makes the businessman unique? Why would the strike have lacked success if all the other men of the mind shrugged, but the businessman did not?

On a practical and visceral level, other professions rely on the businessman for their livelihood. The physicist needs the businessman to recognize the potential value and create commercial markets for his invention. The composer needs the businessman to record and sell his music. The philosophy professor needs the businessman to build and operate the university where he teaches. Even if the professional is engaged in certain business-like activities himself (for example, a self-employed doctor who markets his practice, provides services of value, issues invoices, collects payment, and pays the bills), he relies on others to put up the financing and carry out the construction of buildings that house his practice; to supply and sell the specialized equipment he needs to carry out his profession; to make commercially available new medicines and therapeutic products that will allow his own profession to grow. Who provides all of these elements? The businessman.

In the context of the novel, note that John Galt was temporarily employed by a motor company, Richard Halley performed in concert halls and recorded his music at studios, and Hugh Akston taught at Patrick Henry University. Each of them looked to the businessman for employment or for providing a means of earning an income. The products of their minds had limited exposure and were therefore of limited benefit, until the businessman recognized their value.

But the businessman supplies other professions with much more than employment capital, and industrial products. He is the provider of *material and therefore spiritual wealth,* which makes possible the pursuit of other professions.

Rand, in her discussion of the businessman's role, expanded on what he makes possible: "*He* is the great liberator who, in the short span of a century and a half, has released men from bondage to their physical needs, has released them from the terrible drudgery of an eighteen-hour workday of manual labor for their barest subsistence, has released them from famines, from pestilences, from the stagnant hopelessness and terror in which most of mankind had lived in all the pre-capitalist centuries—and in which most of it still lives, in non-capitalist countries."[6]

Because J. D. Rockefeller refined oil into petroleum and other key materials, new products, including cars, tractors, and bulldozers emerged, freeing men from physical labor and allowing more than a small elite under the protection of patrons to engage in professions such as teaching, painting, or lawyering. Because Thomas Edison manufactured the electric light bulb, men were free to continue their activities after dark, allowing them to produce more in a day, making them wealthier. In their newfound leisure time, they could afford to buy books, listen to recorded performances, and watch movies, resulting in income for authors, musicians, and film directors. Because J. P. Morgan financed corporations, including manufacturing and drug companies, scientists and engineers were able to secure private employment rather than work for the state or under the protection of an aristocratic patron who was entertained by the abstract intellectual work done by the creator.

As *Atlas Shrugged*'s Ellis Wyatt identified:

> What's wealth but the means of expanding one's life? There's two ways one can do that: either by producing more or by producing it faster. And that's what I'm doing, I'm manufacturing time. . . . I'm working to improve my methods, and every hour I save is an hour added to my life. . . . Wealth, Dagny? What greater wealth is there than to own your life and to spend it on growing? Every living thing must grow. It can't stand still. It must grow or perish. (721–22)

Every hour that a man like Ellis Wyatt adds to his life means that more efficient industrial processes and products now exist. With the advent of those comes the growth of many other professions—and the wealth to support them.

The Devastating Effects of the Strike

As the businessmen join the strike, taking their minds and wealth-generating abilities with them, what effect is there?

In the areas of the country where industries have vanished, a regression from modern life to preindustrial conditions takes place. As Rearden and Dagny drive through Michigan's countryside, they visit an abandoned ore mine—and see the "remnants of a crane like a skeleton bending against the sky," a discarded lunch-box at their feet. As they drive through nearby towns, they observe run-down houses, sagging structures—and horse-drawn carriages where cars once traveled. When they reach the area where Dagny finds the abandoned motor, the village of Starnesville, they are met with people dressed in rags with no shoes, drawing wa-ter from wells, living by candlelight in highly unsanitary conditions—who blank-ly stare at their car as if they have appeared from another dimension of space and time. They see the remains of gasoline stations, and isolated telegraph poles. They see chickens loose in the meager vegetable garden, and pigs waddling in refuse. The people appear bedraggled and hopeless. They look much older than their age and as if they are incapable of feeling anything but exhaustion (280–83). What image does this account invoke?

> English peasants in 1086 had little more than enough food to keep them alive, and sometimes not even that. Houses were crude, tempo-rary structures. A peasant owned one set of clothes, best described as rags, and little else. As late as the fifteenth century expenditures of the masses on non-food items such as clothing, heat, light and rent were probably only 13 percent of all expenditures.[7]

When Michigan's industries shut down, its people find themselves living in conditions similar to what eleventh-century peasants endured. They have lost centuries' worth of progress. They are reduced to a state of bare subsistence, and one can no longer afford the luxury of employment as a scientist composer, or philosophy professor. They are on the path to returning to what the West was like prior to Watt, his steam engine, and all of the other advances of the Industrial Revolution: "The hovels of the poor in London and elsewhere were health haz-ards of the highest order. . . . Sanitation was primitive and sewage much the same. In many parts of London, people simply threw their garbage into the street. . . . There were outhouses and cesspools instead of sewers."[8] The tangible effects of the wealth generated through industrialization are plainly visible when looking at how life expectancy has improved as society has become more industrialized.

> The pre-industrial period could generate only minor fluctuations in life expectancy, averaging in the mid-to-high 30s, but the Industrial Revolution created a sustained upward movement. "People lived lon-ger because they were better nourished and sheltered, and cleaner, and thus were less vulnerable to infectious . . . diseases . . . that were pe-culiarly susceptible to improved living standards." The industrial era initiated a gradual but steady march upward regarding English life ex-pectancy, which is currently 74.7 years on average for men and 80.2 for women. "It took thousands of years to increase life expectancy at

birth just over 20 years to the high 20s. Then in just the past two centuries, the length of life . . . in the advanced [i.e., industrialized] countries jumped from less than 30 years to perhaps 75 years."[9]

Starnesville—the town of filthy shacks amongst ruins—provides a stark
reminder of what history has already shown us. It illustrates what happens
when the source of material and spiritual wealth, the industrialist, has withdrawn. Remove the businessman, remove our ability to sustain civilization.
Without the mind, and the businessmen's use of it to create wealth, it is not
possible for others to pursue values beyond those utmost crucial values for
physical survival: food and shelter.

In the absence of industrialists, society returns to a pre-nineteenth-centu-
ry level of existence. Human life shortens in span—death comes more quickly for all. *This* is the result of the mind on strike.

In the days that followed Rearden's strike, what effect was there on the
spirit of the people? A steel shortage causes a number of businesses to fail
and close, shop owners give up their stock to looters, small businessmen commit suicide and panic ensues. In the hours following Dagny's strike, the lights
of New York City go out. All that is left is Wyatt's torch, burning incessant-
ly. There is no mind left to bring the much-needed oil out of the ground. As
Francisco tells Dagny:

> The rebirth of d'Anconia Copper—and of the world—has to start
> here, in the United States. This country was the only country in his-
> tory born, not of chance and blind tribal warfare, but as a rational
> product of man's mind. This country was built on the supremacy of
> reason—and for one magnificent century it redeemed the world. It
> will have to do so again. (771)

WHY THE STRIKE REQUIRED BUSINESSMEN

Given Rand's choice to write a novel about the men of the mind going on strike
in the midst of a collectivist society, her selection of businessmen as the lynchpins
holding the looters' society together was essential. Rand views the businessman
as the "field agent of the army whose lieutenant commander-in-chief is the scientist."[10] She describes her character, Francisco d'Anconia, the industrialist, as being
the perfect blend of his two intellectual fathers, a philosopher and a physicist. In
her view the businessman and the professional intellectual are partners.

Why was the businessman crucial to the strike given its purpose? Because
of all the professions, his mind was the most disdained for being dedicated to
pursuing what is considered the lowest of realms: the material world. Yet his

mind was the one that all others most depended on for the requirements of human flourishing. Industrial civilization and all that it depends on—our release from physical labor, leisure time, art, culture—demands that the businessman be given a special place of honor amongst its "men of the mind." The industrialist not only provides the material means for other professions to exist, his success makes possible our pursuit of spiritual values. Only the businessman is in a position to simultaneously withdraw the material and spiritual wealth that the looters have looted. Only he can sever both sources at once, and with such devastation, simply by uttering one word: "Enough." Only his act of shrugging can figuratively, and literally, turn off the lights of New York City.[11]

Notes

1. Ayn Rand, *For the New Intellectual* (New York: Signet, 1963), p. 88.

2. Ayn Rand, *The Romantic Manifesto: A Philosophy of Literature*, rev. ed. (New York: Signet, 1975), p. 85.

3. B. Reinhard, "McCain blames Wall Street's 'unbridled greed' for economic woes," *Miami Herald* (Sept. 16, 2008), retrieved from www.miamiherald.com.

4. Rand, *For the New Intellectual*, p. 27.

5. *The New Encyclopedia Britannica Micropaedia Ready Reference*, 15th ed., vol. 12 (Chicago: Encyclopedia Britannica, 2002), pp. 528–29.

6. Rand, *For the New Intellectual*, p. 27.

7. J. Simon, *The State of Humanity* (Cambridge, MA: Blackwell, 1995), p. 137.

8. Andrew Bernstein, *The Capitalist Manifesto* (Lanham, Md.: University Press of America, 2005), p. 64.

9. Bernstein, *The Capitalist Manifesto*, p. 120 (see n. 31 for sources cited).

10. Rand, *For the New Intellectual*, 27.

11. I wish to thank the Ayn Rand Institute's Yaron Brook, executive director, and Onkar Ghate, senior fellow, for their insightful editorial advice and their moral support, and its Academic coordinator, Christopher Elsee, whose valuable assistance made it possible for me to have the time to write this essay.

The Money-Making Personality

Ayn Rand

If businessmen are the Atlases, carrying the world on their shoulders and providing the intellectual and productive innovation that makes wealth possible, what makes up the successful businessman? Ayn Rand's tribute to the "money-making personality" was first published in *Cosmopolitan* in April 1963. In this article, she draws a contrast between the men of the mind who make money, and the mindless looters who appropriate it.

The Money-Making Personality

Ayn Rand

Suppose that you have observed two young men on their way through college and, on graduation day, are asked to tell which one of them will make a fortune.

Let us call them Smith and Jones. Both are intelligent, ambitious and come from the same modestly average background. But there are significant differences between them.

Smith is aggressively social and very popular; he belongs to many campus groups and is usually their leader. Jones is quiet, reserved; he does not join group activities; he is usually noticed, but neither liked nor disliked; some people resent him for no apparent reason.

Smith has a wide variety of interests, but is always available for one more undertaking. Jones has chosen an undertaking—the pursuit of some special task or study outside the college curriculum—to which he devotes all of his spare time.

Smith adjusts himself to people easily, but finds it harder to adjust himself to changing circumstances. Jones adjusts himself to circumstances, but is inflexible in regard to people.

Smith's scholastic grades are uniformly excellent. Jones's grades are irregular: he rates "A plus" in some subjects and "C" in others.

Smith's image in people's minds is one of sunny cheerfulness. Jones's image is grimly earnest. But some rare, fleeting signs seem to indicate that in the privacy of their inner worlds their roles are reversed: it is Jones who is serenely cheerful, and Smith who is driven by some grimly nameless dread.

Which one would you choose as the future fortune-maker?

If you subscribe to the currently prevalent ideas, you would choose Smith—and you would be wrong. Jones is the archetype of the Money-Maker, while Smith is a deceptive facsimile who will never *make* money, though he may become rich; to describe him accurately, one would have to call him the "Money-Appropriator."

Prospectors looking for gold know that there exists a mineral which deceives the ignorant by its brilliant glitter: they call it fool's gold. A similar distinction exists between the real producers of wealth and the pseudo-producers, but the mineralogists of the human soul have not learned to differentiate between them.

Most people lump together into the same category all men who become rich, refusing to consider the essential question: the *source* of the riches, the means by which the wealth was acquired.

Money is a tool of exchange; it represents wealth only so long as it can be traded for material goods and services. Wealth does not grow in nature; it has to be produced by men. Nature gives us only the raw materials, but it is man's mind that has to discover the knowledge of how to use them. It is man's thinking and labor that transform the materials into food, clothing, shelter or television sets—into all the goods that men require for their survival, comfort and pleasure.

Behind every step of humanity's long climb from the cave to New York City, there is the man who took that step for the first time—the man who discovered how to make a fire or a wheel or an airplane or an electric light.

When people refuse to consider the source of wealth, what they refuse to recognize is the fact that *wealth is the product of man's intellect*, of his creative ability, fully as much as is art, science, philosophy or any other human value.

The Money-*Maker* is the discoverer who translates his discovery into material goods. In an industrial society with a complex division of labor, it may be one man or a partnership of two: the scientist who discovers new knowledge and the *entrepreneur*—the businessman—who discovers how to use that knowledge, how to organize material resources and human labor into an enterprise producing marketable goods.

The Money-*Appropriator* is an entirely different type of man. He is essentially noncreative—and his basic goal is to acquire an unearned share of the wealth created by others. He seeks to get rich, not by conquering nature, but by manipulating men, not by intellectual effort, but by social maneuvering. He does not produce, he redistributes: he merely switches the wealth already in existence from the pockets of its owners to his own.

The Money-Appropriator may become a politician—or a businessman who "cuts corners"—or that destructive product of a "mixed economy": the businessman who grows rich by means of government favors, such as special privileges, subsidies, franchises; that is, grows rich by means of *legalized force*.

In the present state of our economy, in the chaotic mixture of free enterprise and government controls, it is becoming progressively harder to distinguish the Money-Maker from the Money-Appropriator. When every business is tangled in government regulations, the dividing line between the earned and the unearned grows blurred. Authentic Money-Makers are forced to resort to government help—and some Money-Appropriators are forced, at times, to exercise some productive effort, if only for the sake of their "public image." But if one watches a man's activity over a period of time, one can still see whether his success is due essentially to his productive ability or to political pull.

No single outward characteristic can be taken as a sure sign of the Money-Making personality. The traits ascribed to Smith and Jones may vary. But the net sum of their traits will always add up to the same essentials: the essential characteristic of the Money-Maker is his *independent judgment*; the essential characteristic of the Money-Appropriator is his *social dependence*.

A man of independent judgment is a man of profound self-esteem: he trusts the competence of his own mind to deal with the problems of existence. He looks at the world, wondering: "What can be done?" or "How can things be improved?"

The Money-Maker, above all else, is the originator and innovator. The trait most signally absent from his character is *resignation*, the passive acceptance of the given, the known, the established, the *status quo*. He never says: "What was good enough for my grandfather is good enough for me." He says: "What was good enough for me yesterday will not be good enough tomorrow."

He does not sit waiting for "a break" or for somebody to give him a chance. He makes and takes his own chances. He never whines, "I couldn't help it!"—he *can*, and does.

The men who will never make money are: the hedger who "plays it safe," waiting to follow any trend, and the gambler or plunger who plays blind hunches, on the spur of the moment, on hearsay, on his own unaccountable feelings.

The Money-Maker does neither. He does not wait for trends—he sets them. He does not gamble—he takes calculated risks, assuming the very responsibility which those two attempt to bypass: the responsibility of judgment.

The man who will never make money has an "employee mentality," even in an executive's job; he tries to get away with a minimum of effort, as if any exertion were an imposition; and when he fails to take the proper action, he cries: "But nobody told me to!"

The Money-Maker has an "employer mentality," even when he is only an office boy—which is why he does not remain an office boy for long. In any job he holds, he is committed to a maximum of effort; he learns everything he can about the business, much more than his job requires. He never needs to be told—even when confronting a situation outside his usual duties. These are the reasons why he rises from office boy to company president.

Behind his usually grim, expressionless face, the Money-Maker is committed to his work with the passion of a lover, the fire of a crusader, the dedication of a saint and the endurance of a martyr. As a rule, his creased forehead and his balance sheets are the only evidence of it he can allow the world to see.

Neither space, time nor age can limit the Money-Maker's extravagant energy and drive.

At the age of twenty-two, George Westinghouse observed the frequency of railroad accidents caused by inadequate brakes—and invented the Westinghouse Air Brake which, with some improvements, is used to this day on all trains throughout the world.

At the age of sixty-nine, Cornelius Vanderbilt—who had made a fortune in the shipping business—saw that railroads were to be the chief transportation medium of the future, gave up shipping and became one of the greatest figures in our railroad history, the creator of the New York Central system.

Arthur Vining Davis, who died in 1962 at the age of ninety-five, was the man who built, singlehanded, one of America's greatest industrial concerns: Alcoa (Aluminum Company of America). He joined it at the age of twenty-one, "almost literally as the first hired hand," wrote *Fortune*. "In the decades following the turn of the century, when Alcoa *was* the aluminum industry, A. V. Davis *was* Alcoa." His associates said that he had "absolute confidence in his own business acumen and judgment." He was described as follows: "He has a fierce impatience to get things done . . . is intolerably intolerant of wits less nimble than his own . . . and has a noble temper."

At the age of eighty-nine, with a fortune estimated at $350,000,000, Davis moved to Florida and embarked upon an entirely new career that involved a fantastic variety of new interests: Florida real estate developments, nurseries, airlines, hotels, banks, dairy farms, etc.—all of which he proceeded to manage with splendid efficiency and growing success. When he was questioned about his goals, he answered brusquely, "I buy properties with the thought of making money."

Observe that his new ventures were long-range developments which required decades before they could pay off. The men who dream of winning a fortune on a sweepstakes ticket would never understand his psychology.

It is only the Money-Appropriator who lives and acts short-range, never looking beyond the immediate moment. The Money-Maker lives, thinks and acts long-range. Having complete confidence in his own judgment, he has complete confidence in the future, and only long-range projects can hold his interest. To a Money-Maker, as well as to an artist, work is not a painful duty or a necessary evil, but *a way of life*; to him, productive activity is the essence, the meaning and the enjoyment of existence; it is the state of being alive.

Arthur Vining Davis had created Alcoa by the extraordinary range of his vision. He was a true builder—and, in order to feel alive, he had to remain a builder to his last moment.

That long-range vision is characteristic of all the great Money-Makers. It was characteristic of J. P. Morgan, who made his fortune by his ability to judge which industries held the potential of future growth and to finance, as well as organize, their integration into industrial giants. United States Steel is one of his monuments, as well as the monument of Andrew Carnegie whose company was the central property of that merger and who started out in life as a steelworker.

The Money-Maker's ability to defy established customs, to stand alone against storms of criticism and predictions of failure, was eloquently demonstrated by Henry Ford. Ford was a revolutionary innovator both in technology and in economics. He was the first man to discover the financial advantages of mass production—the first to use an assembly line—the first to refute in practice the theory of "class-warfare" by offering his workers an unsolicited raise in wages, higher than any union scale at the time; which he did, not for an altruistic purpose, but for the honorably rational purpose of attracting the ablest kind of labor and obtaining a higher production efficiency.

In his lifetime, Ford received no recognition of his achievements from the intellectuals who were swimming with the tide of collectivism and indulging in the "robber-barons" type of smears against all great industrialists. Such smears alleged that the men who had created this country's magnificent prosperity had done it by robbing the men who had *not* created it.

Tom M. Girdler, the last living representative of America's great era, who rose from the ranks of labor to the presidency of Republic Steel, was a special victim of the collectivist tide. An intransigent advocate and embodiment of independence, Girdler fought a heroic battle against sundry politicians and intellectuals who singled him out as the object of particularly savage attacks.

Many modern commentators of the collectivist persuasion claim that the day of the great individualist—of the independent mind—is past (and that future progress will be achieved somehow by everybody in general and nobody in particular). But if we look at the Money-Makers of the present who fought their way to success against the barrier of ever-increasing political obstacles and confiscatory taxation, we see the same essential characteristic: the independent judgment that discovers the new and pursues the untried.

"If a man of the Renaissance were alive today," writes *Fortune*, "he might find running an American corporation the most rewarding outlet for his prodigious and manifold talents. In it he could be scientist, artist, inventor, builder and statesman. . . . It would be a company created in a man's image, molded by him in every significant detail, building a product—the embodiment of his genius—that would be unique in all the world. He would gather around him extraordinary associates, selected with meticulous care, who would share his passions and his enthusiasms, who would create and build with him.

"Such a man, as it happens, does exist. He is Edwin H. Land; his company is Polaroid Corporation of Cambridge, Massachusetts, which makes the famous sixty-second camera."

Land's history is the clearest modern example of an authentic Money-Maker's role: like Edison and Westinghouse, he is an inventor-industrialist.

Starting from scratch, he has made a fortune estimated at about one hundred million dollars.

The idea of a camera that would take, develop and produce finished pictures in a single operation lasting a few seconds would have been pronounced impossible by all the experts. The problems seemed insurmountable. Land solved them in six months. "I would be willing to bet," said one of his associates, "that one hundred Ph.D.s would not have been able to duplicate Land's feat in ten years of uninterrupted work."

Land encountered and withstood the opposition of the routine mentalities that greets every great innovator. "Land's revolution was at first derided by all the experts, the people who always know why a revolution cannot succeed. These experts included virtually every camera dealer in the country, every 'advanced' amateur photographer, and nearly everyone on Wall Street."

Land won, as every great innovator does when and if he is left free to win.

It is significant that many of the new millionaires made their fortunes either on new inventions or on their ability to revive old companies perishing from bad management.

One of the most interesting figures in the second group is James E. Robison, president of Indian Head Mills. A true Money-Maker in the stagnant textile industry—an industry stifled by the complex coils of protective tariffs and cotton subsidies—Robison made a fortune by buying run-down textile mills and turning them into lively, profit-making enterprises through his expert management.

His policy rests on opposing all forms of stagnation, and a swift, decisive manner of upsetting traditions or routines. *Fortune* calls him: "the advocate of the un-*status* quo."

At a time when most businessmen are silent, evasive or apologetic about issues of political philosophy, Robison is a militant crusader for pure capitalism. He seems to be fully aware of the fundamental crisis of our age, and he is not afraid to speak.

He wrote a policy manual for Indian Head Mills, which declares: "The objective of this company is to increase the intrinsic value of the common stock"—and explains that the company is in business not "to grow bigger for the sake of size, nor to become more diversified, nor to make the most or best of anything, nor to provide jobs, have the most modern plants, the happiest customers, lead in new product development, or to achieve any other status which has no relationship to the economic use of capital.

"Any or all of these may be, from time to time, a means to our objective, but means and ends must never be confused. Indian Head Mills is in business solely to improve the inherent value of the common shareholder's equity in the company."

That this sounds shocking is a measure of the evasion permeating our cultural atmosphere: this is mere economic common sense, and no productive company can function otherwise.

In his youth, Robison was profoundly influenced by Professor Malcolm P. McNair of the Harvard Business School, who wrote: "The world's work has to be done, and people have to take responsibility for their own work and their own lives. Too much emphasis on human relations encourages people to feel sorry for themselves, makes it easier for them to slough off responsibility, to find excuses for failure, to act like children."

This passage holds a clue to the tragic situation of the Money-Makers. They are the only group of men who fully realize that "the world's work has to be done"— and they go on doing it, under a deluge of abuse, accusations and ever-growing demands. They go on, unable to defend themselves or fully to understand, knowing only that the survival of the world hangs on their unremitting effort.

They are the silent, unknown and forgotten men of our culture.

It is only the Money-Appropriator who hires personal press agents and postures in the public spotlight. It is the Money-Appropriator who flaunts his money in vulgar displays of ostentation, who craves "prestige" and notice and hangs eagerly on the fringes of "cafe society."

The Money-Maker does not care for money as such. Money, to him, is a means to an end—the means for expanding the range of his activity. Most Money-Makers are indifferent to luxury, and their manner of living is startlingly modest in relation to their wealth.

A Wall Street friend once said about Charles Allen, head of the investment banking house of Allen & Company, who has a large fortune and the simplest of wants: "Charlie has no interest in money except making it."

Not all the Money-Makers achieve enormous wealth; their success depends in large measure on the degree of freedom still remaining in their particular field. Some realize only a small fraction of their creative potential; some are never heard of.

In today's conditions, it is impossible to guess their actual number. I once asked Alan Greenspan, president of Townsend-Greenspan & Company, economic consultants, to venture an estimate on what percentage of men in our business world he would regard as authentic Money-Makers—as men of fully sovereign, independent judgment. He thought for a moment and answered, a little sadly: "On Wall Street—about five percent; in industry—about fifteen."

It is this small, lonely minority that carries our world on its shoulders.

Loneliness is the underground to which we have condemned the Money-Maker—a bewildered loneliness that is not erased by his occasional moments of boisterous gaiety. It is the loneliness of sensing that he is the victim of some incomprehensible injustice. His coldly uncommunicative manner hides his enormous, frustrated benevolence, his childlike innocence—and his profoundly earned pride.

Toward the end of his life, Collis P. Huntington—one of the builders of the Central Pacific Railroad, a man of gigantic ability and mixed premises, who had the soul of a Money-Maker, but resorted, at times, to the methods of a Money-Appropriator—made a startling change in his manner of living. He had lived his life in Spartan austerity, contemptuous of all material luxuries and frivolities, but in his sixties he turned to a sudden, frantic orgy of extravagance, indiscriminately buying palatial residences, French furniture, real works of art and costly trash—the sort of things he had condemned his partners for buying.

Among these haphazard acquisitions, there was a painting, depicting an ancient scene, for which he paid $25,000—an action that seemed incomprehensible to his contemporaries. But here is what Huntington wrote about that painting in his autobiographical notes:

> There are seven figures in it—three cardinals of the different orders of their religion. There is an old missionary that has just returned; he is showing his scars, where his hands are cut all over; he is telling a story to these cardinals; they are dressed in luxury. One of them is playing with a dog; one is asleep; there is only one looking at him— looking at him with that kind of an expression saying what a fool you are that you should go out and suffer for the human race when we have such a good time at home. I lose the picture in the story when I look at it. I sometimes sit half an hour looking at that picture.

What story was Huntington seeing? He was seeing a lonely, unappreciated fighter. . . . He was seeing the Money-Maker, the fighter for man's survival in the jungle of inanimate matter—the man who alone remembers that the world's work has to be done.

Part 2

Why Is Business "Public Enemy #1"?

"The victim of the intellectuals' most infamous injustice was the businessman."

—Ayn Rand, "For the New Intellectual," 1960

America's Persecuted Minority: Big Business

Ayn Rand

Ayn Rand demonstrates how political power has been used to quash the earned economic power of businessmen. Since the passage of the Sherman Act in 1890, America's government has persecuted businessmen by subjecting them to special laws not applicable to other citizens, making them the scapegoats for the failures of the mixed economy.

Note: This lecture was originally delivered on November 17, 1961, at the Ford Hall Forum in Boston.

America's Persecuted Minority: Big Business

Ayn Rand

If a small group of men were always regarded as guilty, in any clash with any other group, regardless of the issues or circumstances involved, would you call it persecution? If this group were always made to pay for the sins, errors, or failures of any other group, would you call *that* persecution? If this group had to live under a silent reign of terror, under special laws, from which all other people were immune, laws which the accused could not grasp or define in advance and which the accuser could interpret in any way he pleased—would you call *that* persecution? If this group were penalized, not for its faults, but for its virtues, not for its incompetence, but for its ability, not for its failures, but for its achievements, and the greater the achievement, the greater the penalty—would you call *that* persecution?

If your answer is "yes"—then ask yourself what sort of monstrous injustice you are condoning, supporting, or perpetrating. That group is the American businessmen.

The defense of minority rights is acclaimed today, virtually by everyone, as a moral principle of a high order. But this principle, which forbids discrimination, is applied by most of the "liberal" intellectuals in a *discriminatory* manner: it is applied only to racial or religious minorities. It is not applied to that small, exploited, denounced, defenseless minority which consists of businessmen.

Yet every ugly, brutal aspect of injustice toward racial or religious minorities is being practiced toward businessmen. For instance, consider the evil of condemning some men and absolving others, without a hearing, regardless of the facts. Today's "liberals" consider a businessman guilty in any conflict with a labor union, regardless of the facts or issues involved, and boast that they will not cross a picket line "right or wrong." Consider the evil of judging people by a double standard and of denying to some the rights granted to others. Today's "liberals" recognize the workers' (the majority's) right to their livelihood (their wages), but deny the businessmen's (the minority's) right to *their* livelihood (their profits). If workers struggle for higher wages, this is hailed as "social gains"; if businessmen struggle for higher profits, this is damned as "selfish greed." If the workers' standard of living is low, the "liberals" blame it

79

on the businessmen; but if the businessmen attempt to improve their economic efficacy, to expand their markets, and to enlarge the financial returns of their enterprises, thus making higher wages and lower prices possible, the same "liberals" denounce it as "commercialism." If a noncommercial foundation—i.e., a group which did not have to *earn* its funds—sponsors a television show, advocating its particular views, the "liberals" hail it as "enlightenment," "education," "art," and "public service"; if a businessman sponsors a television show and wants it to reflect *his* views, the "liberals" scream, calling it "censorship," "pressure," and "dictatorial rule." When three locals of the International Brotherhood of Teamsters deprived New York City of its milk supply for fifteen days—no moral indignation or condemnation was heard from the "liberal" quarters; but just imagine what would happen if *businessmen* stopped that milk supply for one hour—and how swiftly they would be struck down by that legalized lynching or pogrom known as "trust-busting."

Whenever, in any era, culture, or society, you encounter the phenomenon of prejudice, injustice, persecution, and blind, unreasoning hatred directed at some minority group—look for the gang that has something to gain from that persecution, look for those who have a vested interest in the destruction of these particular sacrificial victims. Invariably, you will find that the persecuted minority serves as a scapegoat for some movement that does not want the nature of its own goals to be known. Every movement that seeks to enslave a country, every dictatorship or potential dictatorship, needs some minority group as a scapegoat which it can blame for the nation's troubles and use as a justification of its own demands for dictatorial powers. In Soviet Russia, the scapegoat was the bourgeoisie; in Nazi Germany, it was the Jewish people; in America, it is the businessmen.

America has not yet reached the stage of a dictatorship. But, paving the way to it, for many decades past, the businessmen have served as the scapegoat for *statist* movements of all kinds: communist, fascist, or welfare. For whose sins and evils did the businessmen take the blame? For the sins and evils of the bureaucrats.

A disastrous intellectual package-deal, put over on us by the theoreticians of statism, is the equation of *economic* power with *political* power. You have heard it expressed in such bromides as: "A hungry man is not free," or "It makes no difference to a worker whether he takes orders from a businessman or from a bureaucrat." Most people accept these equivocations—and yet they know that the poorest laborer in America is freer and more secure than the richest commissar in Soviet Russia. What is the basic, the essential, the crucial principle that differentiates freedom from slavery? It is the principle of voluntary action *versus* physical coercion or compulsion.

The difference between political power and any other kind of social "power," between a government and any private organization, is the fact that *a government holds a legal monopoly on the use of physical force.* This distinction is so important and so seldom recognized today that I must urge you to keep it in mind. Let me repeat it: *a government holds a legal monopoly on the use of physical force.*

No individual or private group or private organization has the legal power to initiate the use of physical force against other individuals or groups and to compel them to act against their own voluntary choice. Only a government holds that power. The nature of governmental action is: *coercive* action. The nature of political power is: the power to force obedience under threat of physical injury—the threat of property expropriation, imprisonment, or death.

Foggy metaphors, sloppy images, unfocused poetry, and equivocations—such as "A hungry man is not free"—do not alter the fact that *only* political power is the power of physical coercion and that freedom, in a political context, has only one meaning: *the absence of physical coercion.*

The only proper function of the government of a free country is to act as an agency which protects the individual's rights, i.e., which protects the individual from physical violence. Such a government does not have the right to *initiate* the use of physical force against anyone—a right which the individual does not possess and, therefore, cannot delegate to any agency. But the individual does possess the right of self-defense and *that* is the right which he delegates to the government, for the purpose of an orderly, legally defined enforcement. A proper government has the right to use physical force *only* in retaliation and *only* against those who initiate its use. The proper functions of a government are: the police, to protect men from criminals; the military forces, to protect men from foreign invaders; and the law courts, to protect men's property and contracts from breach by force or fraud, and to settle disputes among men according to objectively defined laws.

These, implicitly, were the political principles on which the Constitution of the United States was based; implicitly, but not explicitly. There were contradictions in the Constitution, which allowed the statists to gain an entering wedge, to enlarge the breach, and, gradually, to wreck the structure.

A statist is a man who believes that some men have the right to force, coerce, enslave, rob, and murder others. To be put into practice, this belief has to be implemented by the political doctrine that the government—the state—has the right to *initiate* the use of physical force against its citizens. How often force is to be used, against whom, to what extent, for what purpose and for whose benefit, are irrelevant questions. The basic principle and the ultimate results of all statist doctrines are the same: dictatorship and destruction. The rest is only a matter of time.

Now let us consider the question of economic power.

What is economic power? It is the power to produce and to trade what one has produced. In a free economy, where no man or group of men can use physical coercion against anyone, economic power can be achieved only by *voluntary* means: by the voluntary choice and agreement of all those who participate in the process of production and trade. In a free market, all prices, wages, and profits are determined—not by the arbitrary whim of the rich or of the poor, not by anyone's "greed" or by anyone's need—but by the law of supply and demand. The mechanism of a free market reflects and sums up all the economic choices and decisions made by all the participants. Men trade their goods or services by mutual consent to mutual advantage, according to their own independent, uncoerced judgment. A man can grow rich only if he is able to offer better *values*—better products or services, at a lower price—than others are able to offer.

Wealth, in a free market, is achieved by a free, general, "democratic" vote—by the sales and the purchases of every individual who takes part in the economic life of the country. Whenever you buy one product rather than another, you are voting for the success of some manufacturer. And, in this type of voting, every man votes only on those matters which he is qualified to judge: on his own preferences, interests, and needs. No one has the power to decide for others or to substitute *his* judgment for theirs; no one has the power to appoint himself "the voice of the public" and to leave the public voiceless and disfranchised.

Now let me define the difference between economic power and political power: economic power is exercised by means of a *positive*, by offering men a reward, an incentive, a payment, a value; political power is exercised by means of a *negative*, by the threat of punishment, injury, imprisonment, destruction. The businessman's tool is *values*; the bureaucrat's tool is *fear.*

America's industrial progress, in the short span of a century and a half, has acquired the character of a legend: it has never been equaled anywhere on earth, in any period of history. The American businessmen, as a class, have demonstrated the greatest productive genius and the most spectacular achievements ever recorded in the economic history of mankind. What reward did they receive from our culture and its intellectuals? The position of a hated, persecuted minority. The position of a scapegoat for the evils of the bureaucrats.

A system of pure, unregulated laissez-faire capitalism has never yet existed anywhere. What did exist were only so-called mixed economies, which means: a mixture, in varying degrees, of freedom and controls, of voluntary choice and government coercion, of capitalism and statism. America was the freest country on earth, but elements of statism were present in her economy from the start. These elements kept growing, under the influence of her intellectuals who were predominantly committed to the philosophy of statism. The intellectuals—the ideologists, the interpreters, the assessors of public events—were tempted by the opportunity to seize political power, relinquished by all other social groups, and to establish their own versions of a "good" society at the point of a gun, i.e., by means of legalized physical coercion. They denounced the free businessmen as exponents of "selfish greed" and glorified the bureaucrats as "public servants." In evaluating social problems, they kept damning "economic power" and exonerating political power, thus switching the burden of guilt from the politicians to the businessmen.

All the evils, abuses, and iniquities, popularly ascribed to businessmen and to capitalism, were not caused by an unregulated economy or by a free market, but by government intervention into the economy. The giants of American industry—such as James Jerome Hill or Commodore Vanderbilt or Andrew Carnegie or J. P. Morgan—were self-made men who earned their fortunes by personal ability, by free trade on a free market. But there existed another kind of businessmen, the products of a mixed economy, the men with political pull, who made fortunes by means of special privileges granted to them by the government, such men as the Big Four of the Central Pacific Railroad. It was the political power behind their activities—the power of forced, unearned, economically unjustified privileges—that caused dislocations in the country's economy, hardships, depressions, and mounting public protests. But it was the free market and the free businessmen that took the blame. Every calamitous consequence of government controls was used as a justification for the extension of the controls and of the government's power over the economy.

If I were asked to choose the date which marks the turning point on the road to the ultimate destruction of American industry, and the most infamous piece of legislation in American history, I would choose the year 1890 and the Sherman Act—which began that grotesque, irrational, malignant growth of unenforceable, uncompliable, unjudicable contradictions known as the antitrust laws.

Under the antitrust laws, a man becomes a criminal from the moment he goes into business, no matter what he does. If he complies with one of these laws, he faces criminal prosecution under several others. For instance, if he charges prices which some bureaucrats judge as too high, he can be prosecuted for monopoly, or, rather, for a successful "intent to monopolize"; if he charges prices lower than those of his competitors, he can be prosecuted for "unfair competition" or "restraint of trade"; and if he charges the same prices as his competitors, he can be prosecuted for "collusion" or "conspiracy."

I recommend to your attention an excellent book entitled *The Antitrust Laws of the U.S.A.* by A. D. Neale.[1] It is a scholarly, dispassionate, objective study; the author, a British civil servant, is not a champion of free enterprise; as far as one can tell, he may probably be classified as a "liberal." But he does not confuse facts with interpretations, he keeps them severely apart; and the facts he presents are a horror story.

Mr. Neale points out that the prohibition of "restraint of trade" is the essence of antitrust—and that no exact definition of what constitutes "restraint of trade" can be given. Thus no one can tell what the law forbids or permits one to do; the interpretation of these laws is left entirely up to the courts. A businessman or his lawyer has to study the whole body of the so-called case law—the whole record of court cases, precedents, and decisions—in order to get even a generalized idea of the current meaning of these laws; except that the precedents may be upset and the decisions reversed tomorrow or next week or next year. "The courts in the United States have been engaged ever since 1890 in deciding case by case exactly what the law proscribes. No broad definition can really unlock the meaning of the statute . . ."[2]

This means that a businessman has no way of knowing in advance whether the action he takes is legal or illegal, whether he is guilty or innocent. It means that a businessman has to live under the threat of a sudden, unpredictable disaster, taking the risk of losing everything he owns or being sentenced to jail, with his career, his reputation, his property, his fortune, the achievement of his whole lifetime left at the mercy of any ambitious young bureaucrat who, for any reason, public or private, may choose to start proceedings against him.

Retroactive (or *ex post facto*) law—i.e., a law that punishes a man for an action which was not legally defined as a crime at the time he committed it—is rejected by and contrary to the entire tradition of Anglo-Saxon jurisprudence. It is a form of persecution practiced only in dictatorships and forbidden by every civilized code of law. It is specifically forbidden by the United States Constitution. It is not supposed to exist in the United States and it is not applied to anyone—except to businessmen. A case in which a man cannot know until he is convicted whether the action he took in the past was legal or illegal, is certainly a case of retroactive law.

I recommend to you a brilliant little book entitled *Ten Thousand Commandments* by Harold Fleming.[3] It is written for the layman and presents—in clear, simple, logical terms, with a wealth of detailed, documented evidence—such a picture of the antitrust laws that "nightmare" is too feeble a word to describe it.

> One of the hazards [writes Mr. Fleming] that sales managers must now take into account is that some policy followed today in the light of the best legal opinion may next year be reinterpreted as illegal. In such case the crime and the penalty may be retroactive. . . . Another kind of hazard consists in the possibility of treble damage suits, also possibly retroactive. Firms which, with the best of intentions, run afoul of the law on one of the above counts, are open to treble damage suits under the antitrust laws, even though their offense was a course of conduct that everyone considered, at the time, quite legal as well as ethical, but that a subsequent reinterpretation of the law found to be illegal.[4]

What do businessmen say about it? In a speech entitled "Guilty Before Trial" (May 18, 1950), Benjamin F. Fairless, then President of United States Steel Corporation, said:

> Gentlemen, I don't have to tell you that if we persist in that kind of a system of law—and if we enforce it impartially against all offenders—virtually every business in America, big and small, is going to have to be run from Atlanta, Sing Sing, Leavenworth, or Alcatraz.

The legal treatment accorded to actual criminals is much superior to that accorded to businessmen. The criminal's rights are protected by objective laws, objective procedures, objective rules of evidence. A criminal is presumed to be innocent until he is proved guilty. Only businessmen—the producers, the providers, the supporters, the Atlases who carry our whole economy on their shoulders—are regarded as guilty by nature and are required to prove their innocence, without any definable criteria of innocence or proof, and are left at the mercy of the whim, the favor, or the malice of any publicity-seeking politician, any scheming statist, any envious mediocrity who might chance to work his way into a bureaucratic job and who feels a yen to do some trust-busting.

The better or more honorable kind of government officials have repeatedly protested against the non-objective nature of the antitrust laws. In the same speech, Mr. Fairless quotes a statement made by Lowell Mason, who was then a member of the Federal Trade Commission:

> American business is being harassed, bled, and even blackjacked under a preposterous crazy quilt system of laws, many of which are unintelligible, unenforceable and unfair. There is such a welter of laws governing interstate commerce that the Government literally can find some charge to bring against any concern it chooses to prosecute. I say that this system is an outrage.

Further, Mr. Fairless quotes a comment written by Supreme Court Justice Jackson when he was the head of the Antitrust Division of the Department of Justice:

> It is impossible for a lawyer to determine what business conduct will be pronounced lawful by the Courts. This situation is embarrassing to businessmen wishing to obey the law and to Government officials attempting to enforce it.

That embarrassment, however, is not shared by all members of the government. Mr. Fleming's book quotes the following statement made by Emanuel Celler, Chairman of the House Judiciary Committee, at a symposium of the New York

State Bar Association, in January 1950:

> I want to make it clear that I would vigorously oppose any antitrust
> laws that attempted to particularize violations, giving bills of par-
> ticulars to replace general principles. The law must remain fluid, al-
> lowing for a dynamic society.[5]

I want to make it clear that *"fluid law"* is a euphemism for *"arbitrary power"*—that "fluidity" is the chief characteristic of the law under any dictatorship—
and that the sort of *"dynamic society"* whose laws are so fluid that they flood and
drown the country may be seen in Nazi Germany or Soviet Russia.

The tragic irony of that whole issue is the fact that the antitrust laws were
created and, to this day, are supported by the so-called conservatives, by the
alleged defenders of free enterprise. This is a grim proof of the fact that capitalism has never had any proper, philosophical defenders—and a measure
of the extent to which its alleged champions lacked any political principles,
any knowledge of economics, and any understanding of the nature of political power. The concept of *free* competition *enforced* by law is a grotesque
contradiction in terms. It means: forcing people to be free at the point of a gun.
It means: protecting people's freedom by the arbitrary rule of unanswerable
bureaucratic edicts.

What were the historical causes that led to the passage of the Sherman
Act? I quote from the book by Mr. Neale:

> The impetus behind the movement for the earliest legislation gath-
> ered strength during the 1870's and the 1880's. . . . After the Civil
> War the railways with their privileges, charters, and subsidies be-
> came the main objects of suspicion and hostility. Many bodies with
> revealing names like "The National Anti-Monopoly Cheap Freight
> Railway League" sprang up.[6]

This is an eloquent example of the businessmen serving as scapegoat,
taking the blame for the sins of the politicians. It was the politically granted
privileges—the charters and subsidies of the railroads—that people rebelled
against; it was these privileges that had placed the railroads of the West outside the reach of competition and had given them a monopolistic power, with
all its consequent abuses. But the remedy, written into law by a *Republican*
Congress, consisted of destroying the businessmen's freedom and of extend-
ing the power of political controls over the economy.

If you wish to observe the real American tragedy, compare the ideological motivation of the antitrust laws to their actual results. I quote from Mr. Neale's book:

It seems likely that American distrust of all sources of unchecked power is a more deep-rooted and persistent motive behind the antitrust policy than any economic belief or any radical political trend. This distrust may be seen in many spheres of American life . . . . It is expressed in the theories of "checks and balances" and of "separation of powers." In the United States the fact that some men possess power over the activities and fortunes of others is sometimes recognized as inevitable but never accepted as satisfactory. It is always hoped that any particular holder of power, *whether political or economic*, will be subject to the threat of encroachment by other authorities. . . . [Italics mine.]

At one with this basic motivation of antitrust is its reliance on legal process and judicial remedy rather than on administrative regulation. The famous prescription of the Massachusetts Bill of Rights—"to the end it may be a government of laws and not of men"—is a favourite American quotation and an essential one for understanding antitrust. Without this factor it would be impossible to explain the degree of acceptance—so astonishing to those outside the United States—that is accorded to the antitrust policy by those interests, especially "big business" interests, which are frequently and expensively subject to its discipline.[7]

Here is the tragedy of what happens to human intentions without a clearly defined philosophical theory to guide their practical implementation. The first free society in history destroyed its freedom—in the name of protecting freedom. The failure to differentiate between *political* and *economic* power allowed men to suppose that coercion could be a proper "balance" to production, that both were activities of the same order which could serve as a "check" on each other, that the "authority" of a businessman and the "authority" of a bureaucrat were interchangeable rivals for the same social function. Seeking "a government of laws and not of men," the advocates of antitrust delivered the entire American economy into the power of as arbitrary a government of men as any dictatorship could hope to establish.

In the absence of any rational criteria of judgment, people attempted to judge the immensely complex issues of a free market by so superficial a standard as *"bigness."* You hear it to this day: *"big* business," *"big* government," or *"big* labor" are denounced as threats to society, with no concern for the nature, source, or function of the "bigness," as if *size* as such were evil. This type of reasoning would mean that a *"big"* genius, like Edison, and a *"big"* gangster, like Stalin, were equal malefactors: one flooded the world with immeasurable values and the other with incalculable slaughter, but both did it on a very *big* scale. I doubt whether anyone would care to equate these two—yet *this* is the precise difference between big business and big government. The sole means by which a government can grow big is physical force; the sole means by which a business can grow big, in a free economy, is productive achievement.

The only actual factor required for the existence of free competition is: the unhampered, unobstructed operation of the mechanism of a free market. The only action which a government can take to protect free competition is: *Laissez-faire!*—which, in free translation, means: *Hands off!* But the antitrust laws established exactly opposite conditions—and achieved the exact opposite of the results they had been intended to achieve.

There is no way to legislate competition; there are no standards by which one could define who should compete with whom, how many competitors should exist in any given field, what should be their relative strength or their so-called "relevant markets," what prices they should charge, what methods of competition are "fair" or "unfair." None of these can be answered, because *these* precisely are the questions that can be answered only by the mechanism of a free market.

With no principles, standards, or criteria to guide it, the antitrust case law is the record of seventy years of sophistry, casuistry, and hair-splitting, as absurd and as removed from any contact with reality as the debates of medieval scholastics. With only this difference: the scholastics had better reasons for the questions they raised—and no specific human lives or fortunes hung on the outcome of their debates.

Let me give you a few examples of antitrust cases. In the case of *Associated Press v. United States* of 1945, the Associated Press was found guilty, because its bylaws restricted its membership and made it very difficult for newly established newspapers to join. I quote from Mr. Neale's book:

> It was argued in defense of the Associated Press that there were other news agencies from which new entrants might draw their news. . . . The Court held that . . . Associated Press was collectively organized to secure competitive advantages for members over non-members and, as such, was in restraint of trade, even though the non-members were not necessarily prevented altogether from competing. [The Associated Press news service was considered so important a facility that] by keeping it exclusive to themselves the members of the association impose a real hardship on *would-be competitors*. . . . It is no defense that the members have built up a facility . . . for themselves; new entrants must still be allowed to share it on reasonable terms *unless it is practicable* for them to compete without it. [Italics mine.][8]

Whose *rights* are here being violated? And whose *whim* is being implemented by the power of the law? What qualifies one to be "a would-be competitor"? If I decided to start competing with General Motors tomorrow, what part of their facilities would they have to share with me in order to make it "practicable" for me to compete with them?

In the case of *Milgram v. Loew's*, of 1951, the consistent refusal of the major distributors of motion pictures to grant first-runs to a drive-in theater was held to be a proof of *collusion*. Each company had obviously valid reasons for its refusal, and the defense argued that each had made its own independent decision without knowing the decisions of the others. But the Court ruled that "consciously parallel business practices" are sufficient proof of conspiracy and that "further proof of actual agreement among the defendants is unnecessary." The Court of Appeals upheld this decision, suggesting that evidence of parallel action should transfer the burden of proof to the defendants "to explain away the inference of joint action," which they had not, apparently, explained away.

Consider for a moment the implications of *this* case. If three businessmen reach independently the same blatantly obvious business decision—do they then have to prove that they did *not* conspire? Or if two businessmen observe an intelligent business policy originated by the third—should they refrain from adopting it, for fear of a conspiracy charge? Or if they do adopt it, should he then find himself dragged into court and charged with conspiracy, on the ground of the actions taken by two men he had never heard of? And how, then, is he "to explain away" his presumed guilt and prove himself innocent?

In the case of patents, the antitrust laws seem to respect a patent owner's right—so long as he is alone in using his patent and does not share it with anyone else. But if he decides not to engage in a patent war with a competitor who holds patents of the same general category—if they both decide to abandon that alleged "dog-eat-dog" policy of which businessmen are so often accused—if they decide to pool their patents and to license them to a few other manufacturers of their own choice—*then* the antitrust laws crack down on them both. The penalties, in such patent-pool cases, involve compulsory licensing of the patents to any and all comers—or the outright confiscation of the patents.

I quote from Mr. Neale's book:

> The compulsory licensing of patents—even valid patents lawfully acquired through the research efforts of the company's own employees—is intended not as punishment but as a way in which rival companies may be brought into the market. . . . In the *I.C.I. and duPont* case of 1952, for example, Judge Ryan . . . ordered the compulsory licensing of their existing patents in the fields to which their restrictive agreements applied and improvement patents but not new patents in these fields. In this case an auxiliary remedy was awarded which has become common in recent years. Both I.C.I. and duPont were ordered to provide applicants, at a reasonable charge, with technical manuals which would show in detail how the patents were practiced.[9]

This, mind you, is not regarded as "punitive"!

Whose mind, ability, achievement, and rights are here sacrificed—and for *whose* unearned benefit?

The most shocking court decision in this grim progression (up to, but not including, the year 1961) was written—as one would almost expect—by a distinguished "conservative," Judge Learned Hand. The victim was ALCOA. The case was *United States v. Aluminum Company of America* of 1945.

Under the antitrust laws, monopoly, as such, is not illegal; what *is* illegal is the "intent to monopolize." To find ALCOA guilty, Judge Learned Hand had to find evidence that ALCOA had taken aggressive action to exclude competitors from its market. Here is the kind of evidence which he found and on which he based the ruling that has blocked the energy of one of America's greatest industrial concerns. I quote from Judge Hand's opinion:

> It was not inevitable that it [ALCOA] should always anticipate increases in the demand for ingot and be prepared to supply them. Nothing compelled it to keep doubling and redoubling its capacity before others entered the field. It insists that it never excluded competitors; but we can think of no more effective exclusion than progressively to embrace each new opportunity as it opened, and to face every newcomer with new capacity already geared into a great organization, having the advantage of experience, trade connections and the elite of personnel.[10]

Here, the meaning and purpose of the antitrust laws come blatantly and explicitly into the open, the only meaning and purpose these laws *could* have, whether their authors intended it or not: the penalizing of ability for being ability, the penalizing of success for being success, and the sacrifice of productive genius to the demands of envious mediocrity.

If such a principle were applied to all productive activity, if a man of intelligence were forbidden "to embrace each new opportunity as it opened," for fear of discouraging some coward or fool who might wish to compete with him, it would mean that none of us, in any profession, should venture forward, or rise, or improve, because any form of personal progress—be it a typist's greater speed, or an artist's greater canvas, or a doctor's greater percentage of cures—can discourage the kind of newcomers who haven't yet started, but who expect to start competing at the top.

As a small, but crowning touch, I will quote Mr. Neale's footnote to his account of the ALCOA case:

> It is of some interest to note that the main ground on which economic writers have condemned the aluminum monopoly has been

precisely that ALCOA consistently failed to embrace opportunities for expansion and so underestimated the demand for the metal that the United States was woefully short of productive capacity at the outset of both world wars.[11]

Now I will ask you to bear in mind the nature, the essence, and the record of the antitrust laws, when I mention the ultimate climax which makes the rest of that sordid record seem insignificant: the *General Electric* case of 1961.

The list of the accused in that case reads like a roll call of honor of the electrical-equipment industry: General Electric, Westinghouse, Allis-Chalmers, and twenty-six other, smaller companies. Their crime was that they had provided you with all the matchless benefits and comforts of the electrical age, from bread toasters to power generators. It is for *this* crime that they were punished—because they could not have provided any of it, nor remained in business, without breaking the antitrust laws.

The charge against them was that they had made secret agreements to fix the prices of their products and to rig bids. But without such agreements, the larger companies could have set their prices so low that the smaller ones would have been unable to match them and would have gone out of business, whereupon the larger companies would have faced prosecution, under these same antitrust laws, for "intent to monopolize."

I quote from an article by Richard Austin Smith entitled "The Incredible Electrical Conspiracy," in *Fortune* (April and May 1961): "If G.E. were to drive for 50 per cent of the market, even strong companies like I-T-E Circuit Breaker might be mortally wounded." This same article shows that the price-fixing agreements did not benefit General Electric, that they worked to its disadvantage, that General Electric was, in effect, "the sucker" and that its executives knew it, wanted to leave the "conspiracy," but had no choice (by reason of antitrust and other government regulations).

The best evidence of the fact that the antitrust laws were a major factor in forcing the "conspiracy" upon the electrical industry, can be seen in the aftermath of that case—in the issue of the "consent decree." When General Electric announced that it now intended to charge the lowest prices possible, it was the smaller companies and the government, the Antitrust Division, who objected.

Mr. Smith's article mentions the fact that the meetings of the "conspirators" started as a result of the O.P.A. During the war, the prices of electrical equipment were *fixed by the government*, and the executives of the electrical industry held meetings to discuss a common policy. They continued this practice, after the O.P.A. was abolished.

By what conceivable standard can the policy of price-fixing be a crime, when practiced by businessmen, but a public benefit, when practiced by the government? There are many industries, in peacetime—trucking, for instance—whose prices are fixed by the government. If price-fixing is harmful to competition, to industry, to production, to consumers, to the whole economy, and to the "public interest"—as the advocates of the antitrust laws have claimed—then how can that same harmful policy become beneficial in the hands of the government? Since there is no rational answer to this question, I suggest that you question the economic knowledge, the purpose, and the motives of the champions of antitrust.

The electrical companies offered no defense to the charge of "conspiracy." They pleaded *"nolo contendere,"* which means: *"no contest."* They did it, because the antitrust laws place so deadly a danger in the path of any attempt to defend oneself that defense becomes virtually impossible. These laws provide that a company convicted of an antitrust violation can be sued for *treble damages* by any customer who might claim that he was injured. In a case of so large a scale as the electrical industry case, such treble damage suits could, conceivably, wipe all the defendants out of existence. With that kind of threat hanging over him, who can or will take the risk of offering a defense in a court where there are no objective laws, no objective standards of guilt or innocence, no objective way to estimate one's chances?

Try to project what clamor of indignation and what protests would be heard publicly all around us, if some other group of men, some other minority group, were subjected to a trial in which *defense* was made impossible—or in which the laws prescribed that the more serious the offense, the more dangerous the defense. Certainly the opposite is true in regard to actual criminals: the more serious the crime, the greater the precautions and protections prescribed by the law to give the defendant a chance and the benefit of every doubt. It is only businessmen who have to come to court, bound and gagged.

Now what started the government's investigation of the electrical industry? Mr. Smith's article states that the investigation was started because of complaints by T.V.A. and *demands* by Senator Kefauver. This was in 1959, under Eisenhower's *Republican* Administration. I quote from *Time* of February 17, 1961:

> Often the Government has a hard time gathering evidence in antitrust cases, but this time it got a break. In October 1959, four Ohio businessmen were sentenced to jail after pleading *nolo contendere* in an antitrust case. (One of them committed suicide on the way to jail.) This news sent a chill through the electrical-equipment executives under investigation, and some agreed to testify about their colleagues under the security of immunity. With the evidence gathered from them (most are still with their companies), the Government sewed up its case.

It is not gangsters, racketeers, or dope peddlers that are here being discussed in such terms, but *businessmen*—the productive, creative, efficient, competent members of society. Yet the antitrust laws, *now*, in this new phase, are apparently aimed at transforming business into an underworld, with informers, stool pigeons, double-crossers, special "deals," and all the rest of the atmosphere of *The Untouchables*.

Seven executives of the electrical industry were sentenced to jail. We shall never know what went on behind the scenes of this case or in the negotiations between the companies and the government. Were *these seven* responsible for the alleged "conspiracy"? If it be guilt, were they guiltier than others? Who "informed" on them—and why? Were they framed? Were they double-crossed? Whose purposes, ambitions, or goals were served by their immolation? We do not know. Under a set-up such as the antitrust laws have created, there is no way to know.

When these seven men, who could not defend themselves, came into the courtroom to hear their sentences, their lawyers addressed the judge with pleas for mercy. I quote from the same story in *Time*: "First before the court came the lawyer for . . . a vice president of Westinghouse, to plead for mercy. His client, said the lawyer, was a vestryman of St. John's Episcopal Church in Sharon, Pa., and a benefactor of charities for crippled children." Another defendant's lawyer pleaded that his client was "the director of a boy's club in Schenectady, N.Y., and the chairman of a campaign to build a new Jesuit seminary in Lenox, Mass."

It was not these men's achievements or their productive ability or their executive talent or their intelligence or their *rights* that their lawyers found it necessary to cite—but their altruistic "service" to the "welfare of the needy." The *needy* had a right to welfare—but those who produced and provided it, had not. The welfare and the rights of the producers were not regarded as worthy of consideration or recognition. *This* is the most damning indictment of the present state of our culture.

The final touch on that whole gruesome farce was Judge Ganey's statement. He said: "What is really at stake here is the survival of the kind of economy under which America has grown to greatness, the free-enterprise system." He said it, while delivering the most staggering blow that the free-enterprise system had ever sustained, while sentencing to jail seven of its best representatives and thus declaring that the very class of men who brought America to greatness—the businessmen—are now to be treated, by their nature and profession, as criminals. In the person of these seven men, it is the free-enterprise system that he was sentencing.

These seven men were martyrs. They were treated as sacrificial animals—they were *human sacrifices*, as truly and more cruelly than the human sacrifices offered by prehistorical savages in the jungle.

If you care about justice to minority groups, remember that businessmen are a small minority—a *very small* minority, compared to the total of all the uncivilized hordes on earth. Remember how much you owe to this minority—and what disgraceful persecution it is enduring. Remember also that the smallest minority on earth is the individual. Those who deny individual rights, cannot claim to be defenders of minorities.

What should we do about it? We should demand a reexamination and revision of the entire issue of antitrust. We should challenge its philosophical, political, economic, and *moral* base. We should have a Civil Liberties Union—for businessmen. The repeal of the antitrust laws should be our ultimate goal; it will require a long intellectual and political struggle; but, in the meantime and as a first step, we should demand that the jail-penalty provisions of these laws be abolished. It is bad enough if men have to suffer financial penalties, such as fines, under laws which everyone concedes to be non-objective, contradictory, and undefinable, since no two jurists can agree on their meaning and application; it is obscene to impose prison sentences under laws of so controversial a nature. We should put an end to the outrage of sending men to jail for breaking unintelligible laws which they cannot avoid breaking.

Businessmen are the one group that distinguishes capitalism and the American way of life from the totalitarian statism that is swallowing the rest of the world. All the other social groups—workers, farmers, professional men, scientists, soldiers—exist under dictatorships, even though they exist in chains, in terror, in misery, and in progressive self-destruction. *But there is no such group as businessmen under a dictatorship.* Their place is taken by armed thugs: by bureaucrats and commissars. Businessmen are the symbol of a free society—the symbol of America. If and when they perish, civilization will perish. But if you wish to fight for freedom, you must begin by fighting for its unrewarded, unrecognized, unacknowledged, yet best representatives—the American businessmen.

Notes

1. A. D. Neale, *The Antitrust Laws of the United States of America: A Study of Competition Enforced by Law*, Cambridge, England: Cambridge University Press, 1960.

2. Ibid., p. 13.

3. Harold Fleming, *Ten Thousand Commandments: A Story of the Antitrust Laws*, New York: Prentice Hall, 1951.

4. Ibid., pp. 16–17.

5. Ibid., p. 22.

6. Neale, p. 23.

7. Ibid., pp. 422–423.

8. Ibid., pp. 70–71.

9. Ibid., p. 410.

10. Ibid., p. 114.

11. Ibid.

The Philosophical Origins of Antitrust

John B. Ridpath

What ideas make possible the unjust laws that have resulted in the government's persecution of businessmen? In this essay originally published in 1995, Dr. John Ridpath traces the history of the thought that gave rise to America's antitrust laws. This injustice against businessmen is founded on a belief which reflects a centuries' old tradition of philosophical thought originating in ancient Greece.

The Philosophical Origins of Antitrust

John B. Ridpath

The antitrust laws of the United States are an obscene violation of individual rights that have thrown American business into a no-man's-land of non-objective law. As Ayn Rand states,

> The antitrust laws give the government the power to prosecute and convict any business concern in the country any time it chooses. The threat of sudden destruction, of unpredictable retaliation for unnamed offenses, is a much more potent means of enslavement than explicit dictatorial laws.[1]

Antitrust is a political cancer, clearly alien to the founding principles of this country. Where did it come from?

Unlike most statist measures adopted in this country, antitrust laws were not a European import. They were originated and fostered by Americans—predominantly, by American *conservatives*. In particular, the conceptual underpinnings of American antitrust were supplied by a prominent conservative economist, the founder of the "Chicago School" of economics: Frank H. Knight. It was Frank Knight's theoretical work on competition that, more than any other single factor, gave American antitrust its unparalleled virulence.

The role of Frank Knight's metaphysical and epistemological ideas in the development of his theory of competition amounts to a textbook case in the political impact of basic philosophical premises.

Antitrust was born in the late nineteenth century, with the passage of the Interstate Commerce Act (1887) and the Sherman Act (1890). The movement began as a reaction to the distortions caused by previous government interventions in the market—especially government favors granted to the railroad industry.[2]

In its early years, antitrust had neither an intellectual base nor any justification in economic theory. In fact, most economists of the time favored trusts and other forms of large-scale business combinations. The only intellectual content in the early antitrust campaign derived from a naked equivocation between political power and economic power, as in Senator Sherman's

99

pronouncement: "If we will not endure a king as a political power, we should not endure a king over the production, transportation, and sale of any of the necessaries of life."[3]

Lacking a theoretical base, the early antitrust crusade proceeded somewhat meekly, in an *ad hoc* manner. At this stage, antitrust merely attempted to prescribe limits—however vague—beyond which businesses must not go. Wrong as early antitrust was, it at least did not impose any standard of "proper" business behavior, and businessmen were presumed innocent of the "crime" of "restraining trade," until specific charges of wrongdoing were raised.

But the legal environment for businessmen was to change dramatically in the twentieth century, as antitrust began to embody an (allegedly) pro-competition policy. Now businesses were faced with the task of proving that they were sufficiently competitive. The ominous significance of this re-orientation is explained by A. D. Neale:

> [W]ith a positive aim, even minor [alleged] impairments of competition will tend to be compared with some ideal model that it is hoped to achieve and will look worse in comparison. . . . Economic theory is believed to have established a presumption that any impairment of competition is harmful, and those concerned with enforcing antitrust have come to take this presumption as their rule of thumb.[4]

This "ideal model" that "economic theory" supplied to antitrust is the doctrine of "perfect competition"—the doctrine formalized by Frank Knight. Knight's theory of perfect competition provided antitrust with the theoretical teeth that have made American antitrust unique in its scope and severity. It is Knight's doctrine that has come to serve as the theoretical basis for harassment of businesses, expropriation of property, penalization of success, and imprisonment of businessmen.

What is Knight's doctrine?

The perfect competition model in its full form first appeared in Knight's highly influential work, *Risk, Uncertainty and Profit*, first published in 1921. That work grew out of Knight's interest in the effect of competition upon profit. Knight held that part of a firm's profits—a part he termed "pure profit"—had no actual economic function. This "pure" profit, he wrote, "is *not* properly a 'reward for risk-taking,' . . . [and it] is not the price of the service of its recipient, but a 'residual,' the one true residual."[5]

In this evaluation of "pure" profits, Knight assumed a collectivist standard: "pure" profits, he held, make no contribution to the "general welfare," and this is what marks them as economically superfluous.

Knight went on to ask himself what market conditions would be required to eliminate all "pure" profit, and leave business with only those earnings that are useful to society. Knight constructed in his mind a fantasy world in which all those profit-eliminating conditions obtained. This "ideal" world is the perfect competition model.

The world of perfect competition is described by Knight as having the following characteristics. Everyone is omniscient concerning all economic opportunities, all factors of production are infinitely mobile and infinitely divisible, every market contains an infinite number of buyers and sellers, no one has any "sentimental" (i.e., nonpecuniary) interest in anyone else, all the products of competing firms are identical, and no innovation occurs in any field.

Under these conditions, Knight held, no business would be able to earn more than would be required to cover its operating costs plus an interest return on its capital investment. No part of "society's income" would be withdrawn as "pure" profit.

The most glaringly obvious feature of the world depicted in the perfect competition model is its unreality. As George Reisman has thoroughly demonstrated in his article "Platonic Competition,"[6] the entire theory is neither drawn from nor applicable to reality.

The basic fact of reality is that everything that exists has an identity—everything, including human knowledge, is specific and finite. A world of undifferentiated products, traded by infinitely numerous and infinitely knowledgeable beings is metaphysically impossible. Knight's "ideal" world is one containing entities without identity and men without personal interests and individual judgment—i.e., without selves. Yet, as Dr. Reisman writes,

> This "concept" divorced from reality, this Platonic "ideal of perfection" drawn from non-existence to serve as the "standard" for judging existence . . . is at the base of antitrust prosecutions, which have forced businessmen to operate under conditions approaching a reign of terror.[7]

Had he been confronted with the charge that his theory was totally unrealistic, Knight would have replied, "Exactly. How could it be otherwise?" Knight openly acknowledged that the perfect competition model does not correspond to reality: "such a system is inherently self-defeating and could not exist in the real world."[8]

In general, Knight held that all economic theory is unavoidably severed from the real world: "All 'economic' theory in the proper sense of the word, is purely abstract and formal, without content."[9]

The theory of perfect competition is the product of Knight's basic philosophy, his views concerning reality, causality, concepts, and theory. Knight was no amateur dabbler in philosophy. In graduate school, he first majored, and then minored, in philosophy, and he kept up an active involvement with philosophy throughout his career. He was thoroughly aware of and serious about the philosophical foundations of his work. Knight was quite eclectic philosophically; he showed no complete allegiance to any one school. Overall, however, his outlook is Platonic (this imperfect world is largely closed to reason), with a Kantian twist (reason can create its own world).

In metaphysics, Knight held throughout his life to a single conviction: that reality is permeated by causeless, unpredictable change. The disruptive influence of chance, accidental occurrences swamps whatever tendency toward order and constancy the world might contain. In the preface to the 1957 reprint of *Risk, Uncertainty and Profit*, Knight wrote:

> It is still my conviction that contingency or "chance" is an unanalyzable fact of nature. . . . Chance is more than human ignorance of causality which is "really" absolute; that idea was always a dogma, an intellectual prejudice.[10]

On the surface, reality seems to be made up of thing—entities—each having its own identity, each subject to the law of causality and behaving in orderly, predictable ways. But, Knight believed, this is merely a convenient illusion.

> We have, then, our dogma which is the presupposition of knowledge, in this form; that the world is made up of *things*, which, *under the same circumstances*, always behave *in the same way*.[11]

For Knight, the world is not a place, but a process, a process of continual novelty and transformation in which there is no constancy, no causality, no laws of nature, no enduring facts, and no absolutes other than flux and ignorance. We live in a world where nothing is quite what it is, where everything is either just about to be something, or has just been something, and is now changing from what it wasn't quite, to what it won't quite be.

In taking this view of the world, Knight joined a very old and very wrong tradition in Western philosophy, a tradition founded by the pre-Socratic philosopher, Heraclitus. Heraclitus capsulized this metaphysics in the now-famous phrase "You can't step into the same river twice," a phrase which has created a fetid intellectual current that thinkers have been wading in ever since. Knight was led to plunge into these muddied waters by his study of Henri Bergson, a prominent nineteenth-century Heraclitean.

What of man's nature? Just as lawlessness dominates in physical reality, so irrationality is the major feature of man's nature, according to Knight. Man is dominated by momentary whims; he is unaware of his true motives (chiefly the quest for status and prestige). Man's actions—even in the area of business—are generally not purposeful, but "impulsive and capricious."[12]

But, Knight says, economics cannot deal with the irrational side of man's nature. Economics "assumes that men's acts are ruled by conscious motives,"[13] rather than by unconscious urges. In economics, "Analysis must use the concept of complete rationality—the economic man."[14] This unavoidable divergence between the assumptions of economic science and the facts of man's economic behavior

> raises the fundamental question of how far human behavior is inherently subject to scientific treatment. In his views on this point the author is very much of an irrationalist. In this view the whole interpretation of life as activity directed toward securing anything considered as really wanted, is highly artificial and unreal.[15]

If reality is dominated by Heraclitean contingency, and man's nature is dominated by unconscious motives beyond scientific treatment, what is a theoretician to do? Consistently enough, Knight states that, in the final analysis, theoretical knowledge is impossible. If we understand what such knowledge involves, Knight says, we will see that the human intellect by its very nature is precluded from knowing a world in flux.

> There is however, much question as to how far the world is intelligible at all. . . . In so far as there is "real change" in the Bergsonian (i.e., Heraclitean) sense it seems clear that reasoning is impossible.[16]

Within the context of the dominant philosophies of his time, Knight was not taking a unique or surprising view. He was simply conforming to then-current philosophical trends. Knight had absorbed the basic dichotomy underlying all modern philosophy: the Kantian false dichotomy between reality as it really is, and reality as it appears to us from within the prison of our own minds. For Kant, we are locked inside mental "categories" that are part of our nature and beyond our control, while for Knight, following the neo-Kantians, we, ourselves, arbitrarily fashion our own categories or constructs.

(Like all Kantians, Bergson and Knight did offer a non-rational source of knowledge: a mystical "intuition" which allows the mind to enter into things and grasp them "from the inside."[17] Knight went so far as to announce, "if our feelings tell us nothing about reality, then we know and can know nothing about it."[18])

In his less skeptical moments, Knight allowed a limited role for scientific theory. But it is scientific theory conceived along Kantian lines. Because of the intellect's nature, Knight states, it can deal only with fixed entities, with things which are what they are, and which, accordingly, always behave in a lawful, predictable, noncontradictory way. Bergson had written, "The intellect is never quite at ease, never entirely at home, except when it is working on inert matter." Knight expressed the same idea:

> For if it is the intrinsic nature of a thing to grow and change, it can-
> not serve as a scientific datum. A science must have a "static" sub-
> ject-matter; it must talk about things which will "stay put"; other-
> wise its statements will not remain true after they are made and there
> will be no point in making them.[20]

This leads to Knight's view of what the intellect can do, and what the nature of theory, including the theory of perfect competition, is. The intellect can create *in the mind* the static, stable world it needs as its subject matter. This static construct can then be used as a rough approximation in dealing with the dynamic and unstable real world. Using highly Platonic language, Knight states that the intellect creates an "abstract," "clean," "idealistic" world in the mind, one that is free of "the complex and often unlovely flesh and viscera of reality."[21]

There are at work in the world, according to Knight, certain stable, knowable *tendencies* (e.g., the tendency for competition to eliminate "pure" profit). These tendencies can never manifest themselves in their pure form, because of the overwhelming disruptions caused by the Heraclitean flux. Nevertheless, we can construct in our minds an artificial, lawful world in which these tendencies operate unopposed.

The resulting model, it must be stressed, does not represent an abstraction of essentials from details; it represents a flight into the fantasy world of "what if?" (e.g., "What if every buyer and seller were omniscient?"). Heraclitean contingency and human irrationality are the essentials, according to Knight's philosophy, and these are precisely what "idealizations" such as the perfect competition model must omit.

Thus, for Knight, the perfection involved here is epistemological: when the "unlovely" characteristics of reality are mentally eliminated, the product satisfies perfectly the needs of our mind. Unfortunately, it does so at the price of falsifying reality. Because of the incompatibility between the nature of the world (as flux) and the requirements of the mind (for stability), the best we can do intellectually is to use artificial constructs. In true Kantian fashion, Knight's epistemology proceeds from the assumption that the cognitive requirements of the intellect set it at odds with reality. We must choose between reason and reality. (For details on, and a refutation of, this Kantian premise, see Ayn Rand, *Introduction to Objectivist Epistemology*, chap. 8.)

Knight's perfect competition model was never intended to correspond to reality. It was derived from reality only in the sense that Knight took an alleged tendency from the real world and projected how it would operate in an impossible, unreal world.

In the world of perfect competition, the "pure" profits earned by entrepreneurs would not exist. Knight concluded that these profits must have their source in Heraclitean contingency. Profits, which in fact are the earned reward for intelligently and courageously producing material values, are to Knight nothing more than manna randomly sprinkled by the unknowable flux and human irrationality. This view of the source of profits laid the groundwork, which others later built upon, for taking the existence of high profits as prima facie evidence of uncompetitive behavior in violation of antitrust law.

The perfect competition model furnished a powerful weapon for those who possessed the statist fervor Knight lacked. Knight's pleas to remember that his model was only a theoretical ideal (!) were increasingly ignored. People naturally reasoned: if this is the ideal, then we should try to approach it in practice. Interpreting "perfect competition" in normative terms is virtually unavoidable, psycho-epistemologically. Anyone who automatizes such a term will be led to employ it normatively, even if the term's originator advises against doing so. Even though, for Knight, the "perfection" involved was epistemological, for those who followed him the perfect competition model functioned as a moral and political ideal.

Even those intellectuals who did not share Knight's bizarre Bergsonian premises were attracted to his perfect competition model because of two other Kantian (or neo-Kantian) doctrines: altruism and pragmatism.

Pragmatism has been the dominant philosophical school among American intellectuals in the twentieth century. Pragmatism's scorn of absolutes and of principles (which Knight shared) leads its adherents to take a range-of-the-moment view of the world. Such a view, when applied to economics—a science where the central focus is on long-range consequences—produces disastrous results (the most notable being Keynesianism). A pragmatist approach in economics centers one's attention on the distribution or "allocation" of goods, rather than on their source in production. As Ayn Rand put it in *Atlas Shrugged*:

> The problem of production, they tell you, has been solved and deserves no study or concern; the only problem left for your "reflexes" to solve is now the problem of distribution. Who solved the problem of production? Humanity, they answer. What was the solution? The goods are here. How did they get here? Somehow. What caused it? Nothing has causes.[22]

The implicit premise of the perfect competition theory is that businessmen are to be conceived not as productive creators, but as cogs facelessly involved in a process that spews out undifferentiated goods to impassive throngs—that businessmen can exist and function as selfless automatons with nothing to gain and no power to affect the process. It is the improper focus on distribution and consumption that made possible this notion of a "perfectly competitive" businessman.

Again, quoting from *Atlas Shrugged*:

> Frantic cowards who posture as defenders of industrialists now define the purpose of economics as "an adjustment between the unlimited desires of men and the goods supplied in limited quantity." Supplied—by whom? Blank-out.[23]

Or, in the language of a contemporary economist, Mark S. Massel:

> [Under perfect competition] resources . . . are so allocated that the largest number of consumer wants which can be met are satisfied.[24]

The altruist ideal of unrecorded service to others motivated the acceptance of the perfect competition model and its use as a standard for antitrust. The root reason why lawyers, economists, politicians and businessmen accepted this model and hold it as a virtually unchallengeable standard is that the conduct it depicts *is* perfect according to the altruist morality. The model appeals to altruists because it describes a world in which everyone is acting to best serve the interest of the consuming public—a world in which goods are automatically distributed in such a manner that no one receives any selfish gain "at the expense of" others, and in which everyone participates in a process that gives the most satisfaction equally to all. In Knight's own words:

> Under perfect competition he [the entrepreneur] would of course be completely helpless, a mere automatic registrar of the choices of consumers.[25]

This is the moral meaning of the standard used by modern antitrust. Businessmen are being persecuted for not being sufficiently identityless, passive, altruistic servants of consumers.

Anti-reason, anti-identity, anti-causality, and anti-self—these philosophical poisons have all combined to provide the foundations for modern antitrust's assault on the most productive system man has ever known—capitalism, and on the most productive individuals in human history—the industrialists. This is not surprising. No activity, no individual, no society in this world will ever be deemed good or just when judged by standards drawn from non-existence.

Any theory, such as perfect competition, which is removed from and disdainful of reality, will lead to the immolation of those most capable of dealing with reality. That is both the theory's effect and its ultimate purpose.

Notes

1. "Antitrust: The Rule of Unreason," *The Objectivist Newsletter*, February 1962, p. 8.

2. See Alan Greenspan, "Antitrust," in *Capitalism: The Unknown Ideal*.

3. Quoted in A. D. Neale, *The Antitrust Laws of the U.S.A.* (Cambridge University Press, 1966), p. 25.

4. Ibid., p. 29.

5. *Risk, Uncertainty and Profit* (Augustus Kelley, 1964), p. lix.

6. *The Objectivist*, August–September 1968.

7. *The Objectivist*, September 1968, p. 11.

8. *Risk, Uncertainty and Profit*, p. 193.

9. Ibid., p. xii.

10. Ibid., p. lx.

11. Ibid., p. 204.

12. Ibid., p. 52.

13. Ibid.

14. *Intelligence and Democratic Action* (Harvard University Press, 1960), p. 72.

15. *Risk, Uncertainty and Profit*, pp. 52–3.

16. Ibid., p. 209.

17. *The Ethics of Competition* (Allen & Unwin, 1935), p. 108.

18. Ibid., p. 39.

19. *Creative Evolution* (Holt, 1911), p. 154.

20. *The Ethics of Competition*, p. 21.

21. *The Economic Organization* (Harper & Row, 1965), p. 35.

22. *Atlas Shrugged* (Signet, 1957), p. 968.

23. Ibid.

24. *Competition and Monopoly* (Doubleday, 1964), pp. 196–7.

25. *History and Method of Economics* (University of Chicago Press, 1956), p. 92.

The Morality of Moneylending: A Short History

Yaron Brook

Author's note: This essay is partially based on my lecture "Money-Lending: Its History and Philosophy," delivered at Second Renaissance Conferences, Anaheim, California, July 2001.

In this 2007 article, Dr. Yaron Brook provides a historical account of the practice of moneylending. Since the time of Aristotle, it has been branded as a corrupt and immoral practice, and even during today's economic crisis, moneylenders are blamed as its root cause. Dr. Brook unmasks the errors in the economic arguments and the true meaning of the moral arguments against usury. He further examines the "moral-practical dichotomy" that has plagued the industry's growth since ancient times.

Originally published in The Objective Standard, *vol. 2, no. 3, Fall 2007.*

The Morality of Moneylending: A Short History

Yaron Brook

It seems that every generation has its Shylock—a despised financier blamed for the economic problems of his day. A couple of decades ago it was Michael Milken and his "junk" bonds. Today it is the mortgage bankers who, over the past few years, lent billions of dollars to home buyers—hundreds of thousands of whom are now delinquent or in default on their loans. This "sub-prime mortgage crisis" is negatively affecting the broader financial markets and the economy as a whole. The villains, we are told, are not the borrowers—who took out loans they could not afford to pay back—but the moneylenders—who either deceived the borrowers or should have known better than to make the loans in the first place. And, we are told, the way to prevent such problems in the future is to clamp down on moneylenders and their industries; thus, investigations, criminal prosecutions, and heavier regulations on bankers are in order.

Of course, government policy for decades has been to *encourage* lenders to provide mortgage loans to lower-income families, and when mortgage brokers have refused to make such loans, they have been accused of "discrimination." But now that many borrowers are in a bind, politicians are seeking to lash and leash the lenders.

This treatment of moneylenders is unjust but not new. For millennia they have been the primary scapegoats for practically every economic problem. They have been derided by philosophers and condemned to hell by religious authorities; their property has been confiscated to compensate their "victims"; they have been humiliated, framed, jailed, and butchered. From Jewish pogroms where the main purpose was to destroy the records of debt, to the vilification of the House of Rothschild, to the jailing of American financiers—moneylenders have been targets of philosophers, theologians, journalists, economists, playwrights, legislators, and the masses.

Major thinkers throughout history—Plato, Aristotle, Thomas Aquinas, Adam Smith, Karl Marx, and John Maynard Keynes, to name just a few—considered moneylending, at least under certain conditions, to be a major vice. Dante, Shakespeare, Dickens, Dostoyevsky, and modern and popular novelists depict moneylenders as villains.

Today, anti-globalization demonstrators carry signs that read "abolish usury"

111

or "abolish interest." Although these protestors are typically leftists—opponents of capitalism and anything associated with it—their contempt for moneylending is shared by others, including radical Christians and Muslims who regard charging interest on loans as a violation of God's law and thus as immoral.

Moneylending has been and is condemned by practically everyone. But what exactly is being condemned here? What *is* moneylending or *usury*? And what are its consequences?

Although the term "usury" is widely taken to mean "excessive interest" (which is never defined) or illegal interest, the actual definition of the term is, as the *Oxford English Dictionary* specifies: "The fact or practice of lending money at interest." This is the definition I ascribe to the term throughout this essay.

Usury is a financial transaction in which person A lends person B a sum of money for a fixed period of time with the agreement that it will be returned with interest. The practice enables people *without* money and people *with* money to mutually benefit from the wealth of the latter. The borrower is able to use money that he would otherwise not be able to use, in exchange for paying the lender an agreed-upon premium in addition to the principal amount of the loan. Not only do both interested parties benefit from such an exchange; countless people who are not involved in the trade often benefit too—by means of access to the goods and services made possible by the exchange.

Usury enables levels of life-serving commerce and industry that otherwise would be impossible. Consider a few historical examples. Moneylenders funded grain shipments in ancient Athens and the first trade between the Christians in Europe and the Saracens of the East. They backed the new merchants of Italy and, later, of Holland and England. They supported Spain's exploration of the New World, and funded gold and silver mining operations. They made possible the successful colonization of America. They fueled the Industrial Revolution, supplying the necessary capital to the new entrepreneurs in England, the United States, and Europe. And, in the late 20th century, moneylenders provided billions of dollars to finance the computer, telecommunications, and biotechnology industries.

By taking risks and investing their capital in what they thought would make them the most money, moneylenders and other financiers made possible whole industries—such as those of steel, railroads, automobiles, air travel, air conditioning, and medical devices. Without capital, often provided through usury, such life-enhancing industries would not exist—and homeownership would be impossible to all but the wealthiest people.

Moneylending is the lifeblood of industrial-technological society. When the practice and its practitioners are condemned, they are condemned for furthering and enhancing man's life on earth.

Given moneylenders' enormous contribution to human well-being, why have they been so loathed throughout history, and why do they continue to be distrusted and mistreated today? What explains the universal hostility toward one of humanity's greatest benefactors? And what is required to replace this hostility with the gratitude that is the moneylenders' moral due?

As we will see, hostility toward usury stems from two interrelated sources: certain economic views and certain ethical views. Economically, from the beginning of Western thought, usury was regarded as *unproductive*—as the taking of something for nothing. Ethically, the practice was condemned as *immoral*—as unjust, exploitative, against biblical law, selfish. The history of usury is a history of confusions, discoveries, and evasions concerning the economic and moral status of the practice. Until usury is recognized as both economically productive and ethically praiseworthy—as both practical and moral—moneylenders will continue to be condemned as villains rather than heralded as the heroes they in fact are.

Our brief history begins with Aristotle's view on the subject.

Aristotle

The practice of lending money at interest was met with hostility as far back as ancient Greece, and even Aristotle (384–322 B.C.) believed the practice to be unnatural and unjust. In the first book of *Politics* he writes:

> The most hated sort [of moneymaking], and with the greatest reason, is usury, which makes a gain out of money itself, and not from the natural use of it. For money was intended to be used in exchange, but not to increase at interest. And this term Usury which means the birth of money from money, is applied to the breeding of money, because the offspring resembles the parent. Wherefore of all modes of making money this is the most unnatural.[1]

Aristotle believed that charging interest was immoral because money is not productive. If you allow someone to use your orchard, he argued, the orchard bears fruit every year—it is productive—and from this product the person can pay you rent. But money, Aristotle thought, is merely a medium of exchange. When you loan someone money, he receives no value over and above the money itself. The money does not create more money—it is barren. On this view, an exchange of $100 today for $100 plus $10 in interest a year from now is unjust, because the lender thereby receives more than he gave, and what he gave could not have brought about the 10 percent increase. Making money from money, according to Aristotle, is "unnatural" because money, unlike an orchard, cannot produce additional value.

Aristotle studied under Plato and accepted some of his teacher's false ideas. One such idea that Aristotle appears to have accepted is the notion that every good has some *intrinsic value*—a value independent of and apart from human purposes. On this view, $100 will be worth $100 a year from now and can be worth only $100 to anyone, at any time, for any purpose. Aristotle either rejected or failed to consider the idea that loaned money loses value to the lender over time as his use of it is postponed, or the idea that money can be invested in economic activity and thereby create wealth. In short, Aristotle had no conception of the productive role of money or of the moneylender. (Given the relative simplicity of the Greek economy, he may have had insufficient evidence from which to conclude otherwise.) Consequently, he regarded usury as unproductive, unnatural, and therefore unjust.

Note that Aristotle's conclusion regarding the unjust nature of usury is derived from his view that the practice is *unproductive*: Since usury creates nothing but takes something—since the lender apparently is parasitic on the borrower—the practice is unnatural and immoral. It is important to realize that, on this theory, there is no dichotomy between the economically practical and the morally permissible; usury is regarded as immoral *because* it is regarded as impractical.

Aristotle's economic and moral view of usury was reflected in ancient culture for a few hundred years, but moral condemnation of the practice became increasingly pronounced. The Greek writer Plutarch (46–127 A.D.), for example, in his essay "Against Running In Debt, Or Taking Up Money Upon Usury," described usurers as "wretched," "vulture-like," and "barbarous."[2] In Roman culture, Seneca (ca. 4 B.C.–65 A.D.) condemned usury for the same reasons as Aristotle; Cato the Elder (234–149 B.C.) famously compared usury to murder;[3] and Cicero (106–43 B.C.) wrote that "these profits are despicable which incur the hatred of men, such as those of . . . lenders of money on usury."[4]

As hostile as the Greeks and Romans generally were toward usury, their hostility was based primarily on their economic view of the practice, which gave rise to and was integrated with their moral view of usury. The Christians, however, were another matter, and their position on usury would become the reigning position in Western thought up to the present day.

The Dark and Middle Ages

The historian William Manchester described the Dark and Middle Ages as

> stark in every dimension. Famines and plague, culminating in the Black Death [which killed one in four people at its peak] and its recurring pandemics, repeatedly thinned the population. . . . Among the lost arts were bricklaying; in all of Germany, England, Holland and Scandinavia, virtually no stone buildings, except cathedrals, were raised for ten centuries. . . . Peasants labored harder, sweated

more, and collapsed from exhaustion more often than their animals.[5]

During the Dark Ages, the concept of an economy had little meaning. Human society had reverted to a precivilized state, and the primary means of trade was barter. Money all but disappeared from European commerce for centuries. There was, of course, some trade and some lending, but most loans were made with goods, and the interest was charged in goods. These barter-based loans, primitive though they were, enabled people to survive the tough times that were inevitable in an agrarian society.[6]

Yet the church violently opposed even such subsistence-level lending.

During this period, the Bible was considered the basic source of knowledge and thus the final word on all matters of importance. For every substantive question and problem, scholars consulted scripture for answers—and the Bible clearly opposed usury. In the Old Testament, God says to the Jews: "[He that] Hath given forth upon usury, and hath taken increase: shall he then live? he shall not live . . . he shall surely die; his blood shall be upon him."[7] And:

> Thou shalt not lend upon usury to thy brother; usury of money; usury of victuals; usury of anything that is lent upon usury.

> Unto a stranger thou mayest lend upon usury; but unto thy brother thou shalt not lend upon usury, that the Lord thy God may bless thee in all that thou settest thine hand to in the land whither thou goest to possess it.[8]

In one breath, God forbade usury outright; in another, He forbade the Jews to engage in usury with other Jews but permitted them to make loans at interest to non-Jews.

Although the New Testament does not condemn usury explicitly, it makes clear that one's moral duty is to help those in need, and thus to give to others one's own money or goods without the expectation of anything in return—neither interest nor principal. As Luke plainly states, "lend, hoping for nothing again."[9] Jesus' expulsion of the moneychangers from the temple is precisely a parable conveying the Christian notion that profit is evil, particularly profit generated by moneylending. Christian morality, the morality of divinely mandated altruism, expounds the virtue of self-sacrifice on behalf of the poor and the weak; it condemns self-interested actions, such as profiting—especially profiting from a seemingly exploitative and unproductive activity such as usury.

Thus, on scriptural and moral grounds, Christianity opposed usury from the beginning. And it constantly reinforced its opposition with legal restrictions. In 325 A.D., the Council of Nicaea banned the practice among clerics. Under Charlemagne (768–814 A.D.), the Church extended the prohibition to laymen, defining usury simply as a transaction where more is asked than is given.[10] In 1139, the second Lateran Council in Rome denounced usury as a form of theft, and required restitution from those who practiced it. In the 12th and 13th centuries, strategies that concealed usury were also condemned. The Council of Vienne in 1311 declared that any person who dared claim that there was no sin in the practice of usury be punished as a heretic.

There was, however, a loophole among all these pronouncements: the Bible's double standard on usury. As we saw earlier, read one way, the Bible permits Jews to lend to non-Jews. This reading had positive consequences. For lengthy periods during the Dark and Middle Ages, both Church and civil authorities allowed Jews to practice usury. Many princes, who required substantial loans in order to pay bills and wage wars, allowed Jewish usurers in their states. Thus, European Jews, who had been barred from most professions and from ownership of land, found moneylending to be a profitable, albeit hazardous, profession.

Although Jews were legally permitted to lend to Christians—and although Christians saw some practical need to borrow from them and chose to do so—Christians resented this relationship. Jews appeared to be making money on the backs of Christians while engaging in an activity biblically prohibited to Christians on punishment of eternal damnation. Christians, accordingly, held these Jewish usurers in contempt. (Important roots of anti-Semitism lie in this biblically structured relationship.)

Opposition to Jewish usurers was often violent. In 1190, the Jews of York were massacred in an attack planned by members of the nobility who owed money to the Jews and sought to absolve the debt through violence.[11] During this and many other attacks on Jewish communities, accounting records were destroyed and Jews were murdered. As European historian Joseph Patrick Byrne reports:

> "Money was the reason the Jews were killed, for had they been poor, and had not the lords of the land been indebted to them, they would not have been killed."[12] But the "lords" were not the only debtors: the working class and underclass apparently owed a great deal, and these violent pogroms gave them the opportunity to destroy records of debt as well as the creditors themselves.[13]

In 1290, largely as a result of antagonism generated from their moneylending, King Edward I expelled the Jews from England, and they would not return en masse until the 17th century.

From the Christian perspective, there were clearly problems with the biblical pronouncements on usury. How could it be that Jews were prohibited from lending to other Jews but were allowed to lend to Christians and other non-Jews? And how could it be that God permitted Jews to benefit from this practice but prohibited Christians from doing so? These questions perplexed the thinkers of the day. St. Jerome's (ca. 347–420) "solution" to the conundrum was that it was wrong to charge interest to one's brothers—and, to Christians, all other Christians were brothers—but it was fine to charge interest to one's enemy. Usury was perceived as a weapon that weakened the borrower and strengthened the lender; so, if one loaned money at interest to one's enemy, that enemy would suffer. This belief led Christians to the absurd practice of lending money to the Saracens—their enemies—during the Crusades.[14]

Like the Greeks and Romans, Christian thinkers viewed certain economic transactions as zero-sum phenomena, in which a winner always entailed a loser. In the practice of usury, the lender seemed to grow richer without effort—so it had to be at the expense of the borrower, who became poorer. But the Christians' economic hostility toward usury was grounded in and fueled by biblical pronouncements against the practice—and this made a substantial difference. The combination of economic and biblical strikes against usury—with an emphasis on the latter—led the Church to utterly vilify the usurer, who became a universal symbol for evil. Stories describing the moneylenders' horrible deaths and horrific existence in Hell were common. One bishop put it concisely:

> God created three types of men: peasants and other laborers to assure the subsistence of the others, knights to defend them, and clerics to govern them. But the devil created a fourth group, the usurers. They do not participate in men's labors, and they will not be punished with men, but with the demons. For the amount of money they receive from usury corresponds to the amount of wood sent to Hell to burn them.[15]

Such was the attitude toward usury during the Dark and early Middle Ages. The practice was condemned primarily on biblical/moral grounds. In addition to the fact that the Bible explicitly forbade it, moneylending was recognized as self-serving. Not only did it involve profit; the profit was (allegedly) unearned and exploitative. Since the moneylender's gain was assumed to be the borrower's loss—and since the borrower was often poor—the moneylender was seen as profiting by exploiting the meek and was therefore regarded as evil.

Beginning in the 11th century, however, a conflicting economic reality became increasingly clear—and beginning in the 13th century, the resurgence of respect for observation and logic made that reality increasingly difficult to ignore.

Through trade with the Far East and exposure to the flourishing cultures and economies of North Africa and the Middle East, economic activity was increasing throughout Europe. As this activity created a greater demand for capital and for credit, moneylenders arose throughout Europe to fill the need—and as moneylenders filled the need, the economy grew even faster.

And Europeans were importing more than goods; they were also importing knowledge. They were discovering the Arabic numerical system, double-entry accounting, mathematics, science, and, most importantly, the works of Aristotle.

Aristotle's ideas soon became the focus of attention in all of Europe's learning centers, and his writings had a profound effect on the scholars of the time. No longer were young intellectuals satisfied by biblical references alone; they had discovered reason, and they sought to ground their ideas in it as well. They were, of course, still stifled by Christianity, because, although reason had been rediscovered, it was to remain the handmaiden of faith. Consequently, these intellectuals spent most of their time trying to use reason to justify Christian doctrine. But their burgeoning acceptance of reason, and their efforts to justify their ideas accordingly, would ultimately change the way intellectuals thought about everything—including usury.

Although Aristotle himself regarded usury as unjust, recall that he drew this conclusion from what he legitimately thought was evidence in support of it; in his limited economic experience, usury appeared to be unproductive. In contrast, the thinkers of this era were confronted with extensive use of moneylending all around them—which was accompanied by an ever-expanding economy—a fact that they could not honestly ignore. Thus, scholars set out to reconcile the matter rationally. On Aristotelian premises, if usury is indeed unjust and properly illegal, then there must be a logical argument in support of this position. And the ideas that usury is unproductive and that it necessarily consists in a rich lender exploiting a poor borrower were losing credibility.

Public opinion, which had always been against usury, now started to change as the benefits of credit and its relationship to economic growth became more evident. As support for usury increased, however, the Church punished transgressions more severely and grew desperate for theoretical justification for its position. If usury was to be banned, as the Bible commands, then this new world that had just discovered reason would require new, non-dogmatic explanations for why the apparently useful practice was wrong.

Over the next four hundred years, theologians and lawyers struggled to reconcile a rational approach to usury with Church dogma on the subject. They dusted off Aristotle's argument on the barrenness of money and reasserted that the profit gained through the practice is unnatural and unjust. To this they added that usury entails an artificial separation between the ownership of goods and the use of those same goods, claiming that lending money is like asking two prices for wine—one price for receiving the wine and an additional price for drinking it—one price for its possession and another for its use. Just as this would be wrong with wine, they argued, so it is wrong with money: In the case of usury, the borrower in effect pays $100 for $100, plus another fee, $10, for the use of the money that he already paid for and thus already owns.[16]

In similar fashion, it was argued that usury generates for the lender profit from goods that no longer belong to him—that is, from goods now owned by the borrower.[17] As one Scholastic put it: "[He] who gets fruit from that money, whether it be pieces of money or anything else, gets it from a thing which does not belong to him, and it is accordingly all the same as if he were to steal it."[18]

Another argument against usury from the late Middle Ages went to a crucial aspect of the practice that heretofore had not been addressed: the issue of time. Thinkers of this period believed that time was a common good, that it belonged to no one in particular, that it was a gift from God. Thus, they saw usurers as attempting to defraud God.[19] As the 12th-century English theologian Thomas of Chobham (1160–1233) wrote: "The usurer sells nothing to the borrower that belongs to him. He sells only time, which belongs to God. He can therefore not make a profit from selling someone else's property."[20] Or as expressed in a 13th-century manuscript, "Every man stops working on holidays, but the oxen of usury work unceasingly and thus offend God and all the Saints; and, since usury is an endless sin, it should in like manner be endlessly punished."[21]

Although the identification of the value of time and its relationship to interest was used here in an argument *against* usury, this point is actually a crucial aspect of the argument in *defense* of the practice. Indeed, interest is compensation for a delay in using one's funds. It is compensation for the usurer's time away from his money. And although recognition of an individual's ownership of his own time was still centuries away, this early acknowledgment of the relationship of time and interest was a major milestone.

The Scholastics came to similar conclusions about usury as those reached by earlier Christian thinkers, but they sought to defend their views not only by reference to scripture, but also by reference to their observational understanding of the economics of the practice. The economic worth of usury—its productivity or unproductivity—became their central concern. The question became: Is money barren? Does usury have a productive function? What are the facts?

This is the long arm of Aristotle at work. Having discovered Aristotle's method of observation-based logic, the Scholastics began to focus on reality, and, to the extent that they did, they turned away from faith and away from the Bible. It would take hundreds of years for this perspective to develop fully, but the types of arguments made during the late Middle Ages were early contributions to this crucial development.

As virtuous as this new method was, however, the Scholastics were still coming to the conclusion that usury is unproductive and immoral, and it would not be until the 16th century and the Reformation that usury would be partially accepted by the Church and civil law. For the time being, usury remained forbidden—at least in theory.

Church officials, particularly from the 12th century on, frequently manipulated and selectively enforced the usury laws to bolster the financial power of the Church. When it wanted to keep its own borrowing cost low, the Church enforced the usury prohibition. At other times, the Church itself readily loaned money for interest. Monks were among the earliest moneylenders, offering carefully disguised interest-bearing loans throughout the Middle Ages.

The most common way to disguise loans—and the way in which banking began in Italy and grew to be a major business—was through money exchange. The wide variety of currencies made monetary exchange necessary but difficult, which led to certain merchants specializing in the field. With the rapid growth of international trade, these operations grew dramatically in scale, and merchants opened offices in cities all across Europe and the eastern Mediterranean. These merchants used the complexities associated with exchange of different currencies to hide loans and charge interest. For example, a loan might be made in one currency and returned in another months later in a different location—although the amount returned would be higher (i.e., would include an interest payment), this would be disguised by a new exchange rate. This is one of many mechanisms usurers and merchants invented to circumvent the restrictions. As one commentator notes, "the interest element in such dealings [was] normally . . . hidden by the nature of the transactions either in foreign exchange or as bills of exchange or, frequently, as both."[22] By such means, these merchants took deposits, loaned money, and made payments across borders, thus creating the beginnings of the modern banking system.

Although the merchant credit extended by these early banks was technically interest, and thus usury, both the papal and civic authorities permitted the practice, because the exchange service proved enormously valuable to both. In addition to financing all kinds of trade across vast distances for countless merchants, such lending also financed the Crusades for the Church and various wars for various kings.[23] Everyone wanted what usury had to offer, yet no one understood exactly what that was. So while the Church continued to forbid usury and punish transgressors, it also actively engaged in the practice. What was seen as moral by the Church apparently was not seen as wholly practical by the Church, and opportunity became the mother of evasion.

The Church also engaged in opportunistic behavior when it came to restitution. Where so-called "victims" of usury were known, the Church provided them with restitution from the usurer. But in cases where the "victims" were not known, the Church still collected restitution, which it supposedly directed to "the poor" or other "pious purposes." Clerics were sold licenses empowering them to procure such restitution, and, as a result, the number of usurers prosecuted where there was no identifiable "victim" was far greater than it otherwise would have been. The death of a wealthy merchant often provided the Church with windfall revenue. In the 13th century, the Pope laid claim to the assets of deceased usurers in England. He directed his agents to "inquire concerning living (and dead) usurers and the thing wrongfully acquired by this wicked usury . . . and . . . compel opponents by ecclesiastical censure."[24]

Also of note, Church officials regularly ignored the usury of their important friends—such as the Florentine bankers of the Medici family—while demonizing Jewish moneylenders and others. The result was that the image of the merchant usurer was dichotomized into "two disparate figures who stood at opposite poles: the degraded manifest usurer-pawnbroker, as often as not a Jew; and the city father, arbiter of elegance, patron of the arts, devout philanthropist, the merchant prince [yet no less a usurer!]."[25]

In theory, the Church was staunchly opposed to usury; in practice, however, it was violating its own moral law in myriad ways. The gap between the idea of usury as immoral and the idea of usury as impractical continued to widen as the evidence for its practicality continued to grow. The Church would not budge on the moral status, but it selectively practiced the vice nonetheless.

This selective approach often correlated with the economic times. When the economy was doing well, the Church, and the civil authorities, often looked the other way and let the usurers play. In bad times, however, moneylenders, particularly those who were Jewish, became the scapegoats. (This pattern continues today with anti-interest sentiment exploding whenever there is an economic downturn.)

To facilitate the Church's selective opposition to usury, and to avoid the stigma associated with the practice, religious and civil authorities created many loopholes in the prohibition. Sometime around 1220, a new term was coined to replace certain forms of usury: the concept of interest.[26] Under circumstances where usury was legal, it would now be called the collecting of interest. In cases where the practice was illegal, it would continue to be called usury.[27]

The modern word "interest" derives from the Latin verb *intereo*, which means "to be lost." Interest was considered compensation for a loss that a creditor had incurred through lending. Compensation for a loan was illegal if it was a gain or a profit, but if it was reimbursement for a loss or an expense it was permissible. Interest was, in a sense, "damages," not profit. Therefore, interest was sometimes allowed, but usury never.

So, increasingly, moneylenders were allowed to charge interest as a penalty for delayed repayment of a loan, provided that the lender preferred repayment to the delay plus interest (i.e., provided that it was seen as a sacrifice). Loans were often structured in advance so that such delays were anticipated and priced, and so the prohibition on usury was avoided. Many known moneylenders and bankers, such as the Belgian Lombards, derived their profits from such penalties—often 100 percent of the loan value.[28]

Over time, the view of costs or damages for the lender was expanded, and the lender's time and effort in making the loan were permitted as a reason for charging interest. It even became permissible on occasion for a lender to charge interest if he could show an obvious, profitable alternative use for the money. If, by lending money, the lender suffered from the inability to make a profit elsewhere, the interest was allowed as compensation for the potential loss. Indeed, according to some sources, even risk—economic risk—was viewed as worthy of compensation. Therefore, if there was risk that the debtor would not pay, interest charged in advance was permissible.[29]

These were major breakthroughs. Recognition of the economic need for advanced calculation of a venture's risk and for compensation in advance for that risk were giant steps in the understanding of and justification for moneylending.

But despite all these breakthroughs and the fact that economic activity continued to grow during the later Middle Ages, the prohibition on usury was still selectively enforced. Usurers were often forced to pay restitution; many were driven to poverty or excommunicated; and some, especially Jewish moneylenders, were violently attacked and murdered. It was still a very high-risk profession.

Not only were usurers in danger on Earth; they were also threatened with the "Divine justice" that awaited them after death.[30] They were considered the devil's henchmen and were sure to go to Hell. It was common to hear stories of usurers going mad in old age out of fear of what awaited them in the afterlife.

The Italian poet Dante (1265–1321) placed usurers in the seventh circle of Hell, incorporating the traditional medieval punishment for usury, which was eternity with a heavy bag of money around one's neck: "From each neck there hung an enormous purse, each marked with its own beast and its own colors like a coat of arms. On these their streaming eyes appeared to feast."[31] Usurers in Dante's Hell are forever weighed down by their greed. Profits, Dante believed, should be the fruits of labor—and usury entailed no actual work. He believed that the deliberate, intellectual choice to engage in such an unnatural action as usury was the worst kind of sin.[32]

It is a wonder that anyone—let alone so many—defied the law and their faith to practice moneylending. In this sense, the usurers were truly heroic. By defying religion and taking risks—both financial and existential—they made their material lives better. They made money. And by doing so, they made possible economic growth the likes of which had never been seen before. It was thanks to a series of loans from local moneylenders that Gutenberg, for example, was able to commercialize his printing press.[33] The early bankers enabled advances in commerce and industry throughout Europe, financing the Age of Exploration as well as the early seeds of technology that would ultimately lead to the Industrial Revolution.

By the end of the Middle Ages, although everyone still condemned usury, few could deny its practical value. Everyone "knew" that moneylending was ethically wrong, but everyone could also *see* that it was economically beneficial. Its moral status was divinely decreed and appeared to be supported by reason, yet merchants and businessmen *experienced* its practical benefits daily. The thinkers of the day could not explain this apparent dichotomy. And, in the centuries that followed, although man's understanding of the economic value of usury would advance, his moral attitude toward the practice would remain one of contempt.

Renaissance and Reformation

The start of the 16th century brought about a commercial boom in Europe. It was the Golden Age of Exploration. Trade routes opened to the New World and expanded to the East, bringing unprecedented trade and wealth to Europe. To fund this trade, to supply credit for commerce and the beginnings of industry, banks were established throughout Europe. Genoese and German bankers funded Spanish and Portuguese exploration and the importation of New World gold and silver. Part of what made this financial activity possible was the new tolerance, in some cities, of usury.

The Italian city of Genoa, for example, had a relatively relaxed attitude toward usury, and moneylenders created many ways to circumvent the existing prohibitions. It was clear to the city's leaders that the financial activities of its merchants were crucial to Genoa's prosperity, and the local courts regularly turned a blind eye to the usurious activities of its merchants and bankers. Although the Church often complained about these activities, Genoa's political importance prevented the Church from acting against the city.

The Catholic Church's official view toward usury remained unchanged until the 19th century, but the Reformation—which occurred principally in northern Europe—brought about a mild acceptance of usury. (This is likely one reason why southern Europe, which was heavily Catholic, lagged behind the rest of Europe economically from the 17th century onward.) Martin Luther (1483–1546), a leader of the Reformation, believed that usury was inevitable and should be permitted to some extent by civil law. Luther believed in the separation of civil law and Christian ethics. This view, however, resulted not from a belief in the separation of state and religion, but from his belief that the world and man were too corrupt to be guided by Christianity. Christian ethics and the Old Testament commandments, he argued, are utopian dreams, unconnected with political or economic reality. He deemed usury unpreventable and thus a matter for the secular authorities, who should permit the practice and control it.

However, Luther still considered usury a grave sin, and in his later years wrote:

> [T]here is on earth no greater enemy of man, after the Devil, than a gripe-money and usurer, for he wants to be God over all men. . . . And since we break on the wheel and behead highwaymen, murderers, and housebreakers, how much more ought we to break on the wheel and kill . . . hunt down, curse, and behead all usurers![34]

In other words, usury should be allowed by civil authorities (as in Genoa) because it is inevitable (men will be men), but it should be condemned in the harshest terms by the moral authority. This is the moral-practical dichotomy in action, sanctioned by an extremely malevolent view of man and the universe.

John Calvin, (1509–1564), another Reformation theologian, had a more lenient view than Luther. He rejected the notion that usury is actually banned in the Bible. Since Jews are allowed to charge interest from strangers, God cannot be against usury. It would be fantastic, Calvin thought, to imagine that by "strangers" God meant the enemies of the Jews; and it would be most unchristian to legalize discrimination. According to Calvin, usury does not always conflict with God's law, so not all usurers need to be damned. There is a difference, he believed, between taking usury in the course of business and setting up business as a usurer. If a person collects interest on only one occasion, he is not a usurer. The crucial issue, Calvin thought, is the motive. If the motive is to help others, usury is good, but if the motive is personal profit, usury is evil.

Calvin claimed that the moral status of usury should be determined by the golden rule. It should be allowed only insofar as it does not run counter to Christian fairness and charity. Interest should never be charged to a man in urgent need, or to a poor man; the "welfare of the state" should always be considered. But it could be charged in cases where the borrower is wealthy and the interest will be used for Christian good. Thus he concluded that interest could neither be universally condemned nor universally permitted—but that, to protect the poor, a maximum rate should be set by law and never exceeded.[35]

Although the religious authorities did little to free usury from the taint of immorality, other thinkers were significantly furthering the economic understanding of the practice. In a book titled *Treatise on Contracts and Usury*, Molinaeus, a French jurist, made important contributions to liberate usury from Scholastic rationalism.[36] By this time, there was sufficient evidence for a logical thinker to see the merits of moneylending. Against the argument that money is barren, Molinaeus (1500–1566) observed that everyday experience of business life showed that the use of any considerable sum of money yields a service of importance. He argued, by reference to observation and logic, that money, assisted by human effort, does "bear fruit" in the form of new wealth; the money enables the borrower to create goods that he otherwise would not have been able to create. Just as Galileo would later apply Aristotle's method of observation and logic in refuting Aristotle's specific ideas in physics, so Molinaeus used Aristotle's method in refuting Aristotle's basic objection to usury. Unfortunately, like Galileo, Molinaeus was to suffer for his ideas: The Church forced him into exile and banned his book. Nevertheless, his ideas on usury spread throughout Europe and had a significant impact on future discussions of moneylending.[37]

The prevailing view that emerged in the late 16th century (and that, to a large extent, is still with us today) is that money is not barren and that usury plays a productive role in the economy. Usury, however, is unchristian; it is motivated by a desire for profit and can be used to exploit the poor. It can be practical, but it is not moral; therefore, it should be controlled by the state and subjected to regulation in order to restrain the rich and protect the poor.

This Christian view has influenced almost all attitudes about usury since. In a sense, Luther and Calvin *are* responsible for today's so-called "capitalism." They are responsible for the guilt many people feel from making money and the guilt that causes people to eagerly regulate the functions of capitalists. Moreover, the Protestants were the first to explicitly assert and *sanction* the moral-practical dichotomy—the idea that the moral and the practical are necessarily at odds. Because of original sin, the Protestants argued, men are incapable of being good, and thus concessions must be made in accordance with their wicked nature. Men must be permitted to some extent to engage in practical matters such as usury, even though such practices are immoral.

In spite of its horrific view of man, life, and reality, Luther and Calvin's brand of Christianity allowed individuals who were not intimidated by Christian theology to practice moneylending to some extent without legal persecution. Although still limited by government constraints, the chains were loosened, and this enabled economic progress through the periodic establishment of legal rates of interest.

The first country to establish a legal rate of interest was England in 1545 during the reign of Henry VIII. The rate was set at 10 percent. However, seven years later it was repealed, and usury was again completely banned. In an argument in 1571 to reinstate the bill, Mr. Molley, a lawyer representing the business interests in London, said before the House of Commons:

> Since to take reasonably, or so that both parties might do good, was not hurtful; . . . God did not so hate it, that he did utterly forbid it, but to the Jews amongst themselves only, for that he willed they should lend as Brethren together; for unto all others they were at large; and therefore to this day they are the greatest Usurers in the World. But be it, as indeed it is, evil, and that men are men, no Saints, to do all these things perfectly, uprightly and Brotherly; . . . and better may it be born to permit a little, than utterly to take away and prohibit Traffick; which hardly may be maintained generally without this.
>
> But it may be said, it is contrary to the direct word of God, and therefore an ill Law; if it were to appoint men to take Usury, it were to be disliked; but the difference is great between that and permitting or allowing, or suffering a matter to be unpunished.[38]

Observe that while pleading for a bill permitting usury—on the grounds that it is necessary ("Traffick . . . hardly may be maintained generally without

[it]")—Molley concedes that it is evil. This is the moral-practical dichotomy stated openly and in black-and-white terms, and it illustrates the general attitude of the era. The practice was now widely accepted as practical but still regarded as immoral, and the thinkers of the day grappled with this new context.

One of England's most significant 17th-century intellectuals, Francis Bacon (1561–1626), realized the benefits that moneylending offered to merchants and traders by providing them with capital. He also recognized the usurer's value in providing liquidity to consumers and businesses. And, although Bacon believed that the moral ideal would be lending at 0 percent interest, as the Bible requires, he, like Luther, saw this as utopian and held that "it is better to mitigate usury by declaration than suffer it to rage by connivance." Bacon therefore proposed two rates of usury: one set at a maximum of 5 percent and allowable to everyone; and a second rate, higher than 5 percent, allowable only to certain licensed persons and lent only to known merchants. The license was to be sold by the state for a fee.[39]

Again, interest and usury were pitted against morality. But Bacon saw moneylending as so important to commerce that the legal rate of interest had to offer sufficient incentive to attract lenders. Bacon recognized that a higher rate of interest is economically justified by the nature of certain loans.[40]

The economic debate had shifted from whether usury should be legal to whether and at what level government should set the interest rate (a debate that, of course, continues to this day, with the Fed setting certain interest rates). As one scholar put it: "The legal toleration of interest marked a revolutionary change in public opinion and gave a clear indication of the *divorce of ethics from economics* under the pressure of an expanding economic system."[41]

In spite of this progress, artists continued to compare usurers to idle drones, spiders, and bloodsuckers, and playwrights personified the moneygrubbing usurers in characters such as Sir Giles Overreach, Messrs. Mammon, Lucre, Hoard, Gripe, and Bloodhound. Probably the greatest work of art vilifying the usurer was written during this period—*The Merchant of Venice* by Shakespeare (1564–1616), which immortalized the character of the evil Jewish usurer, Shylock.

In *The Merchant of Venice*, Bassanio, a poor nobleman, needs cash in order to court the heiress, Portia. Bassanio goes to a Jewish moneylender, Shylock, for a loan, bringing his wealthy friend, Antonio, to stand as surety for it. Shylock, who has suffered great rudeness from Antonio in business, demands as security for the loan not Antonio's property, which he identifies as being at risk, but a pound of his flesh.[42]

The conflict between Shylock and Antonio incorporates all the elements of the arguments against usury. Antonio, the Christian, lends money and demands no interest. As Shylock describes him:

> Shy. [Aside.] How like a fawning publican he looks!
> I hate him for he is a Christian;

> But more for that in low simplicity
> He lends out money gratis, and brings down
> The rate of usance here with us in Venice.
> If I can catch him once upon the hip,
> I will feed fat the ancient grudge I bear him.
> He hates our sacred nation, and he rails,
> Even there where merchants most do congregate,
> On me, my bargains, and my well-won thrift,
> Which he calls interest. Cursed be my tribe,
> If I forgive him![43]

Shylock takes usury. He is portrayed as the lowly, angry, vengeful, and greedy Jew. When his daughter elopes and takes her father's money with her, he cries, "My daughter! O my ducats! O my daughter!"[44]—not sure for which he cares more.

It is clear that Shakespeare understood the issues involved in usury. Note Shylock's (legitimate) hostility toward Antonio because Antonio loaned money without charging interest and thus brought down the market rate of interest in Venice. Even Aristotle's "barren money" argument is present. Antonio, provoking Shylock, says:

> If thou wilt lend this money, lend it not
> As to thy friends,—for when did friendship take
> A breed for barren metal of his friend?—
> But lend it rather to thine enemy:
> Who if he break, thou mayst with better face
> Exact the penalty.[45]

Friends do not take "breed for barren metal" from friends; usury is something one takes only from an enemy.

Great art plays a crucial role in shaping popular attitudes, and Shakespeare's depiction of Shylock, like Dante's depiction of usurers, concretized for generations the dichotomous view of moneylending and thus helped entrench the alleged link between usury and evil. As late as 1600, medieval moral and economic theories were alive and well, even if they were increasingly out of step with the economic practice of the time.

The Enlightenment

During the Enlightenment, the European economy continued to grow, culminating with the Industrial Revolution. This growth involved increased activity in every sector of the economy. Banking houses were established to provide credit to a wide array of economic endeavors. The Baring Brothers and the House of Rothschild were just the largest of the many banks that would ultimately help fuel the Industrial Revolution, funding railroads, factories, ports, and industry in general.

Economic understanding of the important productive role of usury continued to improve over the next four hundred years. Yet, the moral evaluation of usury would change very little. The morality of altruism—the notion that self-sacrifice is moral and that self-interest is evil—was embraced and defended by many Enlightenment intellectuals and continued to hamper the acceptability of usury. After all, usury is a naked example of the pursuit of profit—which is patently self-interested. Further, it still seemed to the thinkers of the time that usury could be a zero-sum transaction—that a rich lender might profit at the expense of a poor borrower. Even a better conception of usury—let alone the misconception of it being a zero-sum transaction—is anathema to altruism, which demands the opposite of personal profit: self-sacrifice for the sake of others.

In the mid-17th century, northern Europe was home to a new generation of scholars who recognized that usury served an essential economic purpose, and that it should be allowed freely. Three men made significant contributions in this regard.

Claudius Salmasius (1588–1653), a French scholar teaching in Holland, thoroughly refuted the claims about the "barrenness" of moneylending; he showed the important productive function of usury and even suggested that there should be more usurers, since competition between them would reduce the rate of interest. Other Dutch scholars agreed with him, and, partially as a result of this, Holland became especially tolerant of usury, making it legal at times. Consequently, the leading banks of the era were found in Holland, and it became the world's commercial and financial center, the wealthiest state in Europe, and the envy of the world.[46]

Robert Jacques Turgot (1727–1781), a French economist, was the first to identify usury's connection to property rights. He argued that a creditor has the right to dispose of his money in any way he wishes and at whatever rate the market will bear, because it is *his* property. Turgot was also the first economist to fully understand that the passing of time changes the value of money. He saw the difference between the present value and the future value of money—concepts that are at the heart of any modern financial analysis. According to Turgot: "If . . . two gentlemen suppose that a sum of 1000 Francs and a promise of 1000 Francs possess exactly the same value, they put forward a still more absurd supposition; for if these two things were of equal value, why should any one borrow at all?"[47] Turgot even repudiated the medieval notion that time belonged to God. Time, he argued, belongs to the *individual* who uses it and therefore time could be sold.[48]

During the same period, the British philosopher Jeremy Bentham (1748–1832) wrote a treatise entitled *A Defense of Usury*. Bentham argued that any restrictions on interest rates were economically harmful because they restricted an innovator's ability to raise capital. Since innovative trades inherently involved high risk, they could only be funded at high interest rates. Limits on permissible interest rates, he argued, would kill innovation—the engine of growth. Correcting another medieval error, Bentham also showed that restrictive usury laws actually harmed the borrowers. Such restrictions cause the credit markets to shrink while demand for credit remains the same or goes up; thus, potential borrowers have to seek loans in an illegal market where they would have to pay a premium for the additional risk of illegal trading.

Bentham's most important contribution was his advocacy of contractual freedom:

> My neighbours, being at liberty, have happened to concur among themselves in dealing at a certain rate of interest. I, who have money to lend, and Titus, who wants to borrow it of me, would be glad, the one of us to accept, the other to give, an interest somewhat higher than theirs: Why is the liberty they exercise to be made a pretence for depriving me and Titus of ours.[49]

This was perhaps the first attempt at a moral defense of usury.

Unfortunately, Bentham and his followers undercut this effort with their philosophy of utilitarianism, according to which rights, liberty, and therefore moneylending, were valuable only insofar as they increased "social utility": "the greatest good for the greatest number." Bentham famously dismissed individual rights—the idea that each person should be free to act on his own judgment—as "nonsense upon stilts."[50] He embraced the idea that the individual has a "duty" to serve the well-being of the collective, or, as he put it, the "general mass of felicity."[51] Thus, in addition to undercutting Turgot's major achievement, Bentham also doomed the first effort at a moral defense of usury—which he himself had proposed.

An explicitly utilitarian attempt at a moral defense of usury was launched in 1774 in the anonymously published *Letters on Usury and Interest*. The goal of the book was to explain why usury should be accepted in England of the 18th century, and why this acceptance did not contradict the Church's teachings. The ultimate reason, the author argued, is one of utility:

> Here, then, is a sure and infallible rule to judge of the lawfulness of a practice. Is it useful to the State? Is it beneficial to the individuals that compose it? Either of these is sufficient to obtain a tolerance; but both together vest it with a character of justice and equity. . . . In fact, if we look into the laws of different nations concerning usury, we shall find that they are all formed on the principle of public utility. In those states where usury was found hurtful to society, it was prohibited. In those where it was neither hurtful nor very beneficial, it was tolerated. In those where it was useful, it was authorized. In ours, it is absolutely necessary.[52]

And:

> [T]he practice of lending money to interest is in this nation, and under this constitution, beneficial to all degrees; therefore it is beneficial to society. I say in this nation; which, as long as it continues to be a commercial one, must be chiefly supported by interest; for interest is the soul of credit and credit is the soul of commerce.[53]

Although the utilitarian argument in defense of usury contains some economic truth, it is morally bankrupt. Utilitarian moral reasoning for the propriety of usury depends on the perceived benefits of the practice to the collective or the nation. But what happens, for example, when usury in the form of sub-prime mortgage loans creates distress for a significant number of people and financial turmoil in some markets? How can it be justified? Indeed, it cannot. The utilitarian argument collapses in the face of any such economic problem, leaving moneylenders exposed to the wrath of the public and to the whips and chains of politicians seeking a scapegoat for the crisis.

Although Salmasius, Turgot, and Bentham made significant progress in understanding the economic and political value of usury, not all their fellow intellectuals followed suit. The father of economics, Adam Smith (1723–1790), wrote: "As something can everywhere be made by the use of money, something ought everywhere to be paid for the use of it."[54] Simple and elegant. Yet, Smith also believed that the government must control the rate of interest. He believed that unfettered markets would create excessively high interest rates, which would hurt the economy—which, in turn, would harm society.[55] Because Smith thought that society's welfare was the only justification for usury, he held that the government must intervene to correct the errors of the "invisible hand."

Although Smith was a great innovator in economics, philosophically, he was a follower. He accepted the common philosophical ideas of his time, including altruism, of which utilitarianism is a form. Like Bentham, he justified capitalism only through its social benefits. If his projections of what would come to pass in a fully free market amounted to a less-than-optimal solution for society, then he advocated government intervention. Government intervention is the logical outcome of any utilitarian defense of usury.

(Smith's idea that there need be a "perfect" legal interest rate remains with us to this day. His notion of such a rate was that it should be slightly higher than the market rate—what he called the "golden mean." The chairman of the Federal Reserve is today's very *visible* hand, constantly searching for the "perfect" rate or "golden mean" by alternately establishing artificially low and artificially high rates.)

Following Bentham and Smith, all significant 19th-century economists—such as David Ricardo, Jean Baptiste Say, and John Stuart Mill—considered the economic importance of usury to be obvious and argued that interest rates should be determined by freely contracting individuals. These economists, followed later by the Austrians—especially Carl Menger, Eugen von Böhm-Bawerk, and Ludwig von Mises—developed sound theories of the productivity of interest and gained a significant economic understanding of its practical role. But the moral-practical dichotomy inherent in their altruistic, utilitarian, social justification for usury remained in play, and the practice continued to be morally condemned and thus heavily regulated if not outlawed.

The 19th and 20th Centuries

Despite their flaws, the thinkers of the Enlightenment had created sufficient economic understanding to fuel the Industrial Revolution throughout the 19th century. Economically and politically, facts and reason had triumphed over faith; a sense of individualism had taken hold; the practicality of the profit motive had become clear; and, relative to eras past, the West was thriving.

Morally and philosophically, however, big trouble was brewing. As capitalism neared a glorious maturity, a new, more consistent brand of altruism, created by Kant, Hegel, and their followers, was sweeping Europe. At the political-economic level, this movement manifested itself in the ideas of Karl Marx (1818–1883).

Marx, exploiting the errors of the Classical economists, professed the medieval notion that all production is a result of manual labor; but he also elaborated, claiming that laborers do not retain the wealth they create. The capitalists, he said, take advantage of their control over the means of production—secured to them by private property—and "loot" the laborers' work. According to Marx, moneylending and other financial activities are not productive, but exploitative; moneylenders exert no effort, do no productive work, and yet reap the rewards of production through usury.[56] As one 20th-century Marxist put it: "The major argument against usury is that labor constitutes the true source of wealth."[57] Marx adopted all the medieval clichés, including the notion that Jews are devious, conniving money-grubbers.

> What is the profane basis of Judaism? *Practical* need, *self-interest*. What is the worldly cult of the Jew? *Huckstering*. What is his worldly god? *Money*.
>
> Money is the jealous god of Israel, beside which no other god may exist. Money abases all the gods of mankind and changes them into commodities.[58]

Marx believed that the Jews were evil—not because of their religion, as others were clamoring at the time—but because they pursued their own selfish interests and sought to make money. And Marxists were not alone in their contempt for these qualities.

Artists who, like Marx, resented capitalists in general and moneylenders in particular, dominated Western culture in the 19th century. In Dickens's *A Christmas Carol*, we see the moneygrubbing Ebenezer Scrooge. In Dostoyevsky's *Crime and Punishment*, the disgusting old lady whom Raskolnikov murders is a usurer. And in *The Brothers Karamazov*, Dostoyevsky writes:

> It was known too that the young person had . . . been given to what is called "speculation," and that she had shown marked abilities in the direction, so that many people began to say that she was no better than a Jew. It was not that she lent money on interest, but it was known, for instance, that she had for some time past, in partnership with old Karamazov, actually invested in the purchase of bad debts for a trifle, a tenth of their nominal value, and afterwards had made out of them ten times their value.[59]

In other words, she was what in the 1980s became known as a "vulture" capitalist buying up distressed debt.

Under Marx's influential ideas, and given the culture-wide contempt for moneylenders, the great era of capitalism—of thriving banks and general financial success—was petering out. Popular sentiment concerning usury was reverting to a Dark Ages-type of hatred. Marx and company put the moneylenders back into Dante's *Inferno*, and to this day they have not been able to escape.

The need for capital, however, would not be suppressed by the label "immoral." People still sought to start businesses and purchase homes; thus usury was still seen as practical. Like the Church of the Middle Ages, people found themselves simultaneously condemning the practice and engaging in it.

Consequently, just as the term "interest" had been coined in the Middle Ages to facilitate the Church's selective opposition to usury and to avoid the stigma associated with the practice, so modern man employed the term for the same purpose. The concept of moneylending was again split into two allegedly different concepts: the charging of "interest" and the practice of "usury." Lending at "interest" came to designate lower-premium, lower-risk, less-greedy lending, while "usury" came to mean specifically higher-premium, higher-risk, more-greedy lending. This artificial division enabled the wealthier, more powerful, more influential people to freely engage in moneylending with the one hand, while continuing to condemn the practice with the other. Loans made to lower-risk, higher-income borrowers would be treated as morally acceptable, while those made to higher-risk, lower-income borrowers would remain morally contemptible. (The term "usury" is now almost universally taken to mean "excessive" or illegal premium on loans, while the term "interest" designates tolerable or legal premium.)

From the 19th century onward, in the United States and in most other countries, usury laws would restrict the rates of interest that could be charged on loans, and there would be an ongoing battle between businessmen and legislators over what those rates should be. These laws, too, are still with us.

As Bentham predicted, such laws harm not only lenders but also borrowers, who are driven into the shadows where they procure shady and often illegal loans in order to acquire the capital they need for their endeavors. And given the extra risk posed by potential legal complications for the lenders, these loans are sold at substantially higher interest rates than they would be if moneylending were fully legal and unregulated.

In the United States, demand for high-risk loans has always existed, and entrepreneurs have always arisen to service the demand for funds. They have been scorned, condemned to Hell, assaulted, jailed, and generally treated like the usurers of the Middle Ages—but they have relentlessly supplied the capital that has enabled Americans to achieve unprecedented levels of productiveness and prosperity.

The earliest known advertisement for a small-loan service in an American newspaper appeared in the *Chicago Tribune* in November 1869. By 1872, the industry was prospering. Loans collateralized by furniture, diamonds, warehouse receipts, houses, and pianos were available (called "chattel" loans). The first salary-loan office (offering loans made in advance of a paycheck) was opened by John Mulholland in Kansas City in 1893. Within fifteen years he had offices all across the country. The going rate on a chattel loan was 10 percent a month for loans under $50, and 5–7 percent a month for larger loans. Some loans were made at very high rates, occasionally over 100 percent a month.[60]

The reason rates were so high is because of the number of defaults. With high rates in play, the losses on loans in default could ordinarily be absorbed as a cost of doing business. In this respect, the 19th-century small-loan business was a precursor of the 20th-century "junk" bond business or the 21st-century sub-prime mortgage lender. However, unlike the "junk" bond salesman, who had recourse to the law in cases of default or bankruptcy, these small-loan men operated on the fringes of society—and often outside the law. Because of the social stigmatization and legal isolation of the creditors, legal recourse against a defaulting borrower was generally unavailable to a usurer. Yet these back-alley loans provided a valuable service—one for which there was great demand—and they enabled many people to start their own businesses or improve their lives in other ways.

Of course, whereas most of these borrowers paid off their loans and succeeded in their endeavors, many of them got into financial trouble—and the latter cases, not the former, were widely publicized. The moneylenders were blamed, and restrictions were multiplied and tightened.

In spite of all the restrictions, laws, and persecutions, the market found ways to continue. In 1910, Arthur Morris set up the first bank in America with the express purpose of providing small loans to individuals at interest rates based on the borrower's "character and earning power." In spite of the usury limit of 6 percent that existed in Virginia at the time, Morris's bank found ways, as did usurers in the Middle Ages, to make loans at what appeared to be a 6 percent interest rate while the actual rates were much higher and more appropriate. For instance, a loan for $100 might be made as follows: A commission of 2 percent plus the 6 percent legal rate would be taken off the top in advance; thus the borrower would receive $92. Then he would repay the loan at $2 a week over fifty weeks. The effective compound annual interest rate on such a loan was in excess of 18 percent. And penalties would be assessed for any delinquent payments.[61] Such camouflaged interest rates were a throwback to the Middle Ages, when bankers developed innovative ways to circumvent the restrictions on usury established by the Church. And, as in the Middle Ages, such lending became common as the demand for capital was widespread. Consequently, these banks multiplied and thrived—for a while.

(Today's credit card industry is the successor to such institutions. Credit card lenders charge high interest rates to high-risk customers, and penalties for delinquency. And borrowers use these loans for consumption as well as to start or fund small businesses. And, of course, the credit card industry is regularly attacked for its high rates of interest and its "exploitation" of customers. To this day, credit card interest rates are restricted by usury laws, and legislation attempting to further restrict these rates is periodically introduced.)

In 1913, in New York, a moneylender who issued loans to people who could not get them at conventional banks appeared before a court on the charge of usury. In the decision, the judge wrote:

> You are one of the most contemptible usurers in your unspeakable business. The poor people must be protected from such sharks as you, and we must trust that your conviction and sentence will be a notice to you and all your kind that the courts have found a way to put a stop to usury. Men of your type are a curse to the community, and the money they gain is blood money.[62]

This ruling is indicative of the general attitude toward usurers at the time. The moral-practical dichotomy was alive and kicking, and the moneylenders were taking the blows. Although their practical value to the economy was now clear, their moral status as evil was still common "sense." And the intellectuals of the day would only exacerbate the problem.

The most influential economist of the 20th century was John Maynard Keynes (1883–1946), whose ideas not only shaped the theoretical field of modern economics but also played a major role in shaping government policies in the United States and around the world. Although Keynes allegedly rejected Marx's ideas, he shared Marx's hatred of the profit motive and usury. He also agreed with

Adam Smith that government must control interest rates; otherwise investment and thus society would suffer. And he revived the old Reformation idea that usury is a necessary evil:

> When the accumulation of wealth is no longer of high social importance, there will be great changes in the code of morals. We shall be able to rid ourselves of many of the pseudo-moral principles which have hag-ridden us for two hundred years, by which we have exalted some of the most distasteful of human qualities into the position of the highest virtues. . . . But beware! The time for all this is not yet. For at least another hundred years we must pretend to ourselves and to everyone that fair is foul and foul is fair; for foul is useful and fair is not. Avarice and usury and precaution must be our gods for a little longer still. For only they can lead us out of the tunnel of economic necessity into daylight.[63]

Although Keynes and other economists and intellectuals of the day recognized the need of usury, they universally condemned the practice and its practitioners as foul and unfair. Thus, regardless of widespread recognition of the fact that usury is a boon to the economy, when the Great Depression occurred in the United States, the moneylenders on Wall Street were blamed. As Franklin Delano Roosevelt put it:

> The rulers of the exchange of mankind's goods have failed, through their own stubbornness and their own incompetence, have admitted failure, and have abdicated. Practices of the unscrupulous money changers stand indicted in the court of public opinion, rejected by the hearts and minds of men . . . [We must] apply social values more noble than mere monetary profit.[64]

And so the "solution" to the problems of the Great Depression was greater government intervention throughout the economy—especially in the regulation of interest and the institutions that deal in it. After 1933, banks were restricted in all aspects of their activity: the interest rates they could pay their clients, the rates they could charge, and to whom they could lend. In 1934, the greatest bank in American history, J. P. Morgan, was broken up by the government into several companies. The massive regulations and coercive restructurings of the 1930s illustrate the continuing contempt for the practice of taking interest on loans and the continuing distrust of those—now mainly bankers—who engage in this activity. (We paid a dear price for those regulations with the savings and loan crisis of the 1970s and 1980s, which cost American taxpayers hundreds of billions of dollars.[65] And we continue to pay the price of these regulations in higher taxes, greater financial costs, lost innovation, and stifled economic growth.)

The 21st Century

From ancient Greece and Rome to the Dark and Middle Ages, to the Renaissance and Reformation, to the 19th and 20th centuries, moneylending has been morally condemned and legally restrained. Today, at the dawn of the 21st century, moneylending remains a pariah.

One of the latest victims of this moral antagonism is the business of providing payday loans. This highly popular and beneficial service has been branded with the scarlet letter "U"; consequently, despite the great demand for these loans, the practice has been relegated to the fringes of society and the edge of the law. These loans carry annualized interest rates as high as 1000 percent, because they are typically very short term (i.e., to be paid back on payday). By some estimates there are 25,000 payday stores across America, and it is "a $6 billion dollar industry serving fifteen million people every month."[66] The institutions issuing these loans have found ways, just as banks always have, to circumvent state usury laws. Bank regulators have severely restricted the ability of community banks to offer payday loans or even to work with payday loan offices, more than thirteen states have banned them altogether, and Congress is currently looking at ways to ban all payday loans.[67] This is in spite of the fact that demand for these loans is soaring and that they serve a genuine economic need, that they are a real value for low-income households. As the *Wall Street Journal* reports: "Georgia outlawed payday loans in 2004, and thousands of workers have since taken to traveling over the border to find payday stores in Tennessee, Florida and South Carolina. So the effect of the ban has been to increase consumer credit costs and inconvenience for Georgia consumers."[68]

A story in the *LA Weekly*, titled "Shylock 2000"—ignoring the great demand for payday loans, ignoring the economic value they provide to countless borrowers, and ignoring the fact that the loans are made by mutual consent to mutual advantage—proceeded to describe horrific stories of borrowers who have gone bankrupt. The article concluded: "What's astonishing about this story is that, 400 years after Shakespeare created the avaricious lender Shylock, such usury may be perfectly legal."[69]

What is truly astonishing is that after centuries of moneylenders providing capital and opportunities to billions of willing people on mutually agreed-upon terms, the image of these persistent businessmen has not advanced beyond that of Shylock.

The "Shylocks" du jour, of course, are the sub-prime mortgage lenders, with whom this article began. These lenders provided mortgages designed to enable low-income borrowers to buy homes. Because the default rate among these borrowers is relatively high, the loans are recognized as high-risk transactions and are sold at correspondingly high rates of interest. Although it is common knowledge that many of these loans are now in default, and although it is widely believed that the lenders are to blame for the situation, what is not well known is, as Paul Harvey would say, "the rest of the story."

The tremendous growth in this industry is a direct consequence of government policy. Since the 1930s, the U.S. government has encouraged home ownership among all Americans—but especially among those in lower income brackets. To this end, the government created the Federal Home Loan Banks (which are exempt from state and local income taxes) to provide incentives for smaller banks to make mortgage loans to low-income Americans. Congress passed the Community Reinvestment Act, which requires banks to invest in their local communities, including by providing mortgage loans to people in low-income brackets. The government created Fannie Mae and Freddie Mac, both of which have a mandate to issue and guarantee mortgage loans to low-income borrowers.

In recent years, all these government schemes and more (e.g., artificially low interest rates orchestrated by the Fed) led to a frenzy of borrowing and lending. The bottom line is that the government has artificially mitigated lenders' risk, and it has done so on the perverse, altruistic premise that "society" has a moral duty to increase home ownership among low-income Americans. The consequence of this folly has been a significant increase in delinquent loans and foreclosures, which has led to wider financial problems at banks and at other institutions that purchased the mortgages in the secondary markets.

Any objective evaluation of the facts would place the blame for this disaster on the government policies that caused it. But no—just as in the past, the lenders are being blamed and scapegoated.

Although some of these lenders clearly did take irrational risks on many of these loans, that should be their own problem, and they should have to suffer the consequences of their irrational actions—whether significant financial loss or bankruptcy. (The government most certainly should not bail them out.) However, without the perception of reduced risk provided by government meddling in the economy, far fewer lenders would have been so frivolous.

Further, the number of people benefiting from sub-prime mortgage loans, which make it possible for many people to purchase a home for the first time, is in the millions—and the vast majority of these borrowers are *not* delinquent or in default; rather, they are paying off their loans and enjoying their homes, a fact never mentioned by the media.

It should also be noted that, whereas the mortgage companies are blamed for all the defaulting loans, no blame is placed on the irresponsible borrowers who took upon themselves debt that they knew—or should have known—they could not handle.

After four hundred years of markets proving the incredible benefits generated by moneylending, intellectuals, journalists, and politicians still rail against lenders and their institutions. And, in spite of all the damage done by legal restrictions on interest, regulation of moneylenders, and government interference in financial markets, whenever there is an economic "crisis," there is invariably a wave of demand for *more* of these controls, not less.

Moneylenders are still blamed for recessions; they are still accused of being greedy and of taking advantage of the poor; they are still portrayed on TV and in movies as slick, murderous villains; and they are still distrusted by almost everyone. (According to a recent poll, only 16 percent of Americans have substantial confidence in the American financial industry.[70]) Thus, it should come as no surprise that the financial sector is the most regulated, most controlled industry in America today.

But what explains the ongoing antipathy toward, distrust of, and coercion against these bearers of capital and opportunity? What explains the modern anti-moneylending mentality? Why are moneylenders today held in essentially the same ill repute as they were in the Middle Ages?

The explanation for this lies in the fact that, fundamentally, 21st-century ethics is no different from the ethics of the Middle Ages.

All parties in the assault on usury share a common ethical root: altruism—belief in the notion that self-sacrifice is moral and self-interest is evil. This is the source of the problem. So long as self-interest is condemned, neither usury in particular, nor profit in general, can be seen as good—both will be seen as evil.

Moneylending cannot be defended by reference to its economic practicality alone. If moneylending is to be recognized as a fully legitimate practice and defended accordingly, then its defenders must discover and embrace a new code of ethics, one that upholds self-interest—and thus personal profit—as moral.

Conclusion

Although serious economists today uniformly recognize the economic benefits of charging interest or usury on loans, they rarely, if ever, attempt a philosophical or moral defense of this position. Today's economists either reject philosophy completely or adopt the moral-practical split, accepting the notion that although usury is practical, it is either immoral or, at best, amoral.

Modern philosophers, for the most part, have no interest in the topic at all, partly because it requires them to deal with reality, and partly because they believe self-interest, capitalism, and everything they entail, to be evil. Today's philosophers, almost to a man, accept self-sacrifice as the standard of morality and physical labor as the source of wealth. Thus, to the extent that they refer to moneylending at all, they consider it unquestionably unjust, and positions to the contrary unworthy of debate.

It is time to set the record straight.

Whereas Aristotle *united* productiveness with morality and thereby condemned usury as immoral based on his mistaken belief that the practice is unproductive—and whereas everyone since Aristotle (including contemporary economists and philosophers) has *severed* productiveness from morality and condemned usury on biblical or altruistic grounds as immoral (or at best amoral)—what is needed is a view that again *unifies* productiveness and morality, but that also sees usury as productive, and morality as the means to practical success on earth. What is needed is the economic knowledge of the last millennium *combined with* a new moral theory—one that upholds the morality of self-interest and thus the virtue of personal profit.

Let us first condense the key economic points; then we will turn to a brief indication of the morality of self-interest.

The crucial economic knowledge necessary to a proper defense of usury includes an understanding of why lenders charge interest on money—and why they would do so even in a risk-free, noninflationary environment. Lenders charge interest because their money has alternative uses—uses they temporarily forego by lending the money to borrowers. When a lender lends money, he is thereby unable to use that money toward some benefit or profit for himself. Had he not lent it, he could have spent it on consumer goods that he would have enjoyed, or he could have invested it in alternative moneymaking ventures. And the longer the term of the loan, the longer the lender must postpone his alternative use of the money. Thus interest is charged because the lender views the loan as a better, more profitable use of his money over the period of the loan than any of his alternative uses of the same funds over the same time; he estimates that, given the interest charged, the benefit to him is greater from making the loan than from any other use of his capital.[71]

A lender tries to calculate in advance the likelihood or unlikelihood that he will be repaid all his capital plus the interest. The less convinced he is that a loan will be repaid, the higher the interest rate he will charge. Higher rates enable lenders to profit for their willingness to take greater risks. The practice of charging interest is therefore an expression of the human ability to project the future, to plan, to analyze, to calculate risk, and to act in the face of uncertainty. In a word, it is an expression of man's ability to *reason*. The better a lender's thinking, the more money he will make.

Another economic principle that is essential to a proper defense of usury is recognition of the fact that moneylending is *productive*. This fact was made increasingly clear over the centuries, and today it is incontrovertible. By choosing to whom he will lend money, the moneylender determines which projects he will help bring into existence and which individuals he will provide with opportunities to improve the quality of their lives and his. Thus, lenders make themselves money by rewarding people for the virtues of innovation, productiveness, personal responsibility, and entrepreneurial talent; and they withhold their sanction, thus minimizing their losses, from people who exhibit signs of stagnation, laziness, irresponsibility, and inefficiency. The lender, in seeking profit, does not consider the well-being of society or of the borrower. Rather, he assesses his alternatives, evaluates the risk, and seeks the greatest return on his investment.

And, of course, lent money is not "barren"; it is fruitful: It enables borrowers to improve their lives or produce new goods or services. Nor is moneylending a zero-sum game: Both the borrower and the lender benefit from the exchange (as ultimately does everyone involved in the economy). The lender makes a profit, and the borrower gets to use capital—whether for consumption or investment purposes—that he otherwise would not be able to use.[72]

An understanding of these and other economic principles is necessary to defend the practice of usury. But such an understanding is *not* sufficient to defend the practice. From the brief history we have recounted, it is evident that all commentators on usury from the beginning of time have known that those who charge interest are self-interested, that the very nature of their activity is motivated by personal profit. Thus, in order to defend moneylenders, their institutions, and the kind of world they make possible, one must be armed with a moral code that recognizes rational self-interest and therefore the pursuit of profit as moral, and that consequently regards productivity as a virtue and upholds man's right to his property and to his time.

There is such a morality: It is Ayn Rand's Objectivist ethics, or rational egoism, and it is the missing link in the defense of usury (and capitalism in general).

According to rational egoism, man's life—the life of each individual man—is the standard of moral value, and his reasoning mind is his basic means of living. Being moral, on this view, consists in thinking and producing the values on which one's life and happiness depend—while leaving others free to think and act on their own judgment for their own sake. The Objectivist ethics holds that people should act rationally, in their own long-term best interest; that each person is the proper beneficiary of his own actions; that each person has a moral right to keep, use, and dispose of the product of his efforts; and that each individual is capable of thinking for himself, of producing values, and of deciding whether, with whom, and on what terms he will trade. It is a morality of self-interest, individual rights, and personal responsibility. And it is grounded in the fundamental fact of human nature: the fact that man's basic means of living is his ability to reason.

Ayn Rand identified the principle that the greatest productive, life-serving power on earth is not human muscle but the human mind. Consequently, she regarded profit-seeking—the use of the mind to identify, produce, and trade life-serving values—as the essence of being moral.[73]

Ayn Rand's Objectivist ethics is essential to the defense of moneylending. It provides the moral foundation without which economic arguments in defense of usury cannot prevail. It demonstrates why moneylending is supremely *moral*.

The Objectivist ethics frees moneylenders from the shackles of Dante's inferno, enables them to brush off Shakespeare's ridicule, and empowers them to take an irrefutable moral stand against persecution and regulation by the state. The day that this moral code becomes widely embraced will be the day that moneylenders—and every other producer of value—will be completely free to charge whatever rates their customers will pay and to reap the rewards righteously and proudly.

If this moral ideal were made a political reality, then, for the first time in history, moneylenders, bankers, and their institutions would be legally permitted and morally encouraged to work to their fullest potential, making profits by providing the lifeblood of capital to our economy. Given what these heroes have achieved while scorned and shackled, it is hard to imagine what their productive achievements would be if they were revered and freed.

Notes

Acknowledgments: The author would like to thank the following people for their assistance and comments on this article: Elan Journo, Onkar Ghate, Sean Green, John D. Lewis, John P. McCaskey, and Craig Biddle.

1. Aristotle, *The Politics of Aristotle*, trans. Benjamin Jowett (Oxford: Clarendon Press, 1885), book 1, chap. 10, p. 19.

2. Plutarch, *Plutarch's Morals*, trans. William Watson Goodwin (Boston: Little, Brown & Company, 1874), pp. 412–24.

3. Lewis H. Haney, *History of Economic Thought* (New York: The Macmillan Company, 1920), p. 71.

4. Anthony Trollope, *Life of Cicero* (Kessinger Publishing, 2004), p. 70.

5. William Manchester, *A World Lit Only by Fire* (Boston: Back Bay Books, 1993), pp. 5–6.

6. Glyn Davies, *A History of Money: From Ancient Times to the Present Day* (Cardiff: University of Wales Press, 1994), p. 117.

7. Ezekiel 18:13.

8. Deuteronomy 23:19–20.

9. Luke 6:35.

10. Jacques Le Goff, *Your Money or Your Life* (New York: Zone Books, 1988), p. 26.

11. Edward Henry Palmer, *A History of the Jewish Nation* (London: Society for Promoting Christian Knowledge, 1874), pp. 253–54. And www.routledge-ny.com/ref/middleages/Jewish/England.pdf.

12. Byrne is here quoting Jacob Twinger of Königshofen, a 14th-century priest.

13. Joseph Patrick Byrne, *The Black Death* (Westport: Greenwood Press, 2004), p. 84.

14. Sidney Homer, *A History of Interest Rates* (New Brunswick: Rutgers University Press, 1963), p. 71.

15. Sermon by Jacques de Vitry, "Ad status" 59, 14, quoted in Le Goff, *Your Money or Your Life*, pp. 56–57.

16. See Thomas Aquinas, *Summa Theologica*, part II, section II, question 78, article 1.

17. Ibid.

18. Frank Wilson Blackmar, *Economics* (New York: The Macmillan Company, 1907), p. 178.

19. Le Goff, *Your Money or Your Life*, pp. 33–45.

20. Jeremy Rifkin, *The European Dream* (Cambridge: Polity, 2004), p. 105.

21. Le Goff, *Your Money or Your Life*, p. 30.

22. Davies, *A History of Money*, p. 154.

23. Ibid., pp. 146–74.

24. Robert Burton, *Sacred Trust* (Oxford: Oxford University Press, 1996), p. 118.

25. Ibid., pp. 118–20.

26. Homer, *A History of Interest Rates*, p. 73.

27. As Blackstone's *Commentaries on the Laws of England* puts it: "When money is lent on a contract to receive not only the principal sum again, but also an increase by way of compensation for the use, the increase is called *interest* by those who *think* it lawful, and *usury* by those who do not." p. 1336.

28. Homer, *A History of Interest Rates*, pp. 72–74.

29. Le Goff, *Your Money or Your Life*, p. 74.

30. Ibid., pp. 47–64.

31. Dante Alighieri, *The Inferno*, Canto XVII, lines 51–54.

32. Dorothy M. DiOrio, "Dante's Condemnation of Usury," in *Re: Artes Liberales* V, no. 1, 1978, pp. 17–25.

33. Davies, *A History of Money*, pp. 177–78.

34. Paul M. Johnson, *A History of the Jews* (New York: HarperCollins, 1988), p. 242.

35. Eugen von Böhm-Bawerk, *Capital and Interest: A Critical History of Economical Theory* (London: Macmillan and Co., 1890), trans. William A. Smart, book I, chapter III.

36. Charles Dumoulin (Latinized as Molinaeus), *Treatise on Contracts and Usury* (1546).

37. Böhm-Bawerk, *Capital and Interest*, book I, chapter III.

38. Sir Simonds D'Ewes, "Journal of the House of Commons: April 1571," in *The Journals of all the Parliaments during the reign of Queen Elizabeth* (London: John Starkey, 1682), pp. 155–80. Online: http://www.british-history.ac.uk/report.asp?compid=43684.

39. Francis Bacon, "Of Usury," in *Bacon's Essays* (London: Macmillan and Co., 1892), p. 109.

40. Davies, *A History of Money*, p. 222.

41. Ibid., p. 222, emphasis added.

42. James Buchan, *Frozen Desire* (New York: Farrar, Strauss & Giroux, 1997), p. 87 (synopsis of the play).

43. William Shakespeare, *The Merchant of Venice*, Act 1, Scene 2.

44. Ibid., Act 3, Scene 2.

45. Ibid., Act 1, Scene 3.

46. Böhm-Bawerk, *Capital and Interest*, book I, chapter III.

47. Ibid., book I, p. 56.

48. Ibid., book I, chapter IV.

49. Jeremy Bentham, *A Defence of Usury* (Philadelphia: Mathew Carey, 1787), p. 10.

50. Jeremy Bentham, *The Works of Jeremy Bentham*, edited by John Bowring (Edinburgh: W. Tait; London: Simpkin, Marshall, & Co., 1843), p. 501.

51. Ibid., p. 493.

52. Anonymous, *Letters on Usury and Interest* (London: J. P. Coghlan, 1774).

53. Ibid.

54. Adam Smith, *The Wealth of Nations* (New York: Penguin Classics, 1986), p. 456.

55. Ibid.

56. For a thorough rebuttal of Marx's view, see Böhm-Bawerk, *Capital and Interest*, book I, chapter XII.

57. Gabriel Le Bras, quoted in Le Goff, *Your Money or Your Life*, p. 43.

58. Johnson, *A History of the Jews*, p. 351.

59. Fyodor M. Dostoevsky, *The Brothers Karamazov*, trans. Constance Garnett (Spark Publishing, 2004), p. 316.

60. James Grant, *Money of the Mind* (New York: Noonday Press, 1994), p. 79.

61. Ibid., pp. 91–95.

62. Ibid., p. 83.

63. John Maynard Keynes, "Economic Possibilities for our Grandchildren," in *Essays in Persuasion* (New York: W. W. Norton & Company, 1963), pp. 359, 362. Online: http://www. econ.yale .edu/smith/ econ116a/keynes1.pdf.

64. Franklin D. Roosevelt, First Inaugural Address, March 4, 1933, http://www.historytools.org/ sources/froosevelt1st.html.

65. To understand the link between 1930s regulations and the S&L crisis, see Edward J. Kane, *The S&L Insurance Mess: How Did It Happen?* (Washington, D.C.: The Urban Institute Press, 1989), and Richard M. Salsman, *The Collapse of Deposit Insurance—and the Case for Abolition* (Great Barrington, MA: American Institute for Economic Research, 1993).

66. "Mayday for Payday Loans," *Wall Street Journal*, April 2, 2007, http://online.wsj.com/article/ SB117546964173756271.html.

67. "U.S. Moves Against Payday Loans, Which Critics Charge Are Usurious," *Wall Street Journal*, January 4, 2002, http://online.wsj.com/article/SB1010098721429807840.html.

68. "Mayday for Payday Loans," *Wall Street Journal*.

69. Christine Pelisek, "Shylock 2000," *LA Weekly*, February 16, 2000, http://www.laweekly.com/news/offbeat/shylock-2000/11565/.

70. *Wall Street Journal*, August 2, 2007, p. A4.

71. For an excellent presentation of this theory of interest, see Böhm-Bawerk, *Capital and Interest*, book 2.

72. For a discussion of the productive nature of financial activity, see my taped course "In Defense of Financial Markets," http://www.aynrandbookstore2.com/prodinfo.asp?number=DB46D.

73. For more on Objectivism, see Leonard Peikoff, *Objectivism: The Philosophy of Ayn Rand* (New York: Dutton, 1991); and Ayn Rand, *Atlas Shrugged* (New York: Random House, 1957) and *Capitalism: The Unknown Ideal* (New York: New American Library 1966).

Bibliography

Böhm-Bawerk, Eugen von. *Capital and Interest: A Critical History of Economical Theory*. Books I–III. Trans. William A. Smart. London: Macmillan and Co., 1890.

Buchan, James. *Frozen Desire: The Meaning of Money*. New York: Farrar, Straus & Giroux, 1997.

Cohen, Edward E. *Athenian Economy and Society*. Princeton: Princeton University Press, 1992.

Davies, Glyn. *A History of Money*. Cardiff: University of Wales Press, 1994.

Ferguson, Niall. *The Cash Nexus*. New York: Basic Books, 2001.

Grant, James. *Money of the Mind*. New York: The Noonday Press, 1994.

Homer, Sidney. *A History of Interest Rates*. New Brunswick: Rutgers University Press, 1963.

Le Goff, Jacques. *Your Money or Your Life*. Trans. Patricia Ranum. New York: Zone Books, 1988.

Lewis, Michael. *The Money Culture*. New York: W. W. Norton & Company, 1991.

Lockman, Vic. *Money, Banking, and Usury* (pamphlet). Grants Pass, OR: Westminster Teaching Materials, 1991.

Murray, J. B. C. *The History of Usury*. Philadelphia: J. B. Lippincott & Co., 1866.

Sobel, Robert. *Dangerous Dreamers*. New York: John Wiley & Sons, Inc., 1993.

Why Conservatives Can't Stop the Growth of the State

Alex Epstein and *Yaron Brook*

In this previously unpublished essay, Mr. Alex Epstein and Dr. Yaron Brook analyze the philosophical arguments that undermine the ability of conservatives to slow the growth of government in spite of their rhetoric. Because conservatives have accepted certain philosophical premises as being undeniably true, they have been handicapped in their ability to properly defend business—and until these premises are challenged and rejected, they will be unable to do so.

Why Conservatives Can't Stop
the Growth of the State

Alex Epstein and *Yaron Brook*

When Americans want less government, they typically turn to "conservatives"—politicians, activists, pundits, and intellectuals who advocate "conserving" America's tradition of limited government and free enterprise—and to the Republican Party, conservatives' political home. Conservatives rail against "big government" and demand that individuals and businesses be left freer, keep more of their money, and suffer less from red tape. As conservative icon William F. Buckley declared in his *National Review* mission statement: "It is the job of centralized government (in peacetime) to protect its citizens' lives, liberty and property. All other activities of government tend to diminish freedom and hamper progress. The growth of government (the dominant social feature of this century) must be fought relentlessly."[1]

If we look to history, however, there is a dismaying disconnect between conservative rhetoric and results. For many decades, conservatives have argued and campaigned for a more limited government and talked about the evils of government intervention. They have often been supported by the American people, including businessmen desperate to get government off their backs. And yet the government only grows. Since 1965 inflation-adjusted government spending has sextupled, from $0.6 trillion to over $3.5 trillion annually,[2] and government controls have grown exponentially.[3] Conservatives have not only failed to stop this (indeed, they have never cut spending, even when they were intellectually and politically dominant), they have also been active participants in the growth of "big government."

In 1972 moderate conservative Richard Nixon won a decisive victory against leftist George McGovern, earning a mandate to roll back government. Instead, Nixon expanded government with new regulatory agencies and crippling price controls.[4]

In 1980 Ronald Reagan rose to power during a widely noted "swing to the right," following the "stagflation" brought about by Nixon, Ford, and Carter. Reagan had a reputation as "The Great Communicator," a master of persuasion who would leverage his charisma to limit government. But although he cut income tax rates, he never delivered on his promise to make corresponding cuts in welfare spending. As a result, the man who said "government is not the solution to our problem; government is the problem"[5] presided over an increase in the national debt from $930 billion to $2.6 trillion during his eight years.[6] And when faced with a crisis in Social Security, Reagan's "solution" was not to rein in the massive entitlement but to raise Social Security taxes as a means of entrenching it indefinitely. Reagan also implemented a "big government" trade policy. One of his former economic advisers notes that "the administration added more trade barriers than any administration since Hoover. The share of U.S. imports subject to some form of trade restraint increased from 12 percent in 1980 to 23 percent in 1988."[7]

In 1988 George H. W. Bush, cashing in on Reagan's popularity, was elected president on a campaign promise of "no new taxes." But then he imposed new taxes to finance the continued growth of government.[8]

The Republican Revolution of 1994 swept congressional Republicans into power with a mandate against "big government," prompting President Bill Clinton to declare with resignation: "The era of big government is over."[9] But just as the Republicans appeared poised to make bold cuts in spending, they cowered once Democrats accused them of making cuts in the growth of school lunch programs. The decidedly unrevolutionary Republican Revolution resulted in spending increases at the same rate of growth as before.[10]

The most recent conservative expansion of government was led by President George W. Bush, a self-styled "compassionate conservative," who had the benefit of a conservative Republican majority in Congress from 2000 to 2006. But in the name of affordable prescription drugs for seniors, Bush engineered the largest expansion of the welfare state since the 1960s with his Medicare prescription drug bill.[11] In the name of helping Americans buy homes they couldn't afford, he helped inflate Fannie Mae and Freddie Mac to gargantuan proportions.[12] In response to the accounting scandals of 2001 and 2002, he pushed the nightmarish Sarbanes-Oxley finance law through Congress and instituted a regulatory crackdown throughout American industry.[13] And in response to the financial crisis, he presided over trillions of dollars of bailouts, including the $700 billion TARP bill that initially included a request for more power than even a liberal would hesitate to ask for: "Decisions by the Secretary pursuant to the authority of this Act are non-reviewable and committed to agency discretion, and may not be reviewed by any court of law or any administrative agency."[14]

The upshot: no matter who is elected to the House or Senate, no matter who becomes president, no matter how low Democrats' poll ratings sink, no matter how charismatic the Republican leadership is, or how popular conservative pundits are, or how much the public seems to support limited government, or how much political leaders claim to revere free enterprise, *the conservatives do not reduce, but frequently increase, the size and scope of government.*

The track record of conservatives is more relevant than ever. In 2010, with big government once again on the march, Americans were experiencing the kind of frustration that led them to place trust and confidence in conservatives so many times before. In a January 2010 public opinion poll, after one year of the Obama administration brought annual spending to over $3.5 trillion, annual deficits to over $1 trillion,[15] and government control of business to new heights,[16] Americans said by a 58 percent to 38 percent margin that "they prefer smaller government and fewer services to larger government with more services."[17] Businessmen were particularly frustrated. "I've never seen in general the small business community as depressed as it is today,"[18] said the chairman of a top lender to small businesses. And the CEO of a top manufacturer blamed exploding spending and controls for necessitating 20,000 layoffs at his company. Citing business-unfriendly labor policies, nationalization of health care, cap and trade restrictions on energy, and the threat of enormous future tax increases, the CEO said: "What do you think I am going to do? I'm not going to hire anybody in the United States. I'm moving. They are doing everything possible to destroy jobs." In India and China, where he expected to create new jobs, he noted that "the governments welcome you to actually do something."[19]

As in the past, Americans found themselves turning to conservatives to resist the relentless spread of government controls over the economy. Unfortunately, however, conservatives were no better equipped in 2010 to offer effective resistance than they were during the previous dreary decades.

Those who really want to reverse the growth of government must understand why conservatives always fail.

To this end, it is instructive to note a highly predictable *pattern* by which limited government loses and expanded government wins out in the public debate, and therefore in politics. Conservatives are good at appealing to Americans in abstract, vague, and emotionally loaded terms that "small government" is better than "big government." But when it comes to real, concrete issues in the cultural-political debate, such as whether to let gasoline prices rise (Nixon), whether to rein in Social Security (Reagan), or whether to cut social spending (Republican Revolution), conservatives don't reduce the long-term growth of government intrusion. On the contrary, whatever problems Americans have with "big government" in the abstract, time and again liberals succeed in convincing the country that more government is needed.

This happens because of a conflict in the attitudes most Americans hold. While they have a definite affinity for capitalism, they also have a fundamental discomfort with its central feature: the selfish pursuit of profit by businessmen. Liberals capitalize on this by arguing in case after case that the cause of

Americans' unease, the selfishness of capitalism, is to blame for America's problems, and that more controls and spending are necessary to curb it. This argument takes two major forms: (1) Limited government unleashes the self-ishness, or *greed*, of businessmen, causing massive economic problems, and (2) a limited government fails to make businessmen and other rich individuals serve the *need* of others.

These arguments—the "argument from greed" and the "argument from need"—continue to fuel the growth of government, decade after decade, because *conservatives can't answer them.* But where conservative arguments fail, other arguments can succeed, and open the path to a better, freer future.

The Argument from Greed

Pick an economic problem, any economic problem—the financial crisis, rising health care costs, or the leading story in today's newspaper. Now, answer the following questions: (1) What is the perceived cause of the problem? (2) What is the perceived solution? In almost every case, the answers will boil down to: (1) greedy businessmen, and (2) more government controls to restrain them.

For example, why do we have a financial crisis? The headlines of popular publications tell the prevailing story: "Greed, Stupidity, Delusion—and Some More Greed"[20]; "'human greed' to blame for financial crisis"[21]; "Pope: Greed, selfishness caused crisis"[22]; "The Dalai Lama blames 'greed' for financial crisis."[23] The solution in each article was more government restraint of "greed."

The same pattern holds everywhere:

- Health care: "Consumers Believe Greed Is the Reason for Rising Health Care Costs"[24]; "Health Insurance Industry Exposes Its Insatiable Greed"[25]; "'Greed' Inflates Drug Prices, Democrats Say"[26]
- Jobs: *Take This Job and Ship It: How Corporate Greed and Brain-Dead Politics Are Selling Out America*[27]; "Insurance Company Greed Kills Jobs"[28]
- Gasoline prices: "Oil Company Greed Seen as Major Reason for High Gas Prices"[29]
- Electricity prices: "Greed Fuels Energy Crisis"[30]
- Food prices: "Deadly Greed: The Role of Speculators in the Global Food Crisis"[31]

Read most history books and you'll see greed blamed for economic problems in America's past, from the Great Depression of the 1930s[32] to the accounting scandals of the early 2000s.[33]

Consider: What is "greed," exactly? In all of these cases, it refers not only to criminals' desire for loot but to the profit motive as such—the fundamental motivation of business. When commentators blame higher health care prices on "greed," they are not saying that a substantial portion of insurers, doctors, or hospitals literally stole money, committed fraud, or breached contracts; those would simply be reasons for enforcing basic criminal and civil laws. Instead, commentators are asking us to believe that the profit motive in the health care and health insurance market is inherently destructive—and therefore *forcible interference with voluntary trade*, in the form of government controls, is necessary.

Such controls operate in two basic ways: (1) They allow government to dictate business policies and practices, in opposition to the choices of a business and its customers, and (2) they allow government to continually monitor and investigate businesses with no evidence of criminal behavior, on the grounds of *catching or preempting* the inevitable wrongs of the businessman—a complete reversal of the presumption of innocence.

To see both these features in action, just step into any elevator and notice the regulatory seal of approval issued by a government inspector. Why is it there? On the premise that greedy businesses cannot be trusted to make, buy, or maintain safe elevators—and but for government vigilance, elevators would be plummeting down shafts in building after building. This assumption leaves no room for the idea that if businessmen were left free to act on their own judgment, they would buy functional elevators from reputable manufacturers and have private agencies maintain, inspect, and certify their safety.

On the same premise by which government dictates elevator standards, it forces innocent businesses of many types to submit to regular inspections (i.e., investigations) to make sure they are not violating the law—as if without such inspections, greedy businessmen would be criminally negligent and avoid maintenance at all costs, even at the risk of their employees' lives.

If the profit motive is so corrupting as to make Americans unable to reliably produce even safe elevators, what can they be left free to do? The answer is: fewer and fewer tasks.

For example, all of the alphabet agencies—the Food and Drug Administration, the Federal Aviation Administration, the Environmental Protection Agency, the Securities and Exchange Commission, and dozens more—wield huge, ever-expanding powers in large part because of this view of human nature and of businessmen. Why, for example, is the FDA allowed to dictate what drugs can be sold, and dictate to patients and doctors what drugs can be used—even though hundreds of thousands of patients have died unnecessarily while waiting for non-FDA approved drugs?[34] Because it's believed that if the FDA didn't have this power, unscrupulous drug companies would fleece the irrational public with snake oil or poison. Further, why is the FDA allowed to dictate what testing process a drug must go through before it is sold—even when the companies' scientists believe that a different process would be far more effective and efficient?

Because it's believed that if drug companies were left free, they would not test drugs at all. They would just put dangerous, untested substances on the market and consumers would lap them up. It is such assertions—repeated over and over in response to every new crisis, until they harden into dogma—that have led to the size and scope of our regulatory state.

If the argument from greed is correct, then all this is as it should be. If businessmen pursuing profit necessarily means cutting corners, exploiting customers, and engaging in reckless behavior with nothing but the next day's or the next quarter's profits in mind—if profit-seeking means duping anyone, anyplace, anytime in a mindless quest for dollars at the cost of disaster for millions—then the liberals' response to our economic problems is entirely proper. Indeed, our government has been *too* limited, our enterprise has been *too* free, and government needs to do *more and more* to keep greed in check—by whatever means it deems necessary.

In the face of this logic, one might expect conservatives to mount the barricades against any and all arguments from greed, defending businessmen as a class against such demeaning portrayals. One might expect conservatives to argue powerfully that government intervention, not the profit motive, is the true villain. But they don't. They yell and scream at the liberals who *assert* the argument from greed, but they don't attack the argument itself—and therefore they lose.

Consider the financial crisis. If ever limited government was under attack, it was during the financial crisis, which was widely blamed on a "failure of the free market"—a failure to restrain greed. This claim of a failed free market has been the single biggest justification of President Obama's expansion of government. If ever there was an opportunity for conservatives to shine, it was in September 2008, when Lehman Brothers went bankrupt, the financial system itself was declared to be on the brink, and businessmen's greed was blamed for all the trouble. The conservatives needed to offer an answer.

But they had none.

In fact, many conservatives *agreed* with the liberals and actively supported more controls. This was essentially the response of George W. Bush, who gave a major speech explaining the financial crisis as the product of market forces, while completely evading the market-distorting incentives created by the Fed's artificially low interest rates and by mortgage guarantees from Fannie Mae and Freddie Mac.[35] (In January 2010, speaking at the National Tea Party Convention, Republican Sarah Palin blamed bankers for the economy's ills.[36]) And Republican presidential candidate John McCain (who months earlier had said, "I'm always for less regulation") declared: "Wall Street has betrayed us. They've broken the social contract between capitalism and the average citizen and the worker. . . . This is a result of excess and greed and corruption. And that's exactly what is plaguing Americans today. And we got to fix it and we've got to update our regulatory system."[37]

In short, conservatives complained of having trusted Wall Street to suppress its greed, and now look what they did. When even the self-proclaimed defenders of smaller government admit it's too weak to curb business greed, can anything result besides the massive expansion of government led by the Obama administration?

Other conservatives *evaded* the argument from greed, while vigorously attacking particular liberal policies and personalities. This was essentially the response of more hard-line conservatives, who heaped blame on Democratic politicians such as Christopher Dodd and Barney Frank for their support of Fannie Mae and Freddie Mac, and on the Community Reinvestment Act, passed by Jimmy Carter and expanded by Bill Clinton.[38] Radio personality Rush Limbaugh called the crisis "the Democrat-caused financial crisis."[39] While these accusations had chunks of truth, they were not accompanied by pro-capitalist explanations of how so many on Wall Street, under no direct orders from government, made risky housing investments that the government later bailed out. As a result, a consensus emerged that government needs to exert far more control over financial markets—the lifeblood of capitalism—while conservatives offered little objection or comment.

Agreement and evasion are the typical conservative responses to the argument that greed must be forcibly restrained by government. Conservatives don't defend the financial industry, the insurance industry, the pharmaceutical industry, the food industry, the energy industry, or any other industry demonized for "greed." Nor do they, despite their supposed advocacy of free-market economics, make a compelling case for how government intervention, not industry, is the prime culprit for the economy's never-ending problems.

Why do conservatives so consistently fail?

Because the idea that greed (or the profit motive, or selfishness) causes so many problems and needs to be restrained *makes sense to them*; it is consistent with everything most conservatives (and indeed almost all of us) have been taught about morality and human nature.

As children, the first ethical guidance we get is: "Don't be selfish." Churchgoers quickly learn that "Love of money is the root of all evil" and that a man who earns lots of money for himself has no more chance of entering heaven than a camel has of squeezing through the eye of a needle.[40]

Indeed, the argument from greed is simply one logical implication of the age-old and deeply held view that selfishness as such is evil (and therefore leads to evil results)—a view both liberals and conservatives hold (even when they begrudgingly concede that selfishness, by incentivizing businessmen to produce valuable goods and services, has some socially desirable results). It's because businessmen are eager profit-seekers that they have been viewed negatively for millennia. According to most people's underlying view of human nature (which sometimes takes the form of Original Sin), man's self-ish desires are part of his "lower," immoral nature that drives him to destructive behavior. The ethical implications are straightforward: Morality's job is to restrain our selfish desires, to make us self*less*. The political implications are also straightforward: If individuals won't voluntarily restrain their selfish desires, then society via government must do it for them, by force.

Secular philosophers of the collectivist variety advocate a similar view of selfishness. In this collectivist variant, individuals are inherently inclined to act selfishly, destroying society in the process and making everyone's life, in the words of philosopher Thomas Hobbes, "solitary, poor, nasty, brutish, and short."[41] Hobbes—and sundry socialists and fascists in later centuries—advocated a powerful, interventionist government as the only means of coping with man's selfish nature.

Many conservatives have no compunction about openly damning human nature as selfish and therefore bad. An article in the respected conservative quarterly *City Journal* praises "orthodox Catholic social teaching" as "based on a deeply realistic understanding of man's nature as fallen. For two millennia, the Church has taught that man has a hardwired inclination to sin that, unchecked, leads to drunkenness, envy, lust, selfishness, and a host of other sins. Such a disordered life undermines community and leads to self-destruction."[42]

President Obama couldn't agree more. Observing that "we see here in this country and around the globe violence and want and strife that would seem sadly familiar to those in ancient times," he blames

> the imperfections of man—our selfishness, our pride, our stubbornness, our acquisitiveness, our insecurities, our egos; all the cruelties large and small that those of us in the Christian tradition understand to be rooted in original sin. We too often seek advantage over others. . . . Too many of us view life only through the lens of immediate self-interest and crass materialism.[43]

If man's selfish desires are inherently evil and destructive, then the desire to make and keep money for oneself—the profit motive—must be evil as well. And if that's true, then limited government and capitalism cannot work and should not be allowed. These connections among human nature, morality, politics, and economics were crudely but memorably summarized by filmmaker Michael Moore when discussing his anticapitalist propaganda film, *Capitalism: A Love Story*:

> I started out wanting to explore the premise of capitalism being anti-American, and anti-Jesus, meaning it's not a democratic economy. And it's not run with a moral or ethical code. But when the crash happened,

it added a third plot line: not only is capitalism anti-American and anti-Jesus, it doesn't work.[44]

Taken on his own terms, Moore's logic is unassailable: Why would something that unleashes the worst in human nature work?

The unsustainable contradiction between "selfishness is evil" and "capitalism is good" can sometimes be hidden in seemingly pro-capitalist rhetoric, but it's exposed whenever real-world problems require conservatives to take a stand. At this point, conservatives typically revert to what makes sense according to their view of human nature and morality. It's not that conservatives go looking to expand government—but as soon as there's a scandal, their moral alarm bells go off. They remember that they don't trust human beings, and that we really do need to curb their desire to exploit us. For every new crisis, the conservative will feel the need for more controls—following the example set by George W. Bush, who claimed he had "abandoned free market principles to save the free market system."[45] It is as if conservatives "discover" year by year that freedom for businessmen is less and less desirable. And they are destined to make such "discoveries," so long as they cling to their fundamental view of profit.

Businessmen who struggle to do their jobs despite the restraints imposed by government, and properly resent a government that treats them like criminals, must understand that *conservative* ideas are part of the problem, not part of the solution.

The Virtuous Profit-Motive

What is needed today is a radically different understanding of businessmen and profit—an understanding that can clarify and fortify Americans' real but all-too-vague recognition of the value of limited government and free enterprise—an understanding that can take on and refute the argument from greed.

That new understanding is to be found in the ideas of Ayn Rand, whose works (most notably *Atlas Shrugged*) have already changed the way millions look at business, profits, and capitalism.

The businessman's pursuit of profit, which others regard as both morally suspect and dangerous, is for Rand profoundly moral—even heroic—and the conqueror of danger. In 1960 she wrote:

> The businessman carries scientific discoveries from the laboratory of the inventor to industrial plants, and transforms them into material products that fill men's physical needs and expand the comfort of men's existence. By creating a mass market, he makes these products available to every income level of society. By using machines, he increases the productivity of human labor, thus raising labor's

economic rewards. By organizing human effort into productive enterprises, he creates employment for men of countless professions. *He* is the great liberator who, in the short span of a century and a half, has released men from bondage to their physical needs, has released them from the terrible drudgery of an eighteen-hour workday of manual labor for their barest subsistence, has released them from famines, from pestilences, from the stagnant hopelessness and terror in which most of mankind had lived in all the pre-capitalist centuries—and in which most of it still lives, in non-capitalist countries.[46]

How did businessmen achieve these feats? Not by being the salivating, short-range, exploitative creatures implied by the argument from greed, but by being what she calls "men of the mind"—men who create immense new wealth by creative *thinking*, not plunder or whim.

Based in large part on the businessman's unprecedented record of success from the Industrial Revolution to today, Rand challenged the uncritically accepted, millennia-old ideas about human nature and morality that conservatives and liberals share. Above all, she challenged the common notion that because the profit motive is selfish, it is evil.

The conventional use of the term "selfishness," Rand argued, warps our moral thinking. It does so by falsely equating two types of individual: those who pursue their own interests via production and trade, and the profiteers who seek monetary gain at the expense of others. The conventional usage presents as equally "selfish" both Michael Dell and Bernie Madoff, a productive profit-maker and a parasitical profiteer.

In reality, argued Rand, the only policy that is in one's genuine long-term self-interest, is to pursue profit via production and trade. The Industrial Revolution, she observed, an unprecedented explosion of material wealth, proved once and for all that the wealth men need is *created*, and therefore that one man's gain is not another man's loss. To the contrary, men trading freely pursue profit in productive harmony, benefiting tremendously from one another's achievements. This was evident in the Industrial Revolution, whose result was a soaring, economy-wide increase in standard of living and the growth of tremendous goodwill among men, who came to view one another not as adversaries (though of course they would compete on the market), but as allies who benefited immensely from the intersection of their self-interests.

Rand does not deny that some businessmen attempt to pursue their interests by exploitation. *Atlas Shrugged* contains many incisive, contemptuous portrayals of "businessmen" who make money, not by seeking honest profit, but by gaining political power to exploit others. Rand's view is that such profiteers are not truly acting in their long-range interest, that they give genuine self-interest a bad name, and that they rise to significance only in a highly government-controlled society.

As the famous "Money Speech" from *Atlas Shrugged* says:

> Did you get your money by fraud? By pandering to men's vices or men's stupidity? By catering to fools, in the hope of getting more than your ability deserves? By lowering your standards? By doing work you despise for purchasers you scorn? If so, then your money will not give you a moment's or a penny's worth of joy. Then all the things you buy will become, not a tribute to you, but a reproach; not an achievement, but a reminder of shame. Then you'll scream that money is evil. Evil, because it would not pinch-hit for your self-respect? Evil, because it would not let you enjoy your depravity?[47]

As a modern example of this point, witness the furtive, twisted lives of crooks like Madoff, before and after they get caught—as compared to the productive lives of those who earn profit through mutually beneficial interaction.

Fundamentally, then, we should view the businessman's selfish desire for profit as a desire to live by one's own effort. As an industrialist in *Atlas Shrugged* proclaimed, in a way businessmen today would do well to emulate:

> I am earning my own living, as every honest man must. I refuse to accept as guilt the fact of my own existence and the fact that I must work in order to support it. I refuse to accept as guilt the fact that I am able to do it and do it well. I refuse to accept as guilt the fact that I am able to do it better than most people—the fact that my work is of greater value than the work of my neighbors and that more men are willing to pay me. I refuse to apologize for my ability—I refuse to apologize for my success—I refuse to apologize for my money.[48]

It is the honest, productive businessman who defines capitalism and profit-seeking. In a truly free market, all association is voluntary, and the law does not tolerate theft, fraud, handouts, or bailouts. To achieve one's self-interest—to make good on one's desire for profit—requires that one *create value*, and exchange it for the value created by others. It is in every market participant's interest to offer and to demand the best value in any realm, from mortgage lending standards to accounting standards, to product quality, to health care. It is a marginal phenomenon if an occasional fly-by-night scheme "works" in the short term at the expense of some careless dupes. The dupes are given every motivation to be more careful next time, and if fraud is involved a vigorous police force and judicial system will converge against the schemer and remove him from the market. The normal phenomenon of capitalism is the conscientious building owner who buys and maintains safe elevators—not the landlord who can't be bothered to care whether his elevators are death-traps.

It is only within the "mixed economy"—where freedom to produce and trade is compromised by coercive controls and wealth transfers—that the exploitative pseudo-businessman arises:

> All the evils, abuses, and iniquities, popularly ascribed to businessmen and to capitalism, were not caused by an unregulated economy or by a free market, but by government intervention into the economy. The giants of American industry—such as James Jerome Hill or Commodore Vanderbilt or Andrew Carnegie or J. P. Morgan— were self-made men who earned their fortunes by personal ability, by free trade on a free market. But there existed another kind of businessmen, the products of a mixed economy, the men with political pull, who made fortunes by means of special privileges granted to them by the government, such men as the Big Four of the Central Pacific Railroad. It was the political power behind their activities— the power of forced, unearned, economically unjustified privileges—that caused dislocations in the country's economy, hardships, depressions, and mounting public protests. But it was the free market and the free businessmen that took the blame.[49]

To take a modern case of the same phenomenon, let's look at today's financial crisis, which is falsely considered as today's ultimate validation of the argument from greed.

First, the financial and housing markets that preceded the crisis were the antithesis of a free market. Pre-crisis policy featured record amounts of "oversight"—that is, government control—of housing and finance by the Federal Reserve, Fannie Mae, Freddie Mac, and others, which encouraged excessive lending and borrowing. By contrast, in decades past, a far less controlled housing industry featured financially sound loans made by self-interested lenders without government guarantees to bail out bad risks. Only when the government started pushing government-guaranteed loans did standards decline, and reckless loans become profitable. So long as the Fed kept inflating the housing bubble (housing values were increasing 15 percent a year in the run-up to the crisis[50]), there was no such thing as a bad loan candidate, and so Wall Street and floods of new investors had every incentive to participate. But without government intervention, the ballooning of the housing bubble would never have occurred.

The financial crisis resulted from government perverting the pursuit of profit. Government monetary policy encouraged people to borrow and spend more than they could afford. Government housing policy made some Americans liable for others' risky home loans. Government bailout policy made some Americans liable for others' failed financial institutions. All of this catered to the short-range, exploitative mentality that wants a free (stolen) lunch, be it a subsidized house, or an easy income selling government-guaranteed mortgages, or a hefty profit on housing-bubble mortgage-backed securities.

But government intervention didn't just empower the shady characters; it compromised all productive Americans by forcing them to choose between exploiting others or being exploited—between participating in the government wealth transfer, or abstaining and ending up footing the bill. For example, mortgage brokers who didn't buy into the subprime mania saw their incomes go down—as did banks and financial institutions. "Should I participate?" they had to decide. And if so, for how long? Since government whim was fueling the mania, it was hard to predict when it would bust. What were banks and investors to do? Participate, knowing the ethical and long-term financial problems, or stay away?

This is just one indication of how government intervention, driven by general antipathy toward the profit motive, in fact unleashes the profiteers it purports to oppose and distorts the thinking and decision-making of virtuous profit-seekers.

So long as the argument from greed prevails—so long as its underlying view of businessmen as dangerous animals goes unchallenged—the typical reaction to crisis will always be this question: who let the dogs loose? But a culture armed with Ayn Rand's arguments affirming the virtuous nature of profit-seeking will respond to crises by investigating how government interfered with individuals making free choices on the market. Such is the power of ideas.

The Argument from Need

Just as most arguments for expanding government controls have a common theme, so do most arguments for expanding government spending. The vast majority of such spending is for welfare programs, and has nothing to do with the classic, limited-government functions of the military, police, and courts. Most of that welfare spending is consumed by entrenched government wealth transfer programs: Social Security, Medicare, and Medicaid. These programs alone account for a third of today's federal budget, and some estimates say these programs have piled up $100 trillion in unfunded liabilities for the future.[51]

Virtually all wealth transfer programs are justified by a single basic assertion, put forth as if it's an argument: people *need* the money.

Why do we have Medicare, a program that forces younger Americans to pay for the effectively unlimited medical needs of the elderly? Because the elderly need that medical care, we are told, and therefore, it is taken for granted, everyone else in society, especially "the rich," is obligated to provide those treatments.

Why do we have Social Security, and surrender 12 percent of our income annually to what is in effect a government Ponzi scheme? Because of the need of Americans who are short-sighted or unable to put aside retirement funds—which means the rest of us must pay for their retirement.

Why did we bail out automakers? Because so many employees needed jobs. Why did President Reagan restrict imports from Japanese automakers, making desirable Japanese cars more expensive? Because the U.S. auto industry needed help. Why do we have farm subsidies? Because American farmers need to repeat what their families have been doing for generations, even if they can't make a living at it—and therefore "society" (other taxpayers) should pay premium prices for agricultural products. Why did President Bush encourage government subsidy and bailout programs to increase the rate of home ownership? Because he and his policymakers thought more Americans needed a home in order to achieve the American Dream.

The argument is always the same. Wealth redistribution is the *right* thing to do, because the suffering recipients *need* the money, and wealthy individuals and businesses are able and therefore obligated to alleviate their needs. Often, these arguments are phrased in terms of "society" ("Shouldn't society provide everyone with health care?"), but "society" is just code for the businessmen (and their employees and customers and shareholders) who will actually be paying the bills.

The bottom line: Need is a claim on other people's money. This is the argument from need.

The argument from need creates a spiral of government spending. Since there are always new "needs" to satisfy, and since some people always have more money than others to satisfy needs, one can always argue that the people with more should give a little harder (often, this is done through deficit spending rather than direct taxation). Medicare went *ten times* over budget in its first ten years; it turned out the elderly needed more free health care than the government had thought. Social Security went from a small check for a tiny portion of the population to a large check for a massive portion of the population. And if Medicare and Social Security are right, so is Medicaid, and so is full-fledged national health care. See the pattern? Time after time, the "need" of the person who didn't earn something trumps the "greed" of those who did.

For conservatives to have any impact on spending, they would have to challenge the argument from need. But they don't, because once again that would put them in conflict with prevailing morality.

The most uncontroversial moral ideal in the world is *altruism*: selfless service to others. It is the flip-side of the idea that selfishness is evil. "Altruism" literally means "other-ism"; it holds that one should live one's life in selfless service to the needs of others, that self-sacrifice for others' sake is the highest virtue. To live for one's own sake, to be selfish, according to altruism, is immoral. As a theoretical doctrine, the morality of altruism is descended from Christianity but is accepted today in various forms by both the non-religious and the religious.

Conservatives believe it. John McCain says, "Glory belongs to the act of being constant to something greater than yourself."[52]

Liberals believe it: Barack Obama says, "For if there is one law that we can be most certain of, it is the law that binds people of all faiths and no faith together. . . . The call to serve."[53] One of Michelle Obama's favorite quotes about morality (by Marian Wright Edelman) is: "Service is the rent we pay for living . . . it is the true measure, the only measure of our success."[54]

Businessmen believe it: industrialist Andrew Carnegie said that the rich man should use his "surplus revenues" so as "to produce the most beneficial results for the community—the man of wealth thus becoming the mere agent and trustee for his poorer brethren."[55]

Conservatives have never been willing to challenge the ideal of altruism. Religious conservatives lead the way, holding (correctly) that altruism is required by the Bible. But other conservatives routinely embrace secular forms of altruism, usually collectivism, holding that the individual must serve "the common good"— a malleable term that ends up meaning "the good of everyone else."

If one takes altruism seriously, one must regard a life of profit-seeking and wealth-enjoyment as *immoral*, something that shouldn't exist, especially not on the scale of a rich industrialist. Remember, the purpose of life is to serve others—implying that, as conservative Michael Novak puts it, "the economic and the ethical point of a business corporation is to serve others."[56]

Thus, whatever challenges conservatives have directed toward particular expansions of the welfare state, they have never challenged the moral rightness of its basic goal. They have never condemned wealth transfer programs in the name of protecting the right of a hard-working, ambitious individual (on any scale) to pursue his life to the fullest, using every hour he has and every dollar he earns.

Instead, conservatives typically challenge liberal programs by saying they "won't work" because government programs will retard the overall growth of wealth. But whether something "works" depends on what one is trying to achieve. Liberals are unfazed by the prospect of declining wealth because they're more concerned with a moral question: What is the point of having all this wealth if it is not "justly" distributed—that is, according to need? And the conservatives never have an answer.

To be sure, sometimes conservative criticisms of altruistic programs succeed—for a while. Often it's because Americans think we can't afford the programs or that the prospect of economic destruction is too blatant to ignore. But the long-term trend in spite of all conservative tongue-wagging is more and more welfare spending, and the utter inability to cut spending.

Consider Ronald Reagan. Here was a president who seemed to have a genuine emotional affinity for free markets and who enjoyed great popularity. Yet he was hopeless when it came to making real proposals to shrink the size and scope of government. This is typical of conservatives; they say government is "too big" but can't think of any programs they would cut, because that would mean reducing wealth transfers to the "needy." Reagan, the exception that truly proves this rule, prominently called for cutting the Department of Education early in his presidency[57] but later backed off completely.

The failure of the Republican Revolution of 1994 to cut spending was even more overtly altruistic. A seemingly confident band of free-market conservatives swept into office promising to shrink government. But as soon as specific cuts came up for discussion, President Clinton accused them of being selfish in seeking to reduce government entitlement programs (the only way of cutting spending), and the Republicans retreated with their tails between their legs. Worse, the lesson conservatives took from this was that they were being too selfish. "The budget battle," lamented prominent conservative strategist William Kristol, "played into the two great Republican vulnerabilities: that we are the party of the rich and meanspirited."[58]

The single most prominent politician of the Republican Revolution, former House Speaker Newt Gingrich, now says he has "no particular beef with big government."[59] And the most prominent conservative in the land, the fire-breathing Rush Limbaugh, has publicly agreed in an interview that the government "has a moral obligation to find some way to cover"[60] those without health insurance, by creating a government program to do so.

Some revolution, huh?

A real freedom revolution needs to include a *moral* revolution—a revolution that challenges the idea that the successful owe a duty to the unsuccessful, the idea that businessmen's freedom must be bought by sacrifice to society, the idea of *altruism*. This is exactly the revolution *Atlas Shrugged* makes possible. In that novel, Ayn Rand explains how the whole sacrificial, altruistic approach to morality subverts and punishes the best within all of us—including the best within our businessmen—by calling for profit-seeking producers to be demonized and sacrificed for the needs of others.

For many decades now, liberals have been winning because they confidently argue that expanding government intervention is the *right* thing to do. If those who uphold capitalism are now to start winning, they must proceed with the same moral confidence, armed with the pro-business, self-interested, and guiltless moral philosophy of *Atlas Shrugged*. As Rand wrote: "Capitalism is not the system of the past; it is the system of the future—if mankind is to have a future. Those who wish to fight for it, must discard the title of 'conservatives.'"[61]

Notes

1. William F. Buckley Jr., "Our Mission Statement," *National Review*, November 19, 1955, http://article.nationalreview.com/346187/our-mission-statement/william-f-buckley-jr (accessed February 24, 2010).

2. "2009 Federal Revenue and Spending Book of Charts," The Heritage Foundation, May 2009, http://www.heritage.org/research/features/BudgetChartBook/PDF/BOC_Print_download.pdf (accessed February 24, 2010).

3. James L. Gattuso, "Red Tape Rising," Heritage Foundation, "Backgrounder #2116," March 25, 2008, http://www.heritage.org/rese arch/regulation/bg2116.cfm (accessed March 2, 2010).

4. Robert L. Bradley, Jr., "What Now for U.S. Energy Policy: A Free-Market Perspective," *Policy Analysis* no. 145, January 29, 1991, http://www.cato.org/pub_display.php?pub_id=1005&full=1 (accessed February 24, 2010).

5. Ronald Reagan, Inaugural Address, January 20, 1981, archived at http://www.presidency.ucsb.edu/ws/index.php?pid=43130 (accessed March 1, 2010).

6. Jonathan Weisman, Reagan Policies Gave Green Light to Red Ink, *Washington Post*, June 9, 2004, http://www.washingtonpost.com/wp-dyn/articles/A26402-2004Jun8.html (accessed March 1, 2010).

7. William A. Niskanen, "Reaganonomics," *Concise Encyclopedia of Economics*, edited by David R. Henderson, http://www.econlib.org/library/Enc1/Reaganomics.html (accessed February 24, 2010).

8. "The Presidents," *American Experience*, PBS, http://www.pbs.org/wgbh/amex/presidents/41_g_h_w_bush/index.html (accessed May 17, 2010).

9. "CNN transcript of President Clinton's radio address," January 27, 1996, http://www.cnn.com/US/9601/budget/01-27/clinton_radio/ (accessed February 24, 2010).

10. Office of Management and Budget, *Historical Tables, Budget of the United States Government, Fiscal Year 2006*, table 8.1, p. 125.

11. Daniel J. Mitchell, "Why Medicare Expansion Threatens the Bush Tax Cuts and Undermines Fundamental Tax Reform," The Heritage Foundation, Backgrounder #1672, July 25, 2003, http://www.heritage.org/research/healthcare/bg1672.cfm.

12. "Fannie Mae Pledges Continued Support for President Bush's Nationwide Effort to Increase Minority Homeownership," Business Wire, October 15, 2002, http://findarticles.com/p/articles/mi_m0EIN/is_2002_Oct_15/ai_92843805/ (accessed March 3, 2010).

13. Alex Epstein and Yaron Brook, *Atlanta Journal and Constitution*, October 22, 2002, http://www.aynrand.org/site/News2?page=NewsArticle&id=5455&news_iv_ctrl=1021 (accessed February 24, 2010).

14. Jason Linkins, "Dirty Secret of the Bailout: Thirty-Two Words That None Dare Utter," Huffington Post, September 22, 2008, http://www.huffingtonpost.com/2008/09/22/dirty-secret-of-the-bailo_n_128294.html (accessed February 24, 2010).

15. "2009 Federal Revenue and Spending Book of Charts," The Heritage Foundation, May 2009, http://www.heritage.org/research/features/BudgetChartBook/PDF/BOC_Print_download.pdf (accessed February 24, 2010).

16. Elizabeth Williamson and Melanie Trottman, "Federal Workers, Regulations to Increase," *Wall Street Journal*, May 8, 2009, http://online.wsj.com/article/SB124174004457498761.html (accessed February 24, 2010).

17. Jon Cohen and Jennifer Agiesta, "Poll shows growing disappointment, polarization over Obama's performance," *Washington Post*, January 17, 2010, http://www.washingtonpost.com/wp-dyn/content/article/2010/01/16/AR2010011602828.html (accessed February 24, 2010).

18. John Allison, chairman of BB&T Bank, interviewed on *Stossel*, FOX Business Channel, January 7, 2010.

19. Will Daley, "Emerson's Farr Says U.S. Is Destroying Manufacturing (Update3), Bloomberg.com, November 11, 2009, http://www.bloomberg.com/apps/news?pid=20601103&sid=a_EbBQyskKl0 (accessed February 24, 2010).

20. John Steele Gordon, "Greed, Stupidity, Delusion—and Some More Greed," Freakonomics blog, *New York Times* online, September 22, 2010, http://freakonomics.blogs.nytimes.com/2008/09/22/john-steele-gordon-on-the-financial-mess-greed-stupidity-delusion-and-some-more-greed (accessed February 24, 2010).

21. Ruth Gledhill, "Rowan Williams says 'human greed' to blame for financial crisis," *Times Online*, October 15, 2008, http://www.timesonline.co.uk/tol/comment/faith/article4950733.ece (accessed February 24, 2010).

22. "Pope: Greed, selfishness caused crisis," UPI.com, July 7, 2009, http://www.upi.com/Top_News/2009/07/07/Pope-Greed-selfishness-caused-crisis/UPI-39111246971166/ (accessed February 24, 2010).

23. Tejinder Singh, "The Dalai Lama blames 'greed' for financial crisis," *New Europe* online, December 8, 2008, http://www.neurope.eu/articles/90974.php (accessed February 24, 2010).

24. "Consumers Believe Greed Is the Reason for Rising Health Care Costs," AllBusiness, January 1, 2007, http://www.allbusiness.com/health-care-social-assistance/4014187-1.html (accessed February 24, 2010).

25. Peter Dreier, "Health Insurance Industry Exposes Its Insatiable Greed," Huffington Post, October 12, 2009, http://www.huffingtonpost.com/peter-dreier/health-insurance-industry_b_318066.html (accessed February 24, 2010).

26. Janet Hook, "'Greed' Inflates Drug Prices, Democrats Say," *Los Angeles Times* online, July 17, 2002, http://articles.latimes.com/2002/jul/17/nation/na-drugs17 (accessed February 24, 2010).

27. Byron L. Dorgan, *Take This Job and Ship It: How Corporate Greed and Brain-Dead Politics Are Selling Out America*, (New York: Thomas Dunne Books, 2006).

28. Jason Rosenbaum, "Insurance Company Greed Kills Jobs," Health Care for America NOW!, November 17, 2009, http://blog.healthcareforamericanow.org/2009/11/17/insurance-company-greed-kills-jobs (accessed February 24, 2010).

29. Jeffrey M. Jones, "Oil Company Greed Seen as Major Reason for High Gas Prices; Majority of American expect $4 gas prices this summer, survey," Gallup Poll News Service, May 30, 2007.

30. Dennis Kucinich, "Greed Fuels Energy Crisis," *In These Times* online, April 16, 2001, http://www.inthesetimes.com/article/1477/ (accessed February 24, 2010).

31. Beat Balzli and Frank Horning, "Deadly Greed: The Role of Speculators in the Global Food Crisis," *Spiegel Online*, April 23, 2008, http://www.spiegel.de/international/world/0,1518,549187,00.html (accessed February 24, 2010).

32. V V, "Human Greed and Financial Crisis," *Business Standard,* February 13, 2010, http://www.business-standard.com/india/news/v-v-human-greedfinancial-crises/385561/ (accessed March 1, 2010).

33. Marcia Hughes, "No Accounting for Greed," Global Policy Forum, July 23, 2002, http://www.globalpolicy.org/component/content/article/214/43962.html (accessed March 2, 2010).

34. "Food and Drug Administration," Cato Handbook for Congress, 105th Congress," http://www.cato.org/pubs/handbook/hb105-32.html (accessed March 1, 2010).

35. Associated Press, "Text of President Bush's speech on economic crisis," *OregonLive.com,* September 24, 2008, http://www.oregonlive.com/politics/index.ssf/2008/09/text_of_president_bushs_speech.html (accessed on March 3, 2010).

36. "Sarah Palin Speaks at Tea Party Convention," transcript, CNN Newsroom, February 6, 2010, http://transcripts.cnn.com/TRANSCRIPTS/1002/06/cnr.09.html (accessed February 24, 2010).

37. Ryan Powers, "McCain Flip-Flops on 'Excessive Regulation' in Less Than an Hour," Think Progress, September 16, 2008, http://thinkprogress.org/2008/09/16/mccain-flops-on-regulation/ (accessed February 24, 2010).

38. Howard Husock, "The Trillion-Dollar Bank Shakedown That Bodes Ill for Cities," *City Journal* (Winter 2000), http://www.city-journal.org/html/10_1_the_trillion_dollar.html.

39. Rush Limbaugh, transcript, "There's a Big Idea at Stake in the Democrat-Caused Financial Crisis," *The Rush Limbaugh Show*, September 22, 2008, http://www.rushlimbaugh.com/home/daily/site_092208/content/01125108.guest.html (accessed February 24, 2010).

40. The Bible, Tim. 6:10, Matt. 19:23–24.

41. Thomas Hobbes, *The Leviathan*, "Of the Natural Condition of Mankind, as concerning their Felicity, and Misery," chap. 13, http://oregonstate.edu/instruct/phl302/texts/hobbes/leviathan-contents.html (accessed February 24, 2010).

42. Brian C. Anderson, "How Catholic Charities Lost Its Soul," *City Journal* (Winter 2000), http://www.city-journal.org/html/10_1_how_catholic_charities.html (accessed February 24, 2010).

43. "Obama Notre Dame Speech," full text, http://www.huffingtonpost.com/2009/05/17/obama-notre-dame-speech-f_n_204387.html (accessed February 24, 2010).

44. Scott Cendrowski, "Michael Moore: 'Capitalism is anti-Jesus,'" *Fortune*, September 23, 2009, http://money.cnn.com/2009/09/22/news/economy/michael_moore_capitalism_love.fortune/index.htm?postversion=2009092308 (accessed February 24, 2010).

45. George W. Bush, interview with CNN, December 16, 2008, http://www.youtube.com/watch?v=oetNPJJcuAE.

46. Ayn Rand, "For the New Intellectual," *For the New Intellectual* (USA: Signet, 1963), p. 27.

47. Ayn Rand, *Atlas Shrugged* (New York: Random House, 1957), p. 412.

48. Ayn Rand, *Atlas Shrugged* (USA: Signet, 1996), pp. 444–445.

49. Ayn Rand, "America's Persecuted Minority: Big Business," *Capitalism: The Unknown Ideal*, (New York: New American Library, 1964), p. 48.

50. Ben S. Bernanke, "Monetary Policy and the Housing Bubble," Annual Meeting of the American Economic Association, January 3, 2010, http://www.federalreserve.gov/newsevents/speech/bernanke20100103a.pdf (accessed March 4, 2010).

51. Pamela Villarreal, "Social Security and Medicare Projections: 2009," National Center for Policy Analysis, June 11, 2009, http://www.ncpa.org/pub/ba662 (accessed May 10, 2010).

52. John McCain, quote from *Faith of My Fathers* (HarperCollins: New York, 1999) at http://www.issues2000.org/Archive/Faith_of_My_Fathers_Principles_+_Values.htm (accessed February 24, 2010).

53. Yuval Levin, "Obama's Case Against Obama," *National Review Online*, http://article.national-review.com/394430/obamas-case-against-obama/yuval-levin (accessed February 24, 2010).

54. Michelle Obama, "Michelle Obama's Commencement Address," *New York Times*, May 16, 2009, http://www.nytimes.com/2009/05/16/us/politics/16text-michelle.html?pagewanted=5 (accessed February 24, 2010).

55. Andrew Carnegie, *The Gospel of Wealth* (1889), http://amhist.ist.unomaha.edu/module_files/Carnegie%20Gospel%20of%20Wealth%201889.rtf (accessed February 24, 2010).

56. Michael Novak, quoted at http://www.intentionallyexcellent.com/archive/2006/Vol2Issue31.asp (accessed February 24, 2010).

57. Ronald Reagan, Address Before a Joint Session of the Congress Reporting on the State of the Union, January 26, 1982, archived at http://www.presidency.ucsb.edu/ws/index.php?pid=42687&st=education&st1 (accessed March 1, 2010).

58. Richard Stengel, "Compassion Is Back," *Time*, February 5, 1996, http://www.time.com/time/magazine/article/0,9171,984050,00.html (accessed March 1, 2010).

59. Michael D. Tanner, *Leviathan on the Right* (Washington, D.C.: The Cato Institute, 2007), p. 54.

60. Rush Limbaugh, interviewed by Chris Wallace, Fox News, November 1, 2009, http://www.rushlimbaugh.com/home/daily/site_103009/content/01125118.guest.html (accessed February 24, 2010).

61. Ayn Rand, "Conservatism: An Obituary," *Capitalism: The Unknown Ideal* (New York: New American Library, 1964), p. 201.

The Philosophy of Privation: Environmentalism Unveiled

Peter Schwartz

This essay was first published in 1999 in an anthology titled *Return of the Primitive: The Anti-Industrial Revolution*. On what ideological premises is the environmentalist movement based and what are its ultimate goals? In this article, Mr. Peter Schwartz exposes the true meaning of "environmentalism" and discusses its relationship to religion, science and philosophy more generally. Understanding this movement's philosophical underpinnings helps one understand its hostility toward industry as a whole.

The Philosophy of Privation: Environmentalism Unveiled

Peter Schwartz

The first code of ethics that deliberately and unequivocally divorced man's actions from his interests was Immanuel Kant's. It was Kant who declared that man, to be certain that he is acting morally, must not merely ignore his interests—material or spiritual—but must willfully contradict them. It was Kant who created a formal dichotomy between that which constitutes the good and that which fulfills any need of human life.

Kant's philosophy gradually worked its way into Western culture. Now, some two hundred years later, a political movement has arisen that brazenly endorses this killer creed. It is a movement that seeks to prohibit the pursuit of human values—because of one's moral "duty" to the nonhuman. That movement is: environmentalism.

Many people hold a benign view of environmentalism. They regard it as a salutary force, as a sort of global sanitation department. While critical of certain "excesses," people believe that environmentalism fundamentally seeks to improve man's life by cleaning up the dirt in his water and the pollutants in his air.

But that is a dangerously superficial assessment. If one examines the conflicts between the interests of man and the "interests" of nature, it becomes clear that the former are invariably sacrificed to the latter by environmentalists. Whenever there is a hydroelectric dam to be built, it is the welfare of the snail darter or the Chinook salmon that is inviolate, and the welfare of man that is dispensable. Whenever there is a choice between cutting down trees for human use and leaving them in place for the spotted owl, it is the bird's home that environmentalists save and human habitation that goes unbuilt.

Huge tracts of Arctic land are off-limits to productive enterprises, in order not to disturb the caribou and the ice floes. Mosquito- and alligator-infested swamps (euphemistically called *wetlands*) are deemed sacred, not to be defiled by man-made drainage. (Even land that is actually growing crops can be christened wetlands, if some bureaucrat decides that vegetation typically found in swamps *could* have grown there had the crops not been planted.) The most beneficial projects, from housing developments to science observatories, are halted if there is any danger—if there is any *allegation* of danger—to some piddling species.

The incalculable damage inflicted on human beings by such prohibitions is immaterial to environmentalists. They have abandoned even the pretext of holding human happiness as their ultimate purpose. In its place, as an open secret that the public is unable to take fully seriously, is the premise that nature must remain unchanged *as an end in itself.* It is the premise that nature must be protected, not *for* man, but *from* man.

Several years ago a controversy arose concerning a new cancer-fighting drug, taxol. It was found in the bark of the Pacific yew tree. The director of the National Cancer Institute described taxol as "the most important new drug we have had in cancer for fifteen years."[1] But environmentalists insisted that the trees, which are considered scarce and are home to the spotted owl, remain largely untouched.

Al Gore, in his book *Earth in the Balance,* declares himself incapable of choosing between people and trees: "It seems an easy choice—sacrifice the tree for a human life—until one learns that three trees must be destroyed for each patient treated. . . . Suddenly we must confront some tough questions."[2]

According to an official of the Oregon Natural Resources Council: "The basic issue in our mind is that the yew [tree] is a finite resource. . . . Our concern is that there will not be any left the way we are approaching this."[3] Not be any left—*for whom*? Certainly, his concern was not that the people now dying of cancer would lack trees for their treatment; those were the very people being denied available medicine by the environmentalists. Nor was his concern that future cancer victims would go untreated; for that would imply an endorsement of a crash program to plant new trees—and to cut down every single existing one that was needed for its taxol. Toward whom, then, was this official's concern directed? Toward *no one.* Toward no human being, that is. Environmentalism wants to preserve those trees *for the sake of the trees.* It wants all the people who are suffering from cancer simply to renounce this potential cure. It wants them to accept the inviolability of the yew tree.

Environmentalists view man as the enemy. Their aim is to keep nature pristine, free from the predatory invasions of man. It is not human welfare that sets the standard by which they make their judgments.

For example, author Tom Regan argues that medical research on animals, designed to discover cures for human diseases, should be abolished. He says: "If it means that there are some things we cannot learn, then so be it. We have no basic right not to be harmed by those natural diseases we are heir to."[4]

David Foreman, founder of the organization Earth First, puts it more bluntly: "Wilderness has a right to exist for its own sake, and for the sake of the diversity of the life forms it shelters; we shouldn't have to justify the existence of a wilderness area by saying, 'Well, it protects the watershed, and it's a nice place to backpack and hunt, and it's pretty.'"[5]

David Graber, a biologist with the National Parks Service, revels in execrating human beings as trespassers upon nature. He describes himself as among those who "value wilderness for its own sake, not for what value it confers upon mankind. . . . We are not interested in the utility of a particular species, or free-flowing river, or ecosystem, to mankind. They have intrinsic value, more value—to me—than another human body, or a billion of them. Human happiness, and certainly human fecundity, are not as important as a wild and healthy planet. . . . It is cosmically unlikely that the developed world will choose to end its orgy of fossil-energy consumption, and the Third World its suicidal consumption of landscape. Until such time as Homo sapiens should decide to rejoin nature, some of us can only hope for the right virus to come along.'"

(And speaking of viruses, they too have "rights." According to Rutgers ecologist David Ehrenfeld, the world's remaining supply of the smallpox virus should not be exterminated, since it preys only on human beings.[7])

Taking this illogic one step further, there are now "eco-terrorists," who use violence against loggers and other "intruders" upon nature's domain. A spokesman for the Green Party of Germany says: "We in the Green movement aspire to a cultural model in which the killing of a forest will be considered more contemptible and more criminal than the sale of six-year-old children to Asian brothels."[8] And according to an activist with Earth First, injuring or even murdering such "forest-killers" is justifiable self-defense: "The holocaust against the environment and its species is the same as any holocaust against humans."[9] (Earth First's apt slogan? "Back to the Pleistocene"—the glacial era of one million years ago; it is no accident that the Unabomber was openly sympathetic to the goals of this group.)

But if "wilderness has a right to exist for its own sake"—then man does not. Man survives only by altering nature to satisfy his own needs. Man cannot survive, as animals do, by automatically adapting to the natural surroundings in which he happens to find himself. Nature's vast wilderness, if passively accepted, is *inimical* to his survival. Man must transform the naturally given into a truly *human* environment. He must produce the values his life requires—he must grow food and build supermarkets, chop down trees and erect condominiums, mine ore and design jet planes, isolate organisms and manufacture vaccines. None of these values exists ready-made in nature. Man brings all of them into being only by transmuting his "natural environment."

To live as a human being requires that one regard nature as nothing but a *means* toward one's ends. Every cart, rowboat and space shuttle man has constructed violates the "right" of land, sea and air to maintain their "natural states." Every conscious decision to enhance human life—every attempt to rise above the animals—entails the subduing of nature and the repudiation of environmentalist doctrine. Man's life depends upon his productiveness. In Ayn Rand's words, it depends on a "process by which man's consciousness controls his existence, a constant process of acquiring knowledge and shaping matter to fit one's purpose, of translating an idea into physical form, of remaking the earth in the image of one's values."[10]

But if man lives only by a process of remaking the earth—what is the implication of the environmentalist demand that he renounce this process?

Environmentalism insists that man give up the value of material comfort and the expectation of material progress. He must distrust modern science and modern technology, since they only distance him from nature. He must forgo nuclear power and genetic engineering, luxury cars and food additives, Styrofoam cups and disposable diapers. He must stifle his inventiveness and shrink his cognitive horizons. His ancient ancestors managed to get by without an agglomeration of artificial gadgets—so must he. The essence of this message is that man should accept the only type of existence in true "harmony" with nature: an existence free of the man-made. Which means: for most, an early death; for the others, a life of backbreaking toil and bare subsistence.

The Worldwatch Institute, an environmentalist think tank, offers a stark concretization of this ideal: "The Eskimo's scrupulous use of every scrap of seal or walrus in the face of absolute scarcity might serve as a symbol for all in the years ahead. Conspicuous and excessive consumption of energy and food should be discouraged by law and by social pressure, thus reducing demand."[11]

All the imprecations against "excessive consumption"—all the exhortations to "recycle," to "conserve energy," to "save the earth"—have, as their motivation, a vision of the crudely primitive state of this Eskimo. That is the environmentalist nirvana.

But why do people accept this? Why do the citizens of a modern, industrial society not recoil in horror at the attempt to establish privation as a virtue? Because of two insidious ideas pushed by environmentalists—one metaphysical, the other ethical. The first is that production cannot be "sustained"; the second, that it is unjust to "exploit" nature.

The first idea springs from the old collectivist belief that wealth is created not by the individual, but by the tribe. This belief severs the act of production from the (individual's) faculty of reason. It was updated by Karl Marx, who maintained that the industrial factories and offices are somehow "just here," waiting to be coaxed by proletarian sweat and muscle into discharging their riches.

Environmentalists agree with this view of production as a mindless process. Production, they believe, consists in serendipitously finding the goods—in digging into the earth and uncovering what nature generously yields up. The goods are nature's beneficent gift to us. In the act of production, man is just a bit player, while nature is the star.

But whereas Marx implied that wealth is generated automatically, the environmentalist says it is not. The environmentalist holds that since production is not an act of reason, we cannot assume that the golden eggs will magically continue to appear. Instead, he says, with every scrap of wealth we greedily extract, with every clearing we plow and every bath we run, we "diminish" nature. By persistently trying to improve our environment to suit our ends, we are exceeding nature's willingness to nurture us. We are not allowing her to "replenish" herself. We are not allowing her to set a "sustainable" pace.

Production, therefore, is a hopeless effort. We are running out, the environmentalists cry. Of what? Of everything. The attempt to maintain our present level of wealth—let alone to increase it—is futile. Nature's fragile "ecosystem" simply will not allow it. We must resign ourselves to our impoverishment, because the mother lode is being exhausted.

Marx said the goods are here somehow—so society should seize them. Whereas the environmentalists say the goods are here somehow, but will not be here tomorrow—so society should "conserve" them.

It is not their own policies that are lowering our living standards—environmentalists disingenuously declare. The cause, rather, is the built-in limitations of nature. And the only solution is for us to reconcile ourselves to that fact. That is, since nature has only so much to give, we must stop seeking more. This injunction to make do with less is then resignedly accepted by the public because, it believes, there is no alternative.

Now consider the enormity of what is being evaded by the proponents of this metaphysics of scarcity. The Western world enjoys a material abundance at the end of the twentieth century that is orders of magnitude greater than what existed, say, in the tenth. The population is vastly larger, yet there are vastly more goods per person. Why? Certainly, natural resources have not miraculously multiplied. There is no greater quantity now of iron, or rainfall, or sand or petroleum. Rather, man's *mind* has been at work. Man has taken iron and made it into tools. He has taken waterfalls and made them into generators of electricity. He has transformed grains of sand into computer chips, and oozing black glop into gasoline. A continuous reshaping of nature has occurred. Man has given value to the raw materials that had always existed but had been worthless—worthless, because they had been part of nature's environment, not man's.

This is the essence of production: taking the elements of nature, rearranging their form—and generating prosperity. It is a conceptual, quintessentially *human* process. Wealth does not exist as a fixed, static quantity. It is the creation of a dynamic, boundless mind. And it has no inherent limitations.

The doomsday stories about running out of some "finite resource" (including those coming from the Malthusian predecessors of today's environmentalists) are endless; all of them ignore the causal connection between reason and production. For example, in 1908 the U.S. Geological Survey stated that the maximum future supply of crude oil in the U.S. was 22.5 billion barrels; eighty-seven years' worth of consumption later, there were over 22 billion barrels *just in unused, proven reserves*. In 1914 the U.S. Bureau of Mines said that future American production of oil could total no more than 5.7 billion barrels; in the following eighty years, over 160 billion barrels were produced. In 1939 the Department of the Interior forecast that our oil supplies would last only another thirteen years; some thirty years later, the rate of production alone had almost tripled.[12]

If one recognizes the intellectual root of production, one realizes the arbitrariness of extrapolating from present reserves to a remote future—even with respect to "non-renewable" resources. Goods are produced by rational men acting according to their knowledge and their evaluations. Proven reserves are merely the quantity of some good that it is currently worthwhile to know is available when needed. But the finitude of a given stockpile is no basis for assuming that, when it is used up, scarcities may ensue. There is simply no rational value in locating now all the sources of raw material for the goods that the market will demand only in some far-off future—just as no one would take pains to identify today the particular store from which he will buy a new television set in ten years when his current one wears out. (As the time approaches—*if* television has not been replaced by some superior product—he will make the effort to find a specific outlet from which to purchase what he needs.)

This is why no "finite resources" have ever disappeared, even though they have been in use for millennia. The value of some mineral is not intrinsic in its sheer existence. Its value is a consequence of the fact that man has recognized how it can be made to fill a human need. Every step of creating this value, from discovering how to mine it to inventing new uses for it, is an act of reason. As more of the known quantity of the good is used up and it becomes scarcer, its value grows, and it then becomes rational to search for more supply—it becomes rational to develop improved means of production—it becomes rational to devise better and cheaper substitutes. All of this prevents a good from simply being forever depleted. (Indeed, in a free market the known reserves often *expand* over time. For example, between 1950 and 1994 the U.S. reserves of "finite" zinc rose 271 percent; and of "finite" iron ore, 527 percent.[13])

Only a view of production as mere mechanical motion would make someone believe that what does not exist today will not come into existence tomorrow. That is an unwarranted conclusion, even assuming that the level of knowledge and technology remains unchanged. It is doubly unwarranted given that one cannot know what cognitive advances will be made tomorrow, or what new developments *those* advances will make feasible on the day after tomorrow.

Knowledge is hierarchical. Earlier knowledge makes possible later knowledge. In a continual expansion of thought, every new idea is the key to countless newer ones. Every new thought is another step up the cognitive ladder, providing a wider, more efficient perspective from which to look out on reality—a perspective not attainable from the lower rung. Physical goods are the material product of those thoughts, and will therefore increase as knowledge increases. As long as man is politically free—free to think, and free to act on his ideas— there will be no shortage of physical goods, any more than there can be of intellectual goods.

The irony is that environmentalists sense the connection between reason and production (which is what makes them try to obscure it). This impels them to argue that we are running out of not only physical goods—but *ideas* as well.

The Worldwatch Institute, for example, in discussing "the depletion of physical resources," states: "[Scientific advances in the near future will not be made as frequently or as cheaply as in the past. The known conceptual ground has been worked over pretty thoroughly, and subsequent explorers will find rich research veins less exposed and harder to exploit"[!][14] (One can only be grateful that our genetic engineers and our computer designers—to indicate just two of the many areas that have seen major scientific advances in recent years—were not deterred by such inanity.)

This is a perfectly consistent application of environmentalism. There is no fundamental difference between the act of producing food and the act of producing ideas. The mind is the source of each. To deny its efficacy in the first, therefore, is to deny it in the second.

The contention that a precarious scarcity is our fate—that unless we content ourselves with living in igloos and hunting for walrus, we are endangering the very planet—paves the way for another, more lethal notion.

After arguing that privation is metaphysically inescapable, environmentalists proceed to insist that it is also *desirable*. That is, having maintained that production is not the work of reason, they go on to denounce it as theft—theft from one's neighbors, theft from future generations, theft from the earth itself. And this is the second crucial assertion on which their case depends: namely, that production—the "exploitation" of nature—is morally wrong.

Why, they ask, should you be allowed to extirpate nature's wealth simply to gratify your desires? Who are you to claim such a right for your own selfish purposes? Who are you to declare that you have rights but that nature does not?

According to environmentalism, there is no moral legitimacy to valuing yourself above the rest of nature. "Ecological egalitarianism," as one author hails it, "accords nature ethical status at least equal to that of humans."[15]

In other words, first environmentalism proclaims that the Spartan life of the primitive Eskimo is unavoidable—then, that it is one's moral duty to aspire to it. First you are told that the quest for prosperity is mindless self-destruction— then, that sustaining your measly existence ought not take precedence over some swampland's divine right to wetness.

Only one code of ethics could make such a viewpoint possible: the code of altruism, the code that brands the pursuit of self-interest as evil. This belief is environmentalism's most potent weapon. What, after all, is more manifestly selfish than the act of production itself, in which you remake nature to serve your values? At its core, environmentalism is the demand that you surrender your comfort, your well-being, your *self.* Stop caring about your desire to be happy—it admonishes—and start worrying about how to please the snail darters and the spotted owls.

Altruism is the doctrine that man has no moral right to exist for his own sake. Taken from the Latin *alter* (or "other"), it is the doctrine that the sole justification for your life is your willingness to sacrifice it to others. Environmentalism is altruism unadulterated and uncamouflaged. In the past, the call for sacrifice was made on behalf of other human beings, such as the poor and the sick. Now, in a faithful extension of the altruist maxim, the term "others" is merely being broadened. Now, we are being urged to sacrifice the human to the nonhuman.

And if it *is* evil to live for your own sake, how can you resist such a demand? If self-abnegation is noble, what could be more praiseworthy than to subordinate your existence to that of the bugs, the weeds, and the mud?

The premise of self-sacrifice is embedded in the deceptive meaning now attached to the very term "environment." Logically, there can be no concept of an "environment" that is not the environment *of* someone (or something)—any more than there can be "property" that exists independently of the owner of the property. "Environment" is a relational concept. It properly refers to the surroundings *of* some entity as they relate *to* that entity.

But that is not how the environmentalist employs the term. He subverts it to denote an "environment" severed from any relationship to man—which then enables him to mislead people into *evaluating* it apart from any relationship to man.

That is, he initially counts on its correct meaning, so that people accept a need to care about the fate of the "environment"—which they assume in some way is *their* environment and is linked to *their* fate. This is why the movement's focus is pointedly on the "environment," rather than on the nonrelational concept "nature." But once a confused public has been taken in, environmentalists repackage "environment" to denote something upheld as existing separately from human beings.

Cashing in on the altruist ethics, they condemn as wrong—as selfish—the view that any human value must be a value to *man.* Just as they want you to believe it is wrong to *define* "environment" only in relation to man, they want you to believe it is wrong to *evaluate* it only in relation to man. It is erroneous, they say, to believe that the only "environment" worth protecting is one that is useful to human beings. A vein of iron ore, or a forest, or a sunrise should be regarded as values, they say, not because it benefits man, but because it "benefits" nature. These things have "value"—the environmentalist declares—apart from any connection to, or evaluation by, human beings.

According to the tenets of altruism, you should "value" that which holds no significance for your life—*because* it holds no significance for your life. So while nature's bogs and bugs may not be of any value to you, the precept of self-sacrifice commands: *that* is why you should treat them as though they are.

Thus, even the putative treasures of environmentalists—such as parks set aside as enclaves of uncommercialized, unindustrialized nature—are not permitted to be used as sources of enjoyment for man.

For example, when Yellowstone Park was devastated by fire in 1988, fire-fighting efforts were prohibited for weeks. Park officials allowed the fire to rage out of control, because it had begun naturally (through lightning). By the time firefighters were finally permitted to contain the conflagration, well over one million acres had burned, at a cost of 150 million dollars. What was the motive behind this lunacy? "Fire is a benign rather than a malignant force," explained Yellowstone's chief naturalist. He and other park officials viewed their primary responsibility during the disaster, not as preventing further damage by nature's fire, but as safeguarding the grounds against "unnatural" encroachments. As a news report in the *New York Times* described it: "They said they were trying to protect pristine areas from the destructive effects of bulldozers, fire engines and irrigation pipes."[16]

Yellowstone Park was regarded not as a value to man, but as a "value" to and for its natural self. So why not let it burn down, as long as the flames were part of its "natural" state? The head of the Glacier Institute put the philosophic issue this way: "It comes down to what we expect those lands to be. Is the park primarily for human use or their recreation? Or is the park to be maintained in its original state, letting fires do what they're going to do?"[17]

In other words: is man morally entitled to use nature to benefit himself—or must he become nature's self-sacrificing menial?

It is obvious which alternative environmentalists choose. Technology—which represents the conquest of nature by the human mind—is therefore an object of fear and hatred. It is routinely denounced by environmentalists. They greet every technological advance—from food preservatives to growth hormones to cloning—with a knee-jerkful of scare stories. Technological achievements are psychological threats to the environmentalist. They stand as testimony to the fact that man is both capable and worthy of living. To the nature-venerator, who cries that man can be neither, this is a terrifying reproach. So he reacts by trying to suppress technology (while rationalizing that he harbors only "practical" concerns about human safety).

Environmentalism is a systematic campaign to make man feel puny. It is a screed against self-esteem. It wants man to proclaim his own insignificance and to tremble before the mountains and the mites.

Today's man is told by environmentalists that he—like his primitive ancestors—must hold nature in quivering awe. He is to be, not the ruler of nature, but its obedient thrall. That is, he is to worship nature—*as a God.*

Environmentalism amounts to a modern, secularized form of religion. It is an ideology that instructs man to prostrate himself before a superior, ineffable force. It is an ideology that declares the human mind too feeble to grasp the complexities of an inscrutable world, or "ecosystem." It is an ideology propelled by the desire to have man subordinate himself to a hallowed power—a power which must be placated and paid homage, if man is to receive the gracious bounty upon which his existence depends.

This mysticism is now openly avowed within the environmentalist movement. For instance, New Left mandarin Tom Hayden taught a course at Santa Monica College on "Environment and Spirituality." It began with a discussion of the Bible, and ended with the prospects for what he called a new "earth-oriented religion." Hayden explained: "We need to see nature as having a sacred quality, so we revere it and are in awe of it. That forms a barrier to greed and exploitation and overuse."[18]

The Ecoforestry Institute, in a full-page ad opposing the logging of trees, says about forests: "They have an *intrinsic value* beyond objective measure. A society that sees them only as a resource to be exploited, as a crop to be marketed, has lost its sense of the sacred. Saving America's forests is more than an economic or ecological issue. It is a spiritual one as well."[19] (Emphasis in original.)

This unearthly fusion of religion and environmentalism originated with the New Left. As Paul Ehrlich writes: "It is probably in vain that so many look to science and technology to solve our present ecological crisis. Much more basic changes are needed, perhaps of the type exemplified by the much-despised 'hippie' movement—a movement that adopts most of its religious ideas from the non-Christian East. It is a movement wrapped up in Zen Buddhism, physical love and a disdain for material wealth."[20]

Predictably, the representatives of environmentalism and of religion are forging overt ties. For example, the late scientist Carl Sagan issued "an appeal for joint commitment in science and religion." It was a call for transforming environmentalism into a religious crusade. "We are close to committing—many would say we are already committing—what in religious language is sometimes called Crimes against Creation," he said. Environmentalism "must be recognized from the outset as having a religious as well as scientific dimension. . . . Thus there is a vital role for both religion and science. We hope this appeal will encourage a spirit of common cause and joint action to help preserve the Earth."[21] (This was signed by a number of prominent scientists, including Hans Bethe and Stephen Jay Gould, and by over two hundred religious leaders across the globe—from the dean of the Harvard Divinity School to the Secretary-General of the National Council on Islamic Affairs to the abbot of the Zen Community of New York.)

Even Pope John Paul II has taken up the cause. Contrary to those who regard Christianity as incompatible with environmentalism, the pope sees their fundamental unity. He has declared that world peace is threatened by "a lack of due respect for nature, by the plundering of natural resources and by a progressive decline in the quality of life. . . . Today, the dramatic threat of ecological breakdown is teaching us the extent to which greed and selfishness—both individual and collective[!]—are contrary to the order of creation, an order which is characterized by mutual interdependence. . . . The commitment of believers to a healthy environment for everyone stems from their belief in God the Creator, from their recognition of the effects of original and personal sin, and from the certainty of having been redeemed by Christ."[22]

Both the Church and environmentalism condemn the conception of nature as something to be refashioned by and for man. Both believe that man must repudiate the virtue of productiveness and of pride. Whether the commandment is to make use of nature in service to God or to make use of nature in service to endangered species—man is rendered a servant. Either way, the principle is the same: man must sacrifice his selfish enjoyment of earthly comforts in deference to a "higher" power.

There remains one final issue to be examined in judging environmentalism: its claim to science. In trumpeting the dangers of particular industrial products and activities, environmentalists typically invoke all kinds of empirical evidence. How, then, can their allegations be summarily dismissed? Isn't the honest opponent of environmentalists obligated to investigate, and refute, all their evidence? How can one ignore the copious research, the clinical studies, the laboratory experiments, the complex computer models—all supposedly proving the dire consequences of various technologies? Isn't cold, hard science on the side of environmentalism?

The answer is: no—and the very question reflects the environmentalists' worst perversion of all. Their scientific garb is a masquerade. It is designed to hide the fact that their claims do not rest on scientific evidence, but on the opposite: on a sweeping *rejection* of the methodology of science. Consider, for example, the environmentalists' case against Alar.

Alar is a chemical developed in the early 1960s that improves the appearance of apples and delays their ripening. In 1989, it became the target of a campaign to ban it, orchestrated by the Natural Resources Defense Council. The NRDC announced that it had conducted tests revealing that Alar causes cancer in people. The news media heralded the story of a greedy manufacturer foisting his toxic product upon unsuspecting, apple juice-drinking children. Alarmed farmers, grocers, and parents began avoiding apples. The apple-growing industry lost over 200 million dollars. The manufacturer was compelled to remove Alar from the market.

But what was the scientific basis for these claims? The NRDC tests did indeed show that Alar produced tumors in mice—in doses equivalent to what a human being would absorb by eating fourteen tons of apples a day for seventy years. (And mice fed *half* that amount—the equivalent of seven tons a day for seventy years—produced no tumors at all.)[23]

An earlier study of rodents by the Environmental Protection Agency also supposedly showed a link between Alar and cancer. Yet according to the EPA's own data, the average human exposure to the allegedly carcinogenic chemical was .000047 milligrams per kilogram of body weight (mg/kg); the mice in the ERA study, however, were given doses of 7 mg/kg (for males) and 13 mg/kg (for females)—a level *148,000 to 276,000 times* that of human exposure. (And even at that level, none of the *rats* in the study was stricken with cancer.)[24]

This is considered sufficient grounds for panicking the public and crippling an industry.

Or consider the pesticide DDT. It was banned in the U.S. in 1972, largely because it was said to be carcinogenic. That conclusion was based on studies that found DDT to cause benign liver tumors in mice (and nothing at all in other experimental animals)—and even then, only at doses *100,000 times higher* than what a person would absorb by ingesting DDT through residues in food.[25]

It is now accepted practice in environmentalist circles to assume that if *some* quantity of a substance is harmful, then *any* quantity is. But is there any substance on earth about which this context-dropping claim cannot be made? Everything can become deadly in sufficiently large doses—including water, or air, or organically grown soybeans. If a one-ton piano crashing down on you is fatal, does this imply that a one-ounce feather floating onto your shoulders once a day for eighty-eight years is also a threat? Potatoes contain arsenic; lima beans contain cyanide; nutmeg contains a hallucinogen; broccoli contains a substance that causes cancer in animals.[26] Should these be outlawed? None of the environmental "scientists" cares to publicize an obvious fact: the dosage level makes all the difference between safety and danger.

They don't care to publicize this—because they have an agenda other than the presentation of the truth. Dishonesty, as one of these pseudo-scientists explains, is their best policy: "We have to offer up scary scenarios, make simplified, dramatic statements, and make little mention of any doubts we may have. Each of us has to decide what the right balance is between being effective and being honest."[27]

Virtually any claim about some industrial danger is given instant publicity by environmentalists, while evidence of the benefits (or of the falsehood of the allegation of danger) is systematically disregarded. Paul Ehrlich, for example, has made a living out of issuing apocalyptic statements that the world is running out of food. In 1968 he wrote: "The battle to feed all of humanity is over. In the 1970s the world will undergo famines—hundreds of millions of people are going to starve to death in spite of any crash programs embarked upon now. At this late date nothing can prevent a substantial increase in the world death rate. . . . We must have population control at home, hopefully through a system of incentives and penalties, but *by compulsion if voluntary methods fail*."[28] (Emphasis added.)

Yet reality's repeated debunking of Ehrlich's predictions (to say nothing of the horrifying totalitarianism of his proposed "solution") has not diminished his status as an influential prophet. His regularly updated scenarios of doom are still taken seriously by the environmentalists; his well-known book *The Population Bomb* has gone through more than two dozen printings.

With respect to DDT, the promoters of "eco-hysteria" ignore a study in which *people* were fed DDT every day for up to twenty-seven months—with no harmful results. They ignore the fact that during the period of heaviest DDT use in the United States, from 1944 to 1972, deaths from liver cancer *dropped* 30 percent.[29]

And, most tellingly, they ignore the *benefits* of DDT (and the consequent harm created by its prohibition). They ignore the fact that before the advent of DDT, malaria was rampant. In Sri Lanka (then Ceylon), for example, there were 2.8 million cases of malaria in 1948. By 1963, because DDT killed the insects bearing the disease, the number had dropped to 17! But in the late 1960s, the spraying was halted due to the growing attacks on DDT; by 1969 the number of malaria cases in Sri Lanka had gone back to 2.5 million. In India, about 75 million cases of malaria occurred in 1951; ten years later (after DDT was introduced) the figure had fallen to 50,000; by 1977, however, it had risen to at least 30 million.[30] Today, millions of people a year are dying from malaria as a result of environmentalists' hostility toward pesticides. (But of course the truth about DDT is unimportant when compared with the need for "being effective.")

The environmentalist utilizes science, not to discover the facts, but to obfuscate them. After stripping away the veneer of rationality, one will discover that the hallmark of the catastrophe claim is the half-truth and the out-of-context fact.

When environmental "scientists" claim, for instance, that thousands of highly acidic and fishless lakes in the Northeast (the most severe cases of which are in the Adirondacks) are proof of the destructiveness of "acid rain" caused by coal-burning electric utilities—they neglect to mention: that most of the acidic lakes in the Adirondacks were acidified by natural organic acids; or that the average Adirondack lake is more *alkaline* now than one hundred fifty years ago; or that highly acidic, fishless waters exist naturally in regions with *no* industrial activity, such as the Rio Negro in the Amazon Basin (a river system the size of the Mississippi River).[31]

When environmental "scientists" claim that man-made chlorofluorocarbons (CFCs) have depleted the stratosphere of ozone, leaving us more exposed to the sun's ultraviolet radiation—they neglect to mention: that during the period when the ozone layer was presumably diminishing, the levels of ultraviolet radiation at the earth's surface were *falling*[32]; or that, at its peak, the world output of CFCs was 1.1 million tons annually, while *300* million tons of natural chlorine reach the atmosphere each year through the evaporation of seawater alone[33]; or that a 5 percent drop in ozone—which is of a magnitude that elicits grim calculations of increased skin cancers—would, according to those very calculations, result in a rise in radiation equivalent to that experienced by someone who merely moves sixty miles closer to the equator (say, from Santa Barbara to Los Angeles).[34]

When environmental "scientists" claim that overpopulation is exhausting the earth's capacity to sustain its inhabitants—they neglect to mention: that such conclusive yardsticks as per-capita food production and life expectancy are showing regular *increases*[35]; or that life improves most where industrialization is strongest; or that finding space for a growing population is such a non-problem that if all 5.8 billion earthlings relocated to Texas tomorrow, the resultant population density (22,000 people per square mile) would not be even *half* the current density of, say, Paris.[36]

This whole warped approach is the antithesis of science and objectivity. It is not scientific truth that environmentalists seek to discover—it is not reality that they hold as an absolute—it is not reason that shapes their conclusions. Reason is only an obstacle to the goals of these "scientists"—and some of them readily admit it.

For instance, author Jonathan Schell discusses the nature of the evidence necessary to form conclusions about environmental matters. He writes that scientists should "disavow the certainty and precision they normally insist on. Above all, we need to learn to act decisively to forestall predicted perils, even while knowing that they may never materialize. . . . Scientists need to become connoisseurs and philosophers of uncertainty. . . . The incurable uncertainty of our predicament, far from serving to reassure us, should fill us with unease and goad us to action."[37]

Let's translate this: Despite the lack of rational evidence for some claim of impending doom, we should nonetheless assume that it is true. Certainty and precision may be appropriate in dealing with other issues, but not environmental ones. The knowledge we have about some technology's vast benefits is to be outweighed by the *absence* of knowledge we have about its alleged harmfulness. It does not matter, therefore, that these "philosophers of uncertainty" do not know whether their statements are true. As long as a prediction of theirs can "fill us with unease," it should be acted on, whether it can be scientifically proved or not.

The aim of the environmentalists' studies and experiments, then, is not the identification of accurate, scientific knowledge, but the inculcation of a state of hysterical ignorance. Blind emotion, not reason, is to be our guide in coming to conclusions.

I am not a scientist, and I have not thoroughly investigated these issues. I cannot say that I have conclusive proof that CFCs are not threatening the ozone layer or that factory emissions are not changing the earth's temperature. But what I can say about the environmentalists' claims is something more fundamental: they warrant no cognitive attention—because they are not *attempts* at cognition. They are arbitrary vociferations. They do not represent efforts to reach objective truths. Therefore, as utterances issued not to illuminate reality but to distort it, they should not be admitted into the realm of science.

In this respect, the environmentalist methodology is identical to that of the "Scientific Creationists."

The Creationists' claims about errors in the theory of evolution are not based on science. The Creationists do not want to discover the *facts* about the origin of life. They use science merely as a facade, to disguise the fact that the Bible is the source of their beliefs and that their only agenda is a religious one. They do not seek genuine evidence for their position, because they do not accept any *necessity* for evidence. No facts or arguments will sway them, because their viewpoint does not rest on facts and arguments: it rests on faith. None of their "refutations" of evolution, therefore, qualifies as science.

Once the Creationists' basic method has been discredited, one need not scrutinize every new assertion they come up with. One need not disprove such assertions—indeed, one should not even try to, since it only legitimizes them—in order to defend the validity of evolution. The only rational response to all Creationist "arguments" is to dismiss them as being outside the realm of the rational. They simply deserve no cognitive respect—including even the respect of identifying them as "true" or "false."

The statements of environmentalists ought to be accorded the same *a*scientific status. Just as when you wish to determine the facts about evolution, the pronouncements of Creationists should be irrelevant to your search; so too, if you wish to determine the facts about a particular environmental question, you should do so independently of the declarations made by environmentalists. (Yes, it may turn out that some allegation of theirs happens to be true—by accident, as a parrot's squawkings may coincidentally parallel some fact of reality. If this occurs, and one ascertains it by rational means, appropriate steps should be taken to alleviate the danger—steps that logically *cannot* include any renunciation of technological progress.)

If and when there is genuine evidence that something man-made is harmful to human health or damaging to property, the victim is entitled to legal remedies—on the basis of standard laws that have long existed. These are the same kinds of laws that prevent your neighbor from starting a fire or releasing tear gas in his backyard if it will reach yours. If you can show that you were hurt by someone's actions, your rights should be protected by law. But you must meet one requirement: you must be able to prove your case objectively.

To environmentalists, this requirement is an unacceptable impediment. They do not want to be bound by the strictures of logic and science in their efforts to stifle production. Reason is not the method suited to their ends. They want to "disavow certainty and precision"—and to have government regulators accept their unproved assertions on faith.

The way to assess environmentalism, therefore, is not as a scientific issue, but as a *moral* one. In response to all the claims about the harm posed by various technologies, one must ask a basic question: "Harmful—by what standard?" For according to the standard of man's life here on earth, technology as such is beneficial—wealth as such is beneficial—material progress as such is beneficial. According to a rational standard, no *actual* threats to human welfare could justify the destruction of that upon which man's welfare depends—namely, production, technology, and freedom. The solution to any such threats must embrace improved production, better technology, more capitalism.

But environmentalists do not hold such a standard. What they find "harmful" is man's liberation from a life of primitive toil and bare subsistence. To them, the "harm" lies in the very existence of technology, wealth, and progress; it lies in the fact of industrialization per se. Paul Ehrlich, for instance, declares: "We've already had too much economic growth in the United States. Economic growth in rich countries like ours is the disease, not the cure."[38]

According to the group Earth First. "If radical environmentalists were to invent a disease to bring human populations back to sanity, it would probably be something like AIDS. It has the potential to end industrialism, which is the main force behind the environmental crisis."[39]

This is why environmentalists show no concern for all the suffering and deaths resulting from the *absence* of technology. This is why they do not care about their "ideal" Eskimo's lack of indoor plumbing, central heating, electricity, dentistry, and heart-transplant technology. This is why they are untroubled by the demonstrable evils resulting from all the roads and oil refineries and nuclear plants *not* built—not built, because of the environmentalist desire to protect nature from man.

This is also why, whatever dangers environmentalists claim to find, their answer is always to denounce progress and to search for "nature-friendly" alternatives. If acid rain is supposedly destroying our lakes, they direct us not to neutralize it easily with some alkaline—but to shut down the factories. If topsoil is supposedly being eroded, they direct us not to invent methods of more efficient farming—but to stop harvesting the crops. If there is too much traffic, they direct us not to build better highways—but to stop making the cars. Whatever the alleged problem, their incessant "solution" is: de-industrialize.

Environmentalists believe that "chemicals" are bad, additives are bad, artificial flavoring is bad, preservatives are bad, synthetic fibers are bad—that "interfering" with the processes of nature is inherently immoral. They ban food additives that supposedly cause cancer—yet are indifferent to the natural presence of the identical substances in foods. They condemn DDT—yet disregard the fact that we ingest 10,000 times more naturally produced pesticides than man-made ones.[40] They praise societies that wallow in the filth and disease that characterize a nontechnological "harmony" with nature—yet condemn those that enjoy the cleanliness and health resulting from modern sewage systems, washing machines, refrigeration, and polio vaccines. Whatever is a product of human design, in other words, is by that fact baneful; whatever is natural is by that fact benign.

This view of the man-made as intrinsically noxious is simply the corollary of the premise that nature is intrinsically good. The environmentalists' perverse standard of value is: the human is the harmful—and the way to achieve human "welfare" is to do away with the human.

Environmentalism seeks the renunciation of all progress and pleasure. Its goal is not the elimination of air pollution or filthy water—or anything else actually harmful to man. (If there *are* people animated by such concerns, they should form a new pro-technology/anti-dirt organization; but they should *not* ally themselves with the Paul Ehrlichs, the David Grabers, and the David Foremans, whose dictatorial aims are only abetted by unthinking "fellow-travelers.")

Environmentalists do not want to promote human happiness, or even the "happiness" of other species. Those who are callously indifferent to the millions of people who die annually because DDT has been banned will not be moved to moral outrage at the "injustice" of some spotted owl losing its nest. What environmentalists desire is not the welfare of the nonhuman—but the misery of man.

This is true of all manifestations of altruism. It is not the poor whom altruists wish to lift up (if it were, they would advocate laissez-faire capitalism); it is rather the productive whom they wish to bring down. But when the demand for self-sacrifice takes the form of environmentalism, the desire to destroy becomes more overt. In that form, there is far less pretense of pursuing any human values. There is only the snarling demand for universal deprivation.

The philosophic inspiration for all this is Immanuel Kant. It was Kant, the primary secularizer of religion, whose characteristic approach was to propound a mysticism dressed up as rationality. It is environmentalism that has thoroughly implemented his philosophy.

Kant postulated a "noumenal" world—a nonmaterial world unknowable to man, a world that transcends human perception and human interests, a world that represents "true reality" because it is "unfiltered" by human consciousness. Environmentalism proceeds to postulate an ineffable "ecosystem"—a dimension whose arcane workings are accessible only to those possessing the faculty described by the Ecoforestry Institute as a "sense of the sacred," a dimension in which it is considered "unnatural" for man to engage in what his life requires—productive activity—a dimension that remains "real" only as long as it is unsullied by human values.

Kant maintained that reason can give us only a distorted picture of reality, that the mind is unreliable and can never be in touch with existence "as it really is." Environmentalism too maintains that man's mind is incapable of grasping, and thereby governing, nature, that only if we "disavow certainty and precision" can we apprehend the actual devastation industrialization is sowing, that rational science blinds us to the truth that the squashing of some insect or the trampling of some shrub may bring a fragile planet crashing into oblivion.

And obviously, environmentalism's exhortations to sacrifice for nature—to surrender our self-interest, not for religion's promise of bliss in some afterworld nor for Marx's assurance of prosperity in some indefinable future, but to surrender it as our rewardless obligation to the snail darters and the wetlands, to surrender everything human to anything nonhuman—what is that, but Kant's "categorical imperative" to submit to moral duty, for no reason and for no human end, but for the sake of submission as an end in itself?

The method that Kant instituted, and that environmentalism has adopted, consists of a continual inversion of the rational and the irrational. It consists of Kant's proclamation that whatever man perceives is not real, *because* he perceives it, and that whatever is of value to man is not moral, *because* it is a value. And it consists of environmentalism's final corruption: the declaration that production is destruction—the declaration that whatever wealth we produce makes us poorer, *because* we have produced it.

Kant used the prestige of reason—to undermine reason and objectivity; environmentalism uses the prestige of science—to undermine science and production. Both insidiously pose as advocates of the rational—Kant, by pretending that it is not really reason that he is negating; environmentalists, by pretending that it is not really production (but only "unsustainable" production) that they are attacking. Both, at root, seek to render human life and happiness impossible.

The single basic truth uttered by environmentalists is about themselves: they want to crush what they regard as the evil of self-interest. Their ideology has taken hold not in spite of its opposition to the requirements of man's life—but *because* of it, because it has latched firmly onto the prevailing cultural premise of self-sacrifice. In their campaign for privation, this moral evaluation is their strongest weapon.

It is time to disarm them.

There is only one practical way of fighting environmentalism: by morally defending man. The apologetic attempts to oppose environmentalist laws by showing how much better off the "environment" would be through private, non-bureaucratic efforts, are—like the appeasing attempts to fight the welfare state by arguing that capitalism is more compassionate toward the homeless—doomed to failure. Instead, what needs to be upheld, proudly and unequivocally, is the principle that there is no value in nature apart from that which is of value to man, which means: there *is* no "environment"—other than the environment of man.

The men who live by that premise—the men who make civilization and progress possible—are choking on the philosophic pollution of environmentalism. They need to be freed from the suffocating clutches of the worshipers of a virgin earth. They need to breathe air—the liberating air of industrialization. They need to be left free to produce—to continue creating the magnificent abundance that has lifted humanity out of the caves and jungles of the pre-industrial era. And who are these individuals? Everyone who understands, and glories in, the fact that man lives by reshaping nature to serve his values.

Notes

1. Dr. Samuel Broder, director of the National Cancer Institute, quoted in "Tree Yields a Cancer Treatment, But Ecological Cost May Be High," *New York Times,* May 13, 1991, p. Al.

2. Al Gore, *Earth in the Balance* (Houghton Mifflin, 1992), pp. 105–106.

3. Wendell Wood, quoted in "Tree Yields a Cancer Treatment, But Ecological Cost May Be High," *New York Times,* May 13, 1991, p. A14.

4. Tom Regan, quoted by David Hardy, in *America's New Extremists: What You Need to Know About the Animal Rights Movement* (Washington Legal Foundation, 1990), p. 8.

5. D. Petersen, "The Plowboy Interview," *Mother Earth News,* Jan./Feb. 1985, p. 21.

6. David Graber, "Mother Nature as a Hothouse Flower," Los *Angeles Times Book Review,* Oct. 22, 1989, pp. 1, 9.

7. Cited by Joel Schwartz in "Apocalypse Now," *Commentary,* Aug. 1990, p. 56.

8. Carl Amery, quoted in *Trashing the Planet* (Regnery Gateway, 1990), by Dixy Lee Ray, p. 169.

9. Darryl Cherney, quoted in "Militant Environmentalists Planning Summer Protests to Save Redwoods," *New York Times,* June 19, 1990, p. A18.

10. Ayn Rand, *Atlas Shrugged* (Signet, 1957), p. 946.

11. Robert Fuller, "Inflation: The Rising Cost of Living on a Small Planet," Worldwatch Paper no. 34, Jan. 1980 (Worldwatch Institute).

12. "Doomsday and Inflation," *The Intellectual Activist,* May 1, 1980, p. 4. Oil data from: *U.S. Crude Oil, Natural Gas, and Natural Gas Liquid Reserves* (U.S. Energy Information Administration, 1995); *Historical Statistics of the United States: Colonial Times to 1970* (U.S. Dept. of Commerce, 1975); *Statistical Abstract of the United States* (U.S. Dept. of Commerce, 1996).

13. *Mineral Facts and Problems* (U.S. Dept. of the Interior, 1956); *Mineral Commodity Summaries* (U.S. Dept. of the Interior, 1994).

14. Fuller, op. cit.

15. Roderick Frazier Nash, quoted in "The Rights of Nature and the Death of God," by Joel Schwartz, *The Public Interest,* Fall 1989, pp. 3–4.

16. "Ethic of Protecting Land Fueled Yellowstone Fires," *New York Times,* Sept. 22, 1988, pp. Al, A24.

17. Ibid.

18. "Chronicle," *New York Times*, Aug. 3, 1991, p. 20.

19. Ad by Ecoforestry Institute of the U.S. (Portland, Oregon), *New York Times,* May 25, 1993, p. A9.

20. Paul Ehrlich, *The Population Bomb* (Ballantine, 1968), p. 171.

21. Carl Sagan, "Guest Comment: Preserving and Cherishing the Earth—an Appeal for Joint Commitment in Science and Religion," *American Journal of Physics,* July 1990, p. 615.

22. Pope John Paul II, "World Day of Peace Message," 1990 (published by the Vatican, Dec. 1989).

23. Dixy Lee Ray, *Trashing the Planet* (Regnery Gateway, 1990), pp. 78–79.

24. Eric W. Hagen and James J. Worman, *An Endless Series of Hobgoblins* (Foundation for Economic Education, 1995), pp. 10–11, 19.

25. Ray, op. cit., p. 73.

26. Elizabeth M. Whelan and Frederick J. Stare, *Panic in the Pantry* (Prometheus, 1992), pp. 66–76.

27. Stephen Schneider, quoted in "Our Fragile Earth," by Schell, op. cit.

28. Ehrlich, op. cit., p. xi.

29. Ray, op. cit. pp. 72–73.

30. Ibid., p. 69; also, Julian L. Simon, *The Ultimate Resource 2* (Princeton University, 1996), p. 261.

31. Edward C. Krug, "Acid Rain and Acid Lakes: The Real Story" (published in *Heritage Foundation Backgrounder),* April 19, 1990, p. 13.

32. Michael Sanera and Jane S. Shaw, *Facts, Not Fear* (Regnery, 1996), pp. 167–168.

33. Ray, op. cit, p. 45.

34. Sanera and Shaw, op. cit., pp. 168–169.

35. Simon, op. cit, pp. 87, 320.

36. Calculations based on data in *Encyclopedia Americana*, 1996, vol. 21, p. 430.

37. Jonathan Schell, "Our Fragile Earth," *Discover*, Oct. 1987, pp. 47–50.

38. Paul Ehrlich, quoted in "Journalists and Others for Saving the Planet," by David Brooks, *Wall St. Journal,* Oct. 5, 1989, p. A28.

39. From an Earth First newsletter, cited by Ray, op. cit., p. 168.

40. Hagen and Worman, op. cit., p. 101.

Bibliography

It is difficult for the conscientious reader to find books that treat environmental issues objectively. The following is a list of some titles meeting that standard:

Bailey, Ronald, ed. *The True State of the Planet*. New York: Free Press, 1995.

Fumento, Michael. *Science Under Siege*. New York: William Morrow, 1996.

Hagen, Eric W., and James J. Worman. *An Endless Series of Hobgoblins*. Foundation for Economic Education, 1995.

Lehr, Jay H., ed. *Rational Readings on Environmental Concerns*. New York: Van Nostrand Reinhold, 1992.

Marquardt, Kathleen. *Animal Scam*. Washington, DC: Regnery Gateway, 1993.

Ray, Dixy Lee. *Environmental Overkill*. Washington, DC: Regnery Gateway, 1994.

Ray, Dixy Lee. *Trashing the Planet*. Washington, DC: Regnery Gateway, 1990.

Sanera, Michael, and Jane S. Shaw. *Facts, Not Fear*. Washington, DC: Regnery, 1996.

Simon, Julian L. *The Ultimate Resource 2*. Princeton, NJ: Princeton University Press, 1996.

Simon, Julian L., ed. *The State of Humanity*. Cambridge, MA: Blackwell, 1995.

Whelan, Elizabeth M. *Toxic Terror*. Buffalo, New York: Prometheus Books, 1993.

Whelan, Elizabeth M., and Frederick J. Stare. *Panic in the Pantry*. Buffalo, New York: Prometheus Books, 1992.

Energy Privation:
The Environmentalist Campaign Against Energy

Keith Lockitch

Dr. Keith Lockitch presents a contemporary analysis of the environmentalist movement's true purpose by examining its current arguments against the development and consumption of energy in the name of protecting the climate. This previously unpublished essay serves as a companion piece to the preceding article by Mr. Peter Schwartz and demonstrates that although the targets of the environmentalists' campaign may have shifted, the fundamental goals of this ideological movement remain unchanged.

Energy Privation:
The Environmentalist Campaign Against Energy

Keith Lockitch

In Ayn Rand's novel *Atlas Shrugged*, one of the mysteries driving the plot involves a motor that taps an unusual source of energy: it draws static electricity from the atmosphere and converts it into useable power. Two of the novel's heroes discover the broken remnants of a prototype in an abandoned factory, and then spend much of the novel trying to figure out how the motor works and searching for its unknown inventor.

The motor, and the urgent mystery surrounding its invention, dramatize a crucial idea: *the enormous value of energy to human life*. The characters who find the motor—railroad magnate Dagny Taggart and steel tycoon Hank Rearden—being two of the country's leading business executives, are able immediately to envision its tremendous potential. "Don't you understand what this means?" says Taggart.

> It's the greatest revolution in power motors since the internal-combustion engine—greater than that! It wipes everything out—and makes everything possible. . . . Who'll want to look at a Diesel? Who'll want to worry about oil, coal or refueling stations? Do you see what I see? A brand-new locomotive half the size of a single Diesel unit, and with ten times the power. A self-generator, working on a few drops of fuel, with no limits to its energy. The cleanest, swiftest, cheapest means of motion ever devised. . . . Hank, do you know what that motor would have meant, if built?

"I'd say: about ten years added to the life of every person in this country," replies Rearden,

> if you consider how many things it would have made easier and cheaper to produce, how many hours of human labor it would have released for other work, and how much more anyone's work would have brought him. Locomotives? What about automobiles and ships and airplanes with a motor of this kind? And tractors. And power plants. All hooked to an unlimited supply of energy, with no fuel to

pay for, except a few pennies' worth to keep the converter going. That
motor could have set the whole country in motion and on fire.[1]

While a motor "converting static energy into kinetic power" is an element
of science fiction in *Atlas Shrugged*, what it symbolizes is a fact of the highest
importance. The ability to harness energy on an industrial scale was an unprecedented liberating force, freeing mankind from the unrelenting hardship of brute
physical labor.

Before the Industrial Revolution, survival at the level of barest subsistence
required a backbreaking struggle, powered chiefly by human and animal muscle.
In 1800 more than three quarters of the U.S. labor force worked on farms, toiling
from dawn to dusk to produce quantities of food barely adequate for nutrition,
struggling against drought and pestilence, aided only by crude wooden tools and
the brute strength of draft animals.[2] Today less than 3% of U.S. workers farm
vastly greater quantities (and quality) of food, with the heavy labor done by diesel tractors and combine harvesters, automated irrigation systems, and the ma-
chinery in modern chemical factories that mass-produces highly effective pesticides and fertilizers.[3]

With every new advance in motive power—from the steam engine to the
internal-combustion engine to electric turbines and motors and beyond—came
vast new possibilities for the expansion of human productivity and the improvement of human life. The advent of motive technologies fueled by highly concentrated energy sources blasted the barriers of preindustrial energy—barriers
imposing strict limitations on the productivity of labor and severe restrictions
on travel and trade. In the early nineteenth century, getting across the country,
say from New York to Chicago—a distance we routinely fly today in a matter
of hours—required weeks of grueling travel by stage coach. The production of
goods was limited to the small-scale operations of cottage industries, and shipping was constrained by the endurance of lumbering draft animals or by wind-
powered sailing vessels whose top speed was on the order of ten mph.[4] Today
industrial-scale energy fuels a global trade worth trillions of dollars, with automated factory equipment churning out all manner of life-enhancing goods and
with petroleum-powered trucks, freight trains, and cargo ships carrying them all
over the planet.

Yet even today, large numbers of people still suffer for lack of industrial-scale
energy. About *1.5 billion people* have no electric lighting, refrigeration, computer technology, electronic devices or medical equipment—no access to electricity at all.[5] About *2.5 billion people*—more than one-third of the world's population—have no source of energy for heating or cooking other than biomass fuels
such as wood or animal dung, and the resulting smoke from open fires is a leading cause of death in undeveloped countries.[6] The World Health Organization
estimates that about 1.6 million people die every year from respiratory diseases

directly attributable to indoor air pollution—almost as many as die annually from AIDS.[7]

Similarly, for lack of freshwater and sewage infrastructure built and powered using industrial-scale energy, "over 1 billion people globally lack access to safe drinking-water supplies, while 2.6 billion lack adequate sanitation." Consequently, "diseases related to unsafe water, sanitation and hygiene result in an estimated 1.7 million deaths every year."[8] And for lack of an adequate capacity for food production and distribution, chronic undernourishment affects more than 1 billion people.[9] The result is that in parts of the world today—particularly in parts of Africa—life expectancy is *under forty years*. It hasn't been that low in the industrialized world since the eighteenth century—and today, in industrialized countries life expectancy is closer to eighty years.[10]

Industrial-scale energy is an indispensable, life-saving value. It has completely transformed human life for the better in the industrialized world. And the benefits of industrial development will come to undeveloped countries only if they develop the infrastructure for the large-scale production and use of energy, as India and China are currently doing.

But despite the vital role that energy plays in our lives, most of us tend to take it for granted. We, in the industrialized world, rarely think about the countless benefits it provides, or about how difficult life was (and still is) without it. We have such reliable systems for the production and delivery of energy that we use it without giving it much thought. We are largely ignorant about the sheer scale of the infrastructure and of the continuous investment of capital and resources and brainpower required to discover, extract, transport, process, market and deliver the energy that fuels every aspect of our global economy. We don't think about everything that's involved in keeping the gas flowing out of the pump or the electricity out of the wall.

Because we take the incredible benefits of industrial-scale energy for granted, we much more readily accept the claim, put forward by environmentalists, that our use of energy is a problem desperately in need of a solution. For decades environmentalists have been telling us that man-made emissions of greenhouse gases—especially the burning of fossil fuels in our cars, factories, and power plants—are "interfering" with the earth's climate. The resulting climate change will supposedly disrupt human life and activity, a threat that they insist requires immediate preventative action aimed at reducing greenhouse gas emissions. Almost always absent from the discussion, however, are the enormous values we reap from carbon-based fuels. If human life and happiness are the standard, can we afford to eliminate or even radically reduce our use of these sources of energy? (Of course if you dream up, as many environmentalists do, scare stories like frequent "killer storms worse than Katrina and Gustav," or "drought over half the planet," including a "permanent Dust Bowl" stretching "from Kansas to

California," or rising sea levels displacing "more than 100 million environmental refugees," then even the massive benefits of carbon-based fuels may seem insignificant in comparison.[11])

But, you may be thinking at this point, most environmentalists are not proposing that in reducing greenhouse gas emissions we must do without industrial-scale energy altogether. Rather, we will simply have to shift from carbon-based fuels to "green energy." And because we are ignorant of the huge amount of thought and effort that was necessary to create our current system of industrial-scale energy, we much more readily accept their assertion that this shift is doable, easy, and even economically beneficial. But is there in fact reason to believe this?

Our continued use of industrial-scale energy is literally a matter of life-and-death. It's crucial to examine more closely and carefully the environmentalist movement's proposed transformation of the global energy economy. Just exactly what changes are being proposed to this vital system and just how carefully have they been thought through?

What the environmentalist movement is proposing is not just to tinker with our present system, but to alter it completely. To see this, consider its attitudes toward the energy sources that currently supply most of the world's energy.

Let us begin with oil and coal. These have been utilized on a large scale for only a few hundred years, but they are the fuels which, in a historically brief span of time, have completely transformed human life.

The large-scale production and use of coal began in England in the eighteenth century. As the chief fuel for the newly invented steam engine, coal was the dominant energy source powering the Industrial Revolution, which opened the floodgates for a stream of life-saving benefits unimaginable in the preindustrial era. Today, coal supplies more than a quarter of the world's energy (just over 27%), including nearly half of all the electricity generated in the United States.[12, 13]

Oil was first produced commercially in the 1860s, following Edwin Drake's famous drilling of the first successful oil well in Pennsylvania in 1859. Initially valued for its kerosene content, oil revolutionized the illumination industry, bringing the benefits of inexpensive lighting to the masses of people unable to afford its expensive predecessor, sperm whale oil. When kerosene lamps were supplanted by electric lighting in the late nineteenth century, oil in the form of gasoline and diesel went on to revolutionize the transportation industry, making possible a previously unimaginable degree of personal mobility.[14] Today, oil provides around 36% of the world's primary energy and supplies the overwhelming majority of its transportation fuel.[15, 16]

Together, oil and coal provide nearly two thirds of the world's energy. These are fuels relied on heavily by the five billion people who *do* have access to electricity and the four billion who don't have to cook over an open fire. Yet, they are not merely opposed by environmentalists, but are vilified with a disturbing degree of moral hatred. James Hansen, the NASA climate scientist who has played a leading role in promoting the climate issue, has called for criminal trials against the CEOs of fossil fuel energy companies, such as ExxonMobil and Peabody Coal.[17] Oil is regarded as being in roughly the same category as heroin or crack: a self-destructive addiction that we desperately need to shake, and coal is attacked in even more vitriolic terms. In Hansen's view, the productive activities of the companies and business executives involved in the mining, transportation, and use of coal constitute "high crimes against humanity" on a par with the Nazi Holocaust. "Coal-fired power plants are factories of death," he writes, and the coal trains that supply them are "death trains—no less gruesome than if they were boxcars headed to crematoria."[18, 19]

Were the environmentalists' proposed transformation of the energy system completed, it's safe to say, we no longer would have much access to oil or coal.

While not denounced in quite such incendiary terms, the third major form of fossil fuel energy, natural gas, is also opposed on environmentalist grounds.

Natural gas provides nearly a quarter of the world's energy (23%), and it is less "carbon intensive" than oil or coal—that is, burning it produces about half as much carbon dioxide as coal for the same amount of energy.[20] (This is because each methane molecule has four hydrogen atoms to burn along with every atom of carbon, whereas typical coals have only around one hydrogen atom for every two carbons. [21]) For this reason, some environmentalist groups have expressed qualified support for natural gas as a so-called bridge fuel that could smooth a transition away from coal and oil. (Famously gaffing on NBC's *Meet the Press*, Nancy Pelosi even called natural gas "a clean, cheap alternative to fossil fuels."[22])

But whatever muted support some environmentalists might have for natural gas, that support is highly conditional. As the Natural Resources Defense Council notes, "expanded use of natural gas can result in significantly lower cumulative emissions of carbon dioxide if it is used to displace those higher carbon fuels. However, a greater supply of natural gas in and of itself may or may not result in reduced emissions. . . . If natural gas displaces energy efficiency, renewable resources, or more efficient fuel or vehicle investments, then it would increase cumulative emissions"[23]—in which case they would presumably oppose it.

And ultimately, the environmentalist goal is to eliminate *all* carbon-emitting fossil fuels, including natural gas. A *New York Times* editorial opposing a proposed offshore terminal facility for importing liquefied natural gas explained that one of the "major problems with Broadwater was that the benefits it promised—convenient satisfaction of the region's energy needs—would inevitably shield us from the hard choices that have to be made to develop cleaner energy sources and usher in a world less dependent on traditional fossil fuels of any kind."[24]

But the world's dependence on "traditional fossil fuels" is not really a matter of "convenience." We rely on them substantially to meet our critical energy needs. Most of the world's energy—more than 86%—is supplied by coal, natural gas and oil.[25] Yet, these are the sources we are told we must stop using because of their "footprint" on the atmosphere.

So what "cleaner" options do environmentalists offer as acceptable alternatives?

What about nuclear power or hydroelectricity? These are both sources of energy that contribute significantly to world energy production and neither of them is carbon-based. Nuclear power currently supplies about 6% of the world's energy, or 15% of its electricity. About one-fifth of America's electricity comes from nuclear power plants, while other countries rely on it much more. France, for instance, gets more than three-quarters of its electricity from its fifty-nine nuclear plants. Hydro, too, supplies slightly more than 6% of the world's energy, or more than 16% of its electricity.[26] The sub-atomic processes that release nuclear energy do not emit CO_2, nor does the process of extracting the kinetic energy of water falling through electric turbines. But despite the fact that neither nuclear nor hydro produces greenhouse gas emissions in the process of making energy, neither of these sources is regarded as part of the "solution to global warming."

Three decades before *An Inconvenient Truth*, the smash eco-hit was *The China Syndrome*. The environmentalist movement has been fighting nuclear energy since long before claims about man-made climate change became its dominant crusade. And nuclear power's potential as a safe, proven, *carbon-free* means of providing a substantial portion of the world's electricity has not changed that one bit.

According to the Natural Resources Defense Council, "expanding nuclear power is not a sound strategy for diversifying America's energy portfolio and reducing global warming pollution."[27] WWF "strongly opposes" nuclear power, arguing that "replacing fossil fuel fired power stations with nuclear energy simply replaces one fundamental environmental problem by another"; the group's position is that "the use of nonrenewable energy resources such as fossil fuels and uranium have to eventually be reduced to zero—a phase out of fossil fuel and nuclear power."[28] The Sierra Club calls nuclear power "a bad choice," while Greenpeace calls it "an expensive and dangerous distraction from the real solutions to climate change," adding that "every dollar spent on nuclear power is a dollar stolen from the real solutions to climate change."[29, 30]

As for hydro, environmentalists have opposed hydroelectricity even longer than they have nuclear power. John Muir, the founder of the Sierra Club, famously fought the construction of a dam in Yosemite's Hetch Hetchy Valley.[31] And even though he lost his battle when Congress authorized the dam in 1913, his followers have continued his efforts ever since. The Sierra Club's "History of Accomplishments" proudly lists numerous successful campaigns to block dams.[32]

On environmentalist grounds, the Federal Energy Regulatory Commission, which oversees hydro in the United States, has recently shown more of an interest in *demolishing* small hydro dams than in issuing licenses approving new ones. In 1997 it refused to renew the license for the Edwards Dam, a privately owned 3.5 megawatt hydro facility on Maine's Kennebec river, and took the unprecedented step of ordering the structure demolished against its owner's will. Edwards was torn down in 1999, becoming the first dam destroyed by government edict for environmental reasons.[33] A *New York Times* editorial reflecting on the tenth anniversary of the demolition, celebrated the fact that around 430 dams had been destroyed since Edwards—and looked forward to the anticipated destruction of others.[34]

Oil, coal, natural gas, nuclear power, hydroelectricity. Altogether, these sources provide essentially all of the world's energy—more than 98% of it, to be exact.[35] They collectively supply more than 96% of the world's electricity, while petroleum alone accounts for more than 94% of the world's transportation fuel.[36, 37] These energy sources are what currently power our modern world, and, given their indispensable role in agriculture, manufacturing, transportation, and all the other elements of industrial civilization, it's no exaggeration to say that they are literally keeping us all alive.

Yet, mainstream environmental groups systematically reject each one as unacceptable forms of energy.

Clearly, what is being called for in terms of energy policy is not just a minor adjustment, but a *total transformation* of the whole way we go about producing and using energy: the way we generate electricity, the way we light and heat our buildings, the kinds of cars we drive and the amount of air travel we do, the way we power our factories and businesses, the way we transport goods and products all over the world, and so on and so on. This is a *sweeping and fundamental* transformation that is being proposed. And just how radical a change it would be is significantly under-appreciated in the energy and climate debate.

No one who truly values human life could propose to completely cut off mankind's access to energy. Yet, unless there's a readily available alternative to our current methods of producing energy, that's just what environmentalists seem to be proposing.

What most of us assume is that there is just such an alternative. We assume that environmentalists have a plan for replacing our current forms of energy and for meeting the world's energy needs, despite their rejection of every significant source currently used for that purpose. And environmentalists certainly do claim to have such plans. Indeed, there's no shortage of would-be Energy Czars, each with his own plan for reconfiguring the entire global economy around his particular blend of preferred sources or methods of producing energy. But the sources that all these planners mainly point to as the answer to our energy requirements—the "green" sources they all insist can be exploited economically, and in sufficient quantity, to supply our needs—are those making up the insignificant remaining 2% of world energy production: sources such as wind energy, solar power, geothermal energy, biofuels, etc.

Environmentalists claim that these various forms of energy are abundant sources of cheap, clean power. These are fuels that are "free forever" says Al Gore—in contrast to the "dirty, vulnerable, expensive, polluting fuels" that we currently rely on.[38] Disparaging the "19th-century technologies that depend on dangerous and expensive carbon-based fuels" (electric turbines? the internal-combustion engine?), Gore hails his preferred "renewable" sources as the future of energy, praising the "21st-century technologies" that utilize them (windmills?).[39]

Environmentalists proclaim that the world is on the verge of a "green energy revolution," which, once the vast potential of these renewable sources is unlocked, will power a booming "green economy" with unlimited possibilities. Indeed, to hear the rhetoric describing the promise of these renewables one might think they were talking about something akin to the fictional motor in *Atlas Shrugged*—"the cleanest, swiftest, cheapest means of motion ever devised," "an unlimited supply of energy" that "makes everything possible."[40]

Fred Krupp, the president of Environmental Defense Fund, writes breathlessly about the "Climate Change Opportunity" that awaits. "Solving global warming," he writes,

> will create an historic economic opportunity. Energy is the biggest business in the world, "the mother of all markets," says venture capitalist John Doerr, Google's first funder. The winners of the race to reinvent energy will not only save the planet, but will also make megafortunes. . . . Fixing global warming won't be a drain on the economy. On the contrary, it will unleash one of the greatest floods of new wealth in history.[41]

How do we unleash that flood of wealth? "What if we could use fuels that are not expensive, don't cause pollution and are abundantly available right here at home?" asks Al Gore. "We have such fuels," he declares.

> Scientists have confirmed that enough solar energy falls on the surface of the earth every 40 minutes to meet 100 percent of the entire world's energy needs for a full year. Tapping just a small portion of

this solar energy could provide all of the electricity America uses. And enough wind power blows through the Midwest corridor every day to also meet 100 percent of US electricity demand. Geothermal energy, similarly, is capable of providing enormous supplies of electricity for America." [42]

Unfortunately, however, scientists have confirmed a few other things as well, which undermine Gore's conclusions. While it is true that the *total* quantities of energy available in these sources is large, what he fails to mention is that it is spread out over enormous areas, which dilutes it considerably. For instance, the figure Gore mentions regarding solar energy is accurate, but completely misleading. What he doesn't emphasize, of course, is that all that solar energy is spread out over *half the entire surface of the earth*! The relevant quantity in this context is not the total flux of energy, but the "power density"—that is, the amount of power available per unit area of the earth's surface. And contrary to the implication of Gore's statement, the energy delivered by sunlight and wind is, in fact, extremely weak—these sources have a very low power density. To tap even "just a small portion" and extract a useful flow of energy requires gathering and concentrating all that power over vast areas, and—with today's technology—is, in fact, not "free forever" but forbiddingly expensive.

Consider wind power, for example, which is considered the most promising renewable source and has seen the most rapid growth in recent years. A modern wind turbine generates around 3 megawatts (MW) of electricity when it's running. But this is typically less than a third of the time because wind blows intermittently, so on average one actually gets about 1 MW of usable electricity. By comparison, a typical nuclear plant or a large coal-fired power plant generates around *1,000 MW* of electricity. So to produce the same amount of power of just one nuclear or coal-fired plant takes about 1,000 wind turbines. Note that the United States has around *600* coal-fired plants and around *100* nuclear plants. (700,000 windmills, anyone?) And while a coal or nuclear plant occupies, at most, a few thousand acres of land, the windmills—to collect and concentrate the same amount of energy—would have to be spread out over an area on the order of 200,000 acres. [43]

Note also that each windmill is a tower of steel twenty to forty stories tall that sits on an enormous base of concrete. Various estimates suggest that to build enough windmills to replace just one nuclear power plant would require somewhere between two and ten times more concrete and steel as was used to build the nuclear plant in the first place. [44]

In addition to their low power density, wind and sunlight are also unreliable as a source of stable, readily available power. Subject to the vagaries of shifting clouds and unpredictable breezes, the skittish, intermittent power they supply adds a randomly fluctuating element to a system that, more than anything else, requires a stable, predictable flow of energy. Sudden, unexpected drop-offs

or increases in supply can wreak havoc on an electric grid. Unsuitable for supplying stable, base load power to meet the minimum daily demand on an electric
grid—they are also unavailable to be dispatched at will to meet demand fluctu-
ations. Where fossil-fueled generators can be cycled on or off as needed to supply reserve capacity, sunlight and wind cannot. The more such sources are added
to a grid, the more reserve capacity—typically in natural gas-fired generators—
is needed as back-up.[45]

These are just some of the formidable obstacles to a rapid scale-up of renewable energy. Yet, it is these sources that the would-be planners of our "green energy future" are counting on for their grand schemes. In 2008 Al Gore proposed that
the United States stop using fossil fuels and nuclear power altogether for generating electricity—that we "commit to producing 100 percent of our electricity from
renewable energy and truly clean carbon-free sources within 10 years." This goal,
he insisted, is "achievable, affordable and transformative."[46]

Note first that Gore's proposal would mean—as energy analyst Vaclav Smil
points out—"writing off the entire fossil-fuel and nuclear generation industry, an
enterprise whose power plants alone have a replacement value of at least $1.5
trillion (assuming at least $1,700/installed kW), and spending at least $2.5 trillion to build the new capacity." This would certainly be "transformative." I'm
not so sure about "achievable" or "affordable."[47]

Consider also just how little the sources that Gore names explicitly—wind, solar and geothermal—currently contribute to electricity generation in the United States. According to the most recent data from the U.S.
Energy Information Administration, in the rolling 12-month period ending in
November 2009, these three sources generated about 87 million megawatt-
hours of electricity in the United States. This might seem impressive . . . until
you consider that the total amount of electricity generated in the United States
in that same period was just under 4 *billion* megawatt-hours, so the contribution from Gore's preferred sources was a mere 2.2%.[48]

But aren't these sources expanding rapidly? Between 2005 and 2007, U.S.
wind generating capacity nearly doubled, and it more than doubled again between 2007 and 2009.[49] Indeed, the wind industry is currently crowing about
its growth in 2009. The American Wind Energy Association triumphantly reports that "the U.S. wind industry broke all previous records by installing close
to 10,000 megawatts of new generating capacity in 2009."[50] Again, this might
seem impressive . . . until you consider that the total electric generating capacity in the United States is around 1 *million* MW.[51] The additional 10,000 MW
brings the total installed wind capacity in the United States up to only around
35,000 MW, or 3.5% of total capacity. In the end all that the doubling and re-
doubling meant was that the contribution of wind power to U.S. electric generation went from 0.4% in 2005 to 0.8% in 2007 and then to 1.8% in 2009—and

even this minimal increase was only possible "thanks to Recovery Act incentives" as well as state mandates forcing utilities to expand their reliance on these sources.[52]

Vaclav Smil sums up his assessment of Gore's "plan" in one word: "delusional."[53]

Slightly less delusional, but still dependent on the rapid scale-up of wind power, is the so-called Pickens Plan, the energy plan put forward by oil billionaire T. Boone Pickens. Pickens's idea is to build enough wind generating capacity to displace, not all fossil and nuclear electric generation, à la Gore, but just the natural gas generating capacity. Then, instead of burning natural gas to make electricity, Pickens would use it as a transportation fuel to temporarily displace the oil we burn in our cars and trucks.[54] Of course, in addition to massive new wind capacity this would also require converting America's fleet of some 250 million passenger vehicles to run on natural gas and making that fuel available at the roughly 120,000 gas stations that are not currently built to sell it.[55, 56] Just as with Gore's proposal, the "Pickens Plan" is not really a plan. As the *Wall Street Journal*'s Holman Jenkins Jr. aptly put it:

> Asserting that something would be good to do is not "a plan." Saying how to do it is "a plan." By this standard, what the legendary oil man is devoting $58 million to pitch hardly amounts to a decent slogan.
>
> He would replace natural gas in electricity production with wind, and use the natural gas to power cars. He fails to mention any practical theory of how to get there—that would really be "a plan." Instead, he relies on the deus ex machina of Congress, waving a legislative wand to make people do things they would choose not to do, given the extravagant and unjustified costs involved. . . .
>
> We pick on Boone (and exploit a pun) but his "plan" is emblematic of the brainstorms that always find a market when gasoline hits a cyclical peak. . . . Calls for Manhattan Projects and moon shots invariably decorate the op-ed pages at such times. In a form of social peacockery, the greater the misallocation of resources proposed, the more lavish the ovation—though here Mr. Pickens has already been outdone by Al Gore.
>
> But these plans are fulfillments of ritual, not practical proposals—and their authors indicate as much by the economy of thought they put into them. Mr. Pickens is rightly contemptuous of those who accuse him of merely trying to make money off his natural-gas holdings— if money-making were the goal, he certainly would have invested a more diligent and realistic application of his noggin first. To imply otherwise is to insult the man.[57]

Hiding behind the peppy slogans and cheerleading for the "green energy revolution" are real and formidable obstacles, and an utter lack of anything remotely resembling a realistic plan to overcome them.

Perhaps the most surprising obstacle to "green energy," however, is *opposition from environmentalists*. Just as environmentalists reject nuclear and hydro power despite the emissions-free character of these sources, numerous environmentalists are fighting vehemently against all manner of "green energy" projects intended to displace fossil energy production.

Consider, for instance, the Cape Wind project in Nantucket Sound—a project to build an offshore wind farm consisting of 130 turbines.[58] Cape Wind is viewed as an important test case for offshore wind in America, and yet the opposition to the project from environmentalists and others has been so strong that it's been tied up in the approval process for more than eight years. And who is one of the most vocal and prominent opponents of the wind farm? Robert F. Kennedy Jr., who is a lawyer for the Natural Resources Defense Council and a leading figure in the green movement.

Kennedy and others opposed to the project allege that the turbines will threaten wildlife, will damage the "pristine marine ecosystem" of Nantucket Sound, and will create "noise pollution" and even "light pollution" from the windmills' airplane warning lights. (!) Warning other environmentalists not to be "enticed by Cape Wind," Kennedy writes:

> Cape Wind's proposal involves construction of 130 giant turbines whose windmill arms will reach 417 feet above the water and be visible for up to 26 miles. These turbines are less than six miles from shore and would be seen from Cape Cod, Martha's Vineyard and Nantucket. Hundreds of flashing lights to warn airplanes away from the turbines will steal the stars and nighttime views. The noise of the turbines will be audible onshore. A transformer substation rising 100 feet above the sound would house giant helicopter pads and 40,000 gallons of potentially hazardous oil.
>
> According to the Massachusetts Historical Commission, the project will damage the views from 16 historic sites and lighthouses on the cape and nearby islands. The Humane Society estimates the whirling turbines could every year kill thousands of migrating songbirds and sea ducks.[59]

Raising the specter of "energy companies that are trying to privatize the commons," Kennedy tries to frame the Cape Wind debate as a typical grassroots green battle against industrial "intrusion" upon nature. "Some places," he writes, "should be off limits to any sort of industrial development. I wouldn't build a wind farm in Yosemite National Park. Nor would I build one on Nantucket Sound."[60]

Some additional irony here is that part of the motivation for siting windmills *offshore* is to try to avoid some of the claimed environmental impacts of *onshore* wind farms. Environmentalists have complained about threats to bird populations ever since the first generation of wind turbines was built at Altamont Pass near Oakland, California. From Altamont in the early 1980s to a recent case in West Virginia where a wind developer faced a "lawsuit by environmental groups worried about potential harm to the endangered Indiana bat"—environmental groups have fought against wind projects in every region of the country, from California to Texas to the Allegheny Mountains in the Northeast.[61]

Or consider the trend toward "small hydro"—hydroelectric power plants built on a smaller scale. The reason environmentalists have traditionally fought so vehemently against hydroelectricity is because of the way large-scale hydro dams radically alter waterways, flooding vast areas behind the dam while significantly reducing downstream flows. "Small hydro" is often held up as an alternative to massive dams on major rivers: smaller, less obtrusive dams on streams and tributaries. These facilities typically have a tiny generating capacity: less than 30 megawatts (MW)—enough to supply power to roughly 15,000 to 30,000 households—as compared to, say, the Hoover Dam, which has an installed generating capacity of 2,000 MW, and supplies electricity to 1.3 million people.[62, 63] Power companies have tried to promote small hydro as a win-win alternative to other forms of energy: a source of power with no greenhouse gas emissions, but with a lower impact on local wilderness areas.

But to produce a significant amount of power this way requires large numbers of these "minimal impact" installations. An assessment of the potential for hydroelectricity in Washington state identified 500 feasible sites, but also found that "developing all the state's potential hydro sites, including small ones, would add only 762 megawatts"—i.e., only as much as a *single* large coal-fired power plant.[64] To come even close to the generating capacity of nuclear or hydrocarbon-fueled plants, one would have to build on a large-scale. But building on a large scale is precisely why environmentalists object to Big Hydro in the first place. As the *Wall Street Journal* reports, "the small-hydro trend is beginning to raise eyebrows in environmental and recreation circles."

> "One plant here, one there, maybe we would support that," says Thomas O'Keefe, Northwest regional coordinator of American Whitewater, a rafters' group. "But with so many on the drawing board this really gets to be an issue of cumulative impacts."[65]

And this objection to "cumulative impacts" is having an impact. On the basis of resistance from environmentalists, one company with plans to build nine small-hydro facilities along a thirty-four-mile stretch of the McKenzie River in Oregon was denied preliminary permits by the Federal Energy Regulatory Commission.[66] And, as we've already seen, in addition to blocking the construction of new dams, the commission has overseen the destruction of hundreds of existing dams in just the last decade alone.[67]

Or consider the battles over solar energy in California's Mojave Desert. Being remote and reliably sunny, this region is one of the most plausible places in the world to try to produce solar power. Solar developers also have a captive customer base because of California's regulatory mandate forcing utilities to produce 33% of the state's electricity from renewable sources by 2020.[68] (The original mandate, adopted in 2002, also set a goal of 20% by 2010, but when it became clear that California utilities would not be able to meet it, Governor Schwarzenegger just kicked the can a decade down the road.[69]) The state mandate sparked a boom as companies rushed in to sign contracts with utilities and plan solar power developments, filing hundreds of permit applications with the federal Bureau of Land Management.

But the plans sparked outrage and opposition from local environmental groups seeking to protect the pristine desert. "Deserts don't need to be sacrificed so that people in L.A. can keep heating their swimming pools," says Terry Frewin, a local Sierra Club representative.[70] "It doesn't make any sense," said Terry Weiner, a spokeswoman for a group called the Desert Protective Council, "to slap up big industrial projects hundreds of miles from where the energy's going to be used and put these hideous transmission lines and string those for hundreds of miles. . . . You are destroying habitat and creatures to save the planet?"[71] Similar indignation was expressed by David Myers, executive director of a Southern California environmental group called the Wildlands Conservancy: "How can you say you're going to blade off hundreds of thousands of acres of earth to preserve the Earth?"[72]

Lest one be tempted to write these organizations off as marginal groups whose views are politically insignificant and unrepresentative of the mainstream green perspective, consider that Myers has been a key figure influencing Senator Dianne Feinstein, who has introduced a bill before Congress that would turn a 1 million-acre swath of Mojave into a national monument, blocking all solar and wind projects there.[73] And the mere threat of that legislation has been enough to shut down developers' plans.

For instance, solar developer BrightSource Energy had proposed a 5,130-acre solar power plant in the Broadwell Dry Lake area of Mojave, which falls within Feinstein's proposed monument. But just knowing of Feinstein's opposition, BrightSource scrapped its proposal months before the bill was even introduced and began looking at other locations in the Mojave Desert.[74]

In a statement praising BrightSource for abandoning its Broadwell project, Feinstein said: "It's clear that conservation and renewable energy development are not mutually exclusive goals—there is room enough in the California desert for both."[75] But in fact, that's not clear at all. Kicked out of one solar hotspot, BrightSource indicated that it would try to move ahead with alternative plans for a solar facility in the Ivanpah Valley just south of Las Vegas. But according to the *San Jose Mercury News*:

> BrightSource might have other hurdles to clear at its Ivanpah project, which also could impact tortoise habitats, according to some environmental groups.
>
> "We have concerns about Ivanpah," [the Sierra Club's Barbara] Boyle said. "Ivanpah has some very important tortoise habitats as well as a number of plant species that are sensitive."[76]

Is there really "room enough in the California desert" for the production of energy, as far as environmentalists are concerned? Following Feinstein's introduction of her bill, numerous other companies also dropped their solar projects planned for that region.[77]

The phenomenon of significant green opposition to "green energy" has left Governor Schwarzenegger unsure of whether to laugh or cry:

> Our Department of Fish and Game is slowing approval of a solar facility in Victorville. It's because of an endangered squirrel, an endangered squirrel which has never been seen on that land where they're supposed to build the solar plants. But if such a squirrel were around, this is the kind of area that it would like, they say. . . . So a squirrel that may not exist is holding up environmental progress on a larger and more pressing fight against global warming. What they have here is a case of environmental regulations holding up environmental progress. I don't know whether this is ironic or absurd. But, I mean, if we cannot put solar power plants in the Mojave desert, I don't know where the hell we can put it [*sic*].[78]

Schwarzenegger's exasperation is understandable. How can you claim that the very survival of humanity requires an immediate transition away from fossil fuels and, at the same time, fight tooth and nail against the very projects allegedly capable of effecting that transition? On the premise that human well-being is sacrosanct, and given the indispensability of industrial-scale energy to our lives and happiness, the environmentalists' policies make no sense.

And yet, opposition to solar power plants in the Mojave desert is consistent with everything we have seen so far from the environmentalist movement. What we've seen is that its proponents vehemently oppose every single major source that we currently use for energy—*including* the only two carbon-free sources, nuclear and hydro, that substantially contribute to present world energy; they wildly overstate the present potential of "green energy" sources, such as wind and solar, which are barely utilized today because of their practical limitations; and they blithely put forward, as realistic energy plans, proposals that can only be described as delusional fantasies. So why should it be a surprise that there are even environmentalists who oppose the "green energy" sources required to implement the fantasies?

It is only on the premise that the environmentalist movement is truly driven by a concern for human well-being that one can make no sense of its vehement attacks on carbon-based fuels (without which human life as we know it in the developed world would be impossible), its cavalier lack of any alternative plan, and its active opposition to proposed alternatives (whether real ones like nuclear or hydro, or fantasized ones like solar). If you are willing to question that premise, however, you can make sense of the movement's policies.

As most people see it, there is no inherent conflict between human prosperity and the environmentalist goal of "protecting the environment." Indeed, most people would argue that protecting the environment is a *prerequisite* of human prosperity. With respect to energy and climate, for instance, environmentalists are, in most people's view, simply trying to secure human well-being by preventing large-scale climate change; they are trying to prevent a planetary catastrophe by finding safer ways to power our civilization. People don't see the environmentalist movement as intending to just cut off mankind's access to energy (which truly would be a catastrophe) but to replace our current fuels with better alternatives—to avoid "dangerous anthropogenic interference with the climate system" by finding new ways of meeting man's energy needs.[79]

Yet, nothing we've seen from the environmentalist movement shows any real interest in actually meeting man's energy needs. What's really driving the movement is a basic idea that has animated environmentalism since its inception: the idea that nature is to be protected from human "intrusion."

Environmentalism is a broad social and political movement, with roots stretching back decades and with a diverse array of leaders, groups, institutions, and perspectives. But despite its diversity, it is, in essence, an *intellectual movement* animated by a particular ideology—by a set of philosophic premises that shape its actions and guide its ultimate direction. And the basic moral premise at the root of environmentalism is the premise that nature is something to be left alone—to be preserved untouched by human activity.

To the opponents of small hydro projects, for instance, the possibility of "cumulative impacts" on salmon runs or the habitat of the Furbish lousewort renders irrelevant the numerous homes that could be supplied with electricity. To Myers and his fellow desert activists, if a patch of scorched terrain is favored by the desert tortoise or the bighorn sheep, it should never be "bladed off" for the sake of any sort of industrial development—not even a solar power plant. This moral animus against human "intrusion" upon nature creates a basic conflict between the goals of the environmentalist movement and the needs of human life.

Environmentalists, as Peter Schwartz explains, "have abandoned even the pretext of holding human happiness as their ultimate purpose. In its place, as an open secret that the public is unable to take fully seriously, is the premise that nature must remain unchanged *as an end in itself.* It is the premise that nature must be protected, not *for* man, but *from* man."[80]

Observe that even when environmentalists find themselves on opposite sides of a dispute, they are nevertheless driven by this shared principle. Robert Kennedy Jr., for instance, has been criticized by fellow environmentalists for his opposition to the Cape Wind project. Shortly after he published a *New York Times* op-ed attacking Cape Wind, he was excoriated in the *San Francisco Chronicle* by a pair of angry greens accusing him of "confusion about ecological priorities."[81, 82] The authors of the *Chronicle* piece, Ted Nordhaus and Michael Shellenberger, agree completely with the basic environmentalist injunction against human "intrusions" upon nature, yet they support industrial development in Nantucket Sound. Why? Because, in their view, it is "vitally important to the battle against global warming," which they see as "arguably the greatest of all human intrusions upon nature."[83]

And besides, they assert, "Nantucket Sound is not a pristine wilderness. It is among the busiest shipping channels on the East Coast and is surrounded by heavily populated communities. Cape Wind, at worst, constitutes a relatively minor intrusion upon this already developed landscape."[84] To which Kennedy argues: "The worst trap that environmentalists can fall into is the conviction that the only wilderness worth preserving is in the Rocky Mountains or Alaska. To the contrary, our most important wildernesses are those that are closest to our densest population centers, like Nantucket Sound."[85]

Observe that the standard setting the terms of their dispute is human "interference" with nature. The vital importance of energy to human life is, at best, a secondary consideration. What's really important, on their terms, is determining what constitutes the greater human "intrusion"—the greater threat to "pristine wilderness."

Indeed, the very claims about climate change themselves have more to do with the environmentalist injunction against "interfering" with nature than with any concerns about human well-being.

Environmentalists have long been telling us that our use of carbon-based energy is causing a "planetary emergency"—and that to avoid climate catastrophe we must immediately reduce our greenhouse gas emissions. But what is the nature of the threat we supposedly face from climate change? In essence, it is that we are becoming increasingly vulnerable to climate-related disasters—that we are causing large-scale changes to the Earth's climate that are dramatically increasing the risks that we face from severe climate events: hurricanes, floods, heat waves, drought, etc.

But if the concern is that people are becoming more vulnerable to the climate, then why is there no acknowledgment of the unprecedented degree to which industrial development under capitalism has *reduced* the risk that people face from being harmed by climate extremes? Vulnerability to the climate has been a feature of human existence for all of human history, and it is only in the last two centuries that people have achieved any sort of resilience or protection against it. Compared to undeveloped countries with little political freedom, industrialized nations with relatively free and adaptable markets have little difficulty coping with severe climate events. Compare the horrific death toll from a category 3 cyclone in 1970s Bangladesh, which killed upwards of three hundred thousand people, to that of Hurricane Katrina, which also made landfall as a category 3 storm, but left a still-tragic but much lower toll of around two thousand people dead or missing. Or compare the devastating effects of a severe 1972 drought in the African Sahel, which killed hundreds of thousands of people, to the relatively insignificant effects of a concurrent drought in the United States, which killed no one despite conditions severe enough to rate comparison with the 1930s Dust Bowl.[86]

If the goal is to secure human prosperity and well-being in the face of possible large-scale climate change, what people should be clamoring for is continued economic growth and industrial development—especially the continued production of industrial-scale energy. The notion that we should be cutting off our use of energy in order to reduce carbon emissions in the hope that this might have a salutary effect on the climate is absurd. It is the bizarre notion that people should go without energy—without electricity, without modern hospitals, without fresh water and industrial-scale agriculture—all because there *might* be a slight increase in the intensity of hurricanes. The clamor for reduced energy production only makes sense if the real goal is something other than human well-being. Eliminating man-made emissions into the atmosphere only gets to the heart of the matter if the real issue is to prevent any form of human "interference" with nature.

The real concern that environmentalists have is not man's *vulnerability to* the climate but man's possible *impact on* the climate. What they really object to is not that man-made emissions might be causing changes that are dangerous to people, but that these emissions exist *at all*.

Measurements taken regularly since the late 1950s show that atmospheric CO_2 levels have steadily risen in step with fossil fuel consumption. Similarly, thermometer measurements show that globally averaged temperatures are about 0.5–0.8 degrees Celsius higher than they were when the records began about a century and a half ago. But connection between these two facts is much less clear than environmentalists would have us believe. The start of the thermometer record happens to coincide with the end of a relatively cold period in recent climate history—one characterized by a little ice age, so it's hardly surprising that temperatures are warmer today. The earth's climate is an extremely complex system characterized by significant sources of variability, both internal and external. What has never been established—despite the insistent assertions to the contrary—is the all-important claim that man-made greenhouse gases are the dominant agent driving the changes in temperature.[87]

The lurid projections of climate apocalypse that we're bombarded with on a daily basis are not the result of a sober assessment of scientific fact. Ultimately, what they rest on is the assumption that any human impact on nature has "just got to be bad." It is a mistake to assume that environmentalists oppose human "intrusion" upon nature because they are concerned about its possible harmful consequences. In fact it is the other way around: It is their moral animus against the alleged sin of "tampering" with nature that leads to their hysterical projections of catastrophic doom.

This has been the pattern of the environmentalist movement throughout its history. And it explains why the movement has such a notorious track record of spurious doomsday predictions.

Consider the dire warnings of catastrophic over-population that were issued more than forty years ago. The "unchecked consumption" of our growing populace was, we were told, placing too great a "burden" on the earth and would wipe humanity out in a massive population crash. Paul Ehrlich's 1968 bestseller, *The Population Bomb*, forecast hundreds of millions of deaths per year throughout the 1970s, to be averted, he insisted, only by mass population control "by compulsion if voluntary methods fail."[88] But instead of global-scale famine and death, the 1970s witnessed an agricultural revolution. Despite a near-doubling of world population, food production continues to grow as technological innovation creates more and more food on each acre of farmland.[89] The United States, which has seen its population grow from 200 to 300 million, is more concerned about rampant obesity than a shortage of food.

Or consider the campaign against the insecticide DDT, beginning with Rachel Carson's 1962 book *Silent Spring*.[90] The world had been on the brink of eradicating malaria using DDT—but for Carson and her followers, controlling disease-carrying mosquitoes was an arrogant act of "tampering" with nature. Carson pronounced ominously that nature was "capable of striking back in unexpected ways" unless people showed more "humility before [its] vast forces."[91] She asserted, baselessly, that continued DDT use would unleash a cancer epidemic, generating a panicked fear of the pesticide that endures as public opinion to this day. But the scientific case against DDT was, and still is, nonexistent. Almost sixty years have passed since the malaria-spraying campaigns began—with hundreds of millions of people exposed to large concentrations of DDT—yet, according to international health scholar Amir Attaran, the scientific literature "has not even one peer reviewed, independently replicated study linking exposure to DDT with any adverse health outcome."[92] Indeed, in a 1956 study, human volunteers ate DDT every day for over two years with no ill effects then or since.[93] Carson's book led to such a public outcry that, despite its life-saving benefits and mountains of scientific evidence supporting its continued use, DDT was banned in the United States in 1972. Thanks to environmentalist opposition, DDT was almost completely phased out worldwide. And while there is still zero evidence of a DDT cancer risk, the deaths of over a million people a year from malaria's resurgence are all too real.

Environmentalist doomsday projections repeatedly turn out to be wild exaggerations because they are not rooted in objective scientific facts, but on the cowering fear that "tampering" with nature will unleash metaphysical punishment. Just as the Christian faith expects apocalyptic judgment for man's sins against God, environmentalism has its own eschatology predicting Armageddon caused by man's sins against nature. "In their cosmology," Ayn Rand explains,

> man is infinitely malleable, controllable and dispensable, nature is sacrosanct. It is only man—and his work, his achievement, his mind— that can be violated with impunity, while nature is not to be defiled by a single bridge or skyscraper. . . .
>
> In confrontation with nature, their plea is: "Leave well enough alone." Do not upset the balance of nature—do not disturb the birds, the forests, the swamps, the oceans—do not rock the boat (or even build one)—do not experiment—do not venture out—what was good enough for our anthropoid ancestors is good enough for us—adjust to the winds, the rains, the man-eating tigers, the malarial mosquitoes, the tsetse flies—do not rebel—do not anger the unknowable demons who rule it all.[94]

In the end, what we find is that the environmentalist climate campaign is, in fact, a campaign against energy as such—not a crusade to replace carbon-based fuels with something else, but a crusade to methodically eliminate any practical means of producing energy on an industrial scale. What environmentalism opposes is any alteration of pristine nature that results from the production of useful quantities of energy, whatever the means used.

Industrial-scale energy has lifted mankind out of preindustrial poverty and made possible all the life-giving benefits of our modern civilization. But the ugly truth is that environmentalists oppose it not in spite of the incredible benefits it brings us, but *precisely because* it brings us those benefits at the cost of "interfering" with nature.

The environmentalist movement continues to grow in prominence partly because people are unable or unwilling to recognize its corrupt intellectual core. They mistakenly assume that it values human flourishing and well-being. They assume that if some genius like the mysterious inventor in *Atlas Shrugged* were to come along and discover a means of exploiting a cheap, clean, unlimited supply of energy—which would be the greatest, most life-enhancing discovery in all of human history—environmentalists would rejoice in that discovery along with everyone else. But the grisly truth is that environmentalists would condemn it as an *environmental* catastrophe. "Giving society cheap, abundant energy at this point," says Paul Ehrlich, "would be the moral equivalent of giving an idiot child a machine gun."[95] Or as alternative energy guru Amory Lovins has said: "If you ask me, it'd be little short of disastrous for us to discover a source of clean, cheap, abundant energy *because of what we would do with it*. We ought to be looking for energy sources that are adequate for our needs, but that won't give us the excesses of concentrated energy with which we could do mischief to the earth . . . ."[96]

Despite the life-and-death importance of energy to human well-being, the environmentalist movement is on a crusade to cut it off. It's up to each one of us to grasp this inconvenient truth. For if the movement succeeds in its climate and energy policy goals, the result will not be a booming "green economy" powered by abundant, cheap, "green" energy—but the universal devastation and misery of forced energy privation.

Notes

Acknowledgements: I am grateful to Onkar Ghate for his invaluable editorial guidance. I would also like to thank Jeff Scialabba and Donna Montrezza for their assistance with fact-checking and references.

1. Ayn Rand, *Atlas Shrugged* (New York: Dutton, 1992), pp. 289, 290.

2. Richard J. Sullivan, "Trends in the Agricultural Labor Force," in Julian L. Simon, *State of Humanity* (Cambridge, MA: Blackwell Publishers, 1995), p. 126; see also Vaclav Smil, *Energy: A Beginner's Guide* (Oxford: Oneworld Publications), p. 68.

3. National Institute of Food and Agriculture, "About Us," http://www.csrees.usda.gov/qlinks/extension.html.

4. Smil, *Energy*, p. 78.

5. International Energy Agency, "Access to Electricity," *World Energy Outlook* (2009), http://www.iea.org/weo/electricity.asp.

6. International Energy Agency, "Transition to Modern Energy Services, *World Energy Outlook* (2009), http://www.iea.org/weo/energy_services.asp.

7. World Health Organization, "Indoor Air Pollution and Health," fact sheet no. 292 (June 2005), http://www.who.int/mediacentre/factsheets/fs292/en/index.html.

8. World Health Organization, "Water, Health and Ecosystems," http://www.who.int/heli/risks/water/water/en/index.html.

9. Food and Agriculture Organization of the United Nations, "The State of Food Insecurity in the World," ftp://ftp.fao.org/docrep/fao/012/i0876e/i0876e_flyer.pdf.

10. Stephen Olmecher, "41 Nations top U.S. life expectancy," *Seattle Times*, August 12, 2007, http://seattletimes.nwsource.com/html/health/2003832640_life12.html.

11. Joseph Romm, "An introduction to global warming impacts: Hell and High Water," March 22, 2009, http://climateprogress.org/2009/03/22/an-introduction-to-global-warming-impacts-hell-and-high-water/

12. U.S. Energy Information Administration, "World Energy Overview: 1996–2006," *International Energy Annual 2006*, http://www.eia.doe.gov/iea/overview.html.

13. U.S. Energy Information Administration, "Net Generation by Energy Source: Total (All Sectors)," April 20, 2010, table 1.1, http://www.eia.doe.gov/cneaf/electricity/epm/table1_1.html.

14. Alex Epstein, "Energy at the Speed of Thought: The Original Alternative Energy Market," *The Objective Standard* 4, no. 2 (Summer 2009): p. 47.

15. U.S. Energy Information Administration, "World Energy Overview: 1996–2006," *International Energy Annual 2006*, http://www.eia.doe.gov/iea/overview.html.

16. International Energy Agency, "World Energy Outlook 2008," calculated from 2006 figures in World Reference Scenario, p. 506; report available at http://www.worldenergyoutlook.org/2008.asp

17. James Hansen, "Global Warning Twenty Years Later," World Watch Institute (June 23, 2008), http://www.worldwatch.org/node/5798.

18. James Hansen, "Coal-fired power stations are death factories. Close them," *UK Guardian*, February 15, 2009, http://www.guardian.co.uk/commentisfree/2009/feb/15/james-hansen-power-plants-coal

19. James Hansen quoted in Andrew C. Revkin, "Climate, Coal and Crematoria," *New York Times*, November 6, 2007, http://dotearth.blogs.nytimes.com/2007/11/26/holocausts/.

20. U.S. Energy Information Administration, "World Energy Overview: 1996–2006," *International Energy Annual 2006*, http://www.eia.doe.gov/iea/overview.html.

21. S. Pacala and R. Socolow, "Stabilization Wedges: Solving the Climate Problem for the Next 50 Years with Current Technologies," *Science* 305 (August 13, 2004): p. 969; See also Jesse H. Ausubel, "Renewable and Nuclear Heresies," *Int. J. Nuclear Governance, Economy and Ecology* I, no. 3 (2007): p. 230.

22. John D. McKinnon, "Pelosi on Natural Gas: Fossil Fuel or Not?" *Wall Street Journal* Washington Wire blog (August 24, 2008), http://blogs.wsj.com/washwire/2008/08/24/pelosi-on-natural-gas-fossil-fuel-or-not/tab/article/.

23. Natural Resources Defense Council, "Finding the Balance: The Role of Natural Gas in America's Energy Future," January 2010, www.nrdc.org/energy/naturalgas/files/balance.pdf.

24. Editorial, "Sinking Broadwater," *New York Times*, April 15, 2009, http://www.nytimes.com/2009/04/16/opinion/16thu3.html.

25. U.S. Energy Information Administration, "World Energy Overview: 1996–2006," *International Energy Annual2006*, http://www.eia.doe.gov/iea/overview.html.

26. For world energy figures, see U.S. Energy Information Administration, "World Energy Overview: 1996–2006," *International Energy Annual 2006*, http://www.eia.doe.gov/iea/overview.html; U.S. Energy Information Administration, "World Electricity Data," *International Energy Annual 2006*, table 6.3, http://www.eia.doe.gov/iea/elec.html. See also data from U.S. Energy Information Administration, "World Energy Production in British Thermal Units (Quadrillion Btu)," *International Energy Annual 2006*, especially table 2.9, http://www.eia.doe.gov/iea/wepbtu.html. For US electricity generation figures, see U.S. Energy Information Administration, "Net Generation by Energy Source: Total (All Sectors)," April 20, 2010, table 1.1, http://www.eia.doe.gov/cneaf/electricity/epm/table1_1.html. For France figures, see World Nuclear Association, "Nuclear Power in France," page updated April 13, 2010, http://www.world-nuclear.org/info/inf40.htm.

27. Natural Resources Defense Council, "New Nuclear Plants Are Not a Solution to America's Energy Needs," February 2007, http://www.nrdc.org/nuclear/plants/plants.pdf.

28. WWF, "Position Paper: Nuclear Power," May 2003, http://assets.panda.org/downloads/wwf_position_statement_nuclear_power.pdf.

29. Sierra Club, "The Basics of Nuclear Power," April 2008, http://www.sierraclub.org/energy/factsheets/basics-nuclearpower.pdf.

30. Greenpeace, "Nuclear Power: Undermining Action on Climate Change," December 1, 2007, http://www.greenpeace.org/usa/press-center/reports4/nuclear-power-undermining-ac.

31. Thomas R. Wellock, "The Battle for Hetch Hetchy," *Preserving the Nation* (Wheeling, Ill: Harlan Davidson, 2007), pp. 60–65; See also Sierra Club, "Hetch Hetchy: Time to Redeem a Historic Mistake," http://www.sierraclub.org/ca/hetchhetchy/.

32. Sierra Club, "History of Accomplishments," http://www.sierraclub.org/parks/downloads/

Accomp_2009.pdf.

33. Carey Goldberg, "Fish Are Victorious over Dam as U.S. Agency Orders Shutdown," *New York Times*, November 26, 1997, http://www.nytimes.com/1997/11/26/us/fish-are-victorious-over-dam-as-us-agency-orders-shutdown.html.

34. Editorial, "10 Years, 430 Dams," *New York Times*, July 3, 2009, http://www.nytimes.com/2009/07/04/opinion/04sat3.html?_r=1.

35. U.S. Energy Information Administration, "World Energy Overview: 1996–2006," *International Energy Annual 2006*, http://www.eia.doe.gov/iea/overview.html.

36. U.S. Energy Information Administration, "World Electricity Data," *International Energy Annual 2006*, table 6.3 http://www.eia.doe.gov/iea/elec.html.

37. International Energy Agency, "World Energy Outlook 2008," calculated from 2006 figures in World Reference Scenario, p. 506; report available at http://www.worldenergyoutlook.org/2008.asp.

38. Ted Johnson, "Al Gore Brings Climate Change Message to Beverly Hills," *Variety*, November 13, 2009, http://www.wilshireandwashington.com/2009/11/al-gore-took-his-climate-change-message-to-beverly-hills-on-thursday-night.html.

39. Al Gore, "The Climate for Change," *New York Times*, November 9, 2008, http://www.nytimes.com/2008/11/09/opinion/09gore.html.

40. *Atlas Shrugged*, pp. 289, 290.

41. Fred Krupp, "Climate Change Opportunity," *Wall Street Journal*, April 8, 2008, http://online.wsj.com/article/SB120761565455196769.html.

42. Al Gore, "A Generational Challenge to Repower America," July 17, 2008, http://blog.algore.com/2008/07/a_generational_challenge_to_re.html.

43. Robert Bryce, *Power Hungry: The Myths of "Green" Energy and the Real Fuels of the Future* (Public Affairs, 2010), p. 86; see also Ausubel, "Renewable and Nuclear Heresies," p. 233.

44. Scott W. White and Gerald L. Kulcinski, "Birth to Death" Analysis of the Energy Payback Ratio and CO2 Gas Emission Rates from Coal, Fission, Wind, and DT Fusion Electrical Power Plants" (paper presented at the 6th IAEA meeting on fusion power plant design and technology, Culham, England, March 23–27, 1998 [rev. February 1999]), http://www.colorado.edu/physics/phys3070/phys3070_sp05/docs/wisc1998.pdf; see also Ausubel, "Renewable and Nuclear Heresies," p.234, and Benjamin K. Sovacool, "Valuing the Greenhouse Gas Emissions from Nuclear Power: A Critical Survey," *Energy Policy* 36 (2008): 2940–2953, http://www.nirs.org/climate/background/sovacool_nuclear_ghg.pdf.

45. See, e.g., Bryce, *Power Hungry*.

46. Gore, "A Generational Challenge," http://blog.algore.com/2008/07/a_generational_challenge_to_re.html.

47. Vaclav Smil, "Moore's Curse and the Great Energy Delusion," *The American*, November 19, 2008, http://www.american.com/archive/2008/november-december-magazine/moore2019s-curse-and-the-great-energy-delusion.

48. U.S. Energy Information Administration, "Net Generation by Energy Source: Total (All Sectors)," *Electric Power Monthly*, table 1.1, http://www.eia.doe.gov/cneaf/electricity/epm/table1_1.html; and U.S. Energy Information Administration, "Net Generation by Other

Renewables: Total (All Sectors," *Electric Power Monthly*, table 1.1.A, http://www.eia.doe.gov/cneaf/electricity/epm/table1_1_a.html.

49. U.S. Energy Information Administration, "U.S. Electric Net Summer Capacity," report released July 2009, http://www.eia.doe.gov/cneaf/alternate/page/renew_energy_consump/table4.html.

50. American Wind Energy Association, "Year End 2009 Market Report," January 2010, http://www.awea.org/publications/reports/4Q09.pdf.

51. U.S. Energy Information Administration, "Electricity Explained," data for 2008, http://tonto.eia.doe.gov/energyexplained/index.cfm?page=electricity_home#tab2.

52. American Wind Energy Association, "Year End 2009 Market Report," January 2010, http://www.awea.org/publications/reports/4Q09.pdf.

53. Smil, "Moore's Curse," http://www.american.com/archive/2008/november-december-magazine/moore2019s-curse-and-the-great-energy-delusion.

54. Pickens Plan, "America Is Addicted to Foreign Oil," http://www.pickensplan.com/theplan/.

55. Bureau of Transportation Statistics, "Table 1-11: Number of U.S. Aircraft, Vehicles, Vessels, and Other Conveyances," http://www.bts.gov/publications/national_transportation_statistics/html/table_01_11.html.

56. Vaclav Smil, "A Reality Check on the Pickens Energy Plan," *Yale Environment 360* (August 25, 2008), http://e360.yale.edu/content/feature.msp?id=2058.

57. Holman W. Jenkins Jr., "Boone Doggle," *Wall Street Journal*, August 6, 2008, http://online.wsj.com/article/SB121797900578415011.html.

58. Cape Wind, press conference video clip streaming from Park Plaza Hotel, Boston, Mass., April 28, 2010, http://www.capewind.org/.

59. Robert F. Kennedy Jr., "An Ill Wind off Cape Cod, *New York Times*, December 16, 2005, http://www.nytimes.com/2005/12/16/opinion/16kennedy.html.

60. Ibid., http://www.nytimes.com/2005/12/16/opinion/16kennedy.html.

61. Industrial Wind Action Group, "Md. Wind Farm Developer to Forgo 24 Turbines," by Vicki Smith in ABC News, January 28, 2010, http://www.windaction.org/news/25324; also, Felicity Barringer, "Debate over Wind Power Creates Environmental Rift," *New York Times*, June 6, 2006, http://www.nytimes.com/2006/06/06/us/06wind.html.

62. Jim Carlton, "Deep in the Wilderness, Power Companies Wade In," *Wall Street Journal*, August 21, 2009, U.S. edition, http://online.wsj.com/article_email/SB125080811184347787-lMyQjAxMDI5NTIwMTgyMDE4Wj.html. See also http://www.small-hydro.com/.

63. U.S. Department of the Interior, "Hydropower at Hoover Dam," *Reclamation* (last reviewed February 2009), http://www.usbr.gov/lc/hooverdam/faqs/powerfaq.html.

64. Carlton, "Deep in the Wilderness, Power Companies Wade In," http://online.wsj.com/article_email/SB125080811184347787-lMyQjAxMDI5NTIwMTgyMDE4Wj.html.

65. Ibid.

66. Ibid.

67. Editorial, "10 Years, 430 Dams," http://www.nytimes.com/2009/07/04/opinion/04sat3.html?_r=1.

68. Office of the Governor of the State of California, *Executive Order S-21-09*, September 15,

2009, http://gov.ca.gov/executive-order/13269.

69. Celia Lamb, "Report: Power Giants Likely to Miss California Renewable Energy Goal," *San Francisco Business Times*, August 5, 2008, http://losangeles.bizjournals.com/eastbay/stories/2008/08/04/daily18.html.

70. Felicity Barringer, "Environmentalists in a Clash of Goals," *New York Times*, March 23, 2009, http://www.nytimes.com/2009/03/24/science/earth/24ecowars.html?_r=1.

71. Transcript, "Solar Plan Ignites Some Environmental Concerns," NPR, September 28, 2009, http://www.npr.org/templates/transcript/transcript.php?storyId=112860913.

72. Barringer, "Environmentalists in a Clash," http://www.nytimes.com/2009/03/24/science/earth/24ecowars.html?_r=1.

73. Todd Woody, "Desert Vistas vs. Solar Power," *New York Times*, December 21, 2009, http://www.nytimes.com/2009/12/22/business/energy-environment/22solar.html?_r=1.

74. Louis Sahagun, "Solar Energy Firm Drops Plan for Project in Mojave Desert," *Los Angeles Times*, September 18, 2009, http://articles.latimes.com/2009/sep/18/business/fi-solar18.

75. Ibid., http://articles.latimes.com/2009/sep/18/business/fi-solar18.

76. George Avalos, "Calif. Solar firm hits desert storm," *Physorg.com*, September 29, 2009, http://www.physorg.com/news173461215.html.

77. Woody, "Desert Vistas vs. Solar Power," http://www.nytimes.com/2009/12/22/business/energy-environment/22solar.html; see also Rebecca Smith, "Green Battle Rages in Desert," *Wall Street Journal*, December 23, 2009, http://online.wsj.com/article/SB126144129302900923.html.

78. Office of the Governor of the State of California, Governor Schwarzenegger's keynote address at Yale Climate Change Conference, April 18, 2008, http://gov.ca.gov/speech/9360/.

79. United Nations Framework Convention on Climate Change, May 1992, http://unfccc.int/resource/docs/convkp/conveng.pdf.

80. Peter Schwartz, "The Philosophy of Privation," previous essay in this volume.

81. Kennedy, "An Ill Wind," http://www.nytimes.com/2005/12/16/opinion/16kennedy.html.

82. Michael Shellenberger and Ted Nordhaus, "Arctic Battle Should Move to Hyannis Port," *SFGate.com*, December 21, 2005, http://articles.sfgate.com/2005-12-21/opinion/17404260_1_cape-wind-cape-cod-wind-farm.

83. Ibid., http://articles.sfgate.com/2005-12-21/opinion/17404260_1_cape-wind-cape-cod-wind-farm.

84. Ibid., http://articles.sfgate.com/2005-12-21/opinion/17404260_1_cape-wind-cape-cod-wind-farm.

85. Kennedy, "An Ill Wind," http://www.nytimes.com/2005/12/16/opinion/16kennedy.html.

86. For further discussion of this point, see Keith Lockitch, "Climate Vulnerability and the Indispensible Value of Industrial Capitalism," *Energy and Environment* 20, no. 5 (2009): pp. 733-745; available online at http://www.aynrand.org/site/DocServer/ee_climate_vulnerability_keith_lockitch.pdf?docID=2221

87. Richard Lindzen, "The Climate Science Isn't Settled," *Wall Street Journal*, November 30, 2009, http://online.wsj.com/article/SB10001424052748703939404574567423917025400.html; also Richard Lindzen, "Global Warming - Sensibilities and Science," (Paper presented at

the Third International Conference on Climate Change, Washington, D.C., June 2, 2009), http://www.heartland.org/events/WashingtonDC09/PDFs/Lindzen.pdf

88. Paul Ehrlich, prologue to *The Population Bomb* (New York: Ballantine Books, 1968), p. 11.

89. Julian L. Simon, *The Ultimate Resource 2* (Princeton, NJ: Princeton University Press, 1996), chap. 6.

90. Rachel Carson, *Silent Spring* (New York: Mariner Books, 2002).

91. Ibid., p. 297.

92. Amir Attaran and Rajendra Maharaj, "DDT for malaria control should not be banned," *British Medical Journal* 321 (2000): p. 1403.

93. W. J. Hayes, Jr., W. F. Durham, and C. Cuerto, Jr., "The effect of known repeated oral doses of chlorophenothane (DDT) in man," *J. Am. Med. Assoc.* 162 (1956): pp. 890-897; and W.J. Hayes, Jr., W.E. Dale, and C.I. Pirkle, "Evidence of safety of long-term, high, oral doses of DDT for man," *Arch. Environ. Health* 22 (1971): pp. 119-135.

94. Ayn Rand, "The Anti-Industrial Revolution," *Return of the Primitive: The Anti-Industrial Revolution* (New York: Meridian, 1999), p. 287.

95. Paul R. Ehrlich, "An Ecologist's Perspective on Nuclear Power," *Federation of American Scientists Public Interest Report* 28, no. 5–6 (May–June, 1975): p. 5.

96. Amory Lovins, Plowboy interview, *Mother Earth News*, November–December 1977, http://www.motherearthnews.com/Renewable-Energy/1977-11-01/Amory-Lov

Part 3

Doesn't Business Require Compromise?

"There can be no compromise on basic principles or on fundamental issues. What would you regard as a 'compromise' between life and death? Or between truth and falsehood? . . . Today, however, when people speak of 'compromise,' what they mean is not a legitimate mutual concession or a trade, but precisely the betrayal of one's principles. . . . Integrity does not consist of loyalty to one's subjective whims, but of loyalty to rational principles."

—Ayn Rand, "Doesn't Life Require Compromise?" 1962

The Anatomy of Compromise

Ayn Rand

One often hears that "business requires compromise." Is that true? Ayn Rand's essay outlining three rules for helping one understand how principles work in practice and their relationship to one's goals was first published in 1966 in *Capitalism: The Unknown Ideal.* She offers this analysis as a starting point for anyone interested in understanding how principles operate and what outcomes are inevitable in situations of both conflict and collaboration.

The Anatomy of Compromise

Ayn Rand

A major symptom of a man's—or a culture's—intellectual and moral disintegration is the shrinking of vision and goals to the concrete-bound range of the immediate moment. This means: the progressive disappearance of abstractions from a man's mental processes or from a society's concerns. The manifestation of a disintegrating consciousness is the inability to think and act in terms of *principles*.

A principle is "a fundamental, primary, or general truth, on which other truths depend." Thus a principle is an abstraction which subsumes a great number of concretes. It is only by means of principles that one can set one's long-range goals and evaluate the concrete alternatives of any given moment. It is only principles that enable a man to plan his future and to achieve it.

The present state of our culture may be gauged by the extent to which principles have vanished from public discussion, reducing our cultural atmosphere to the sordid, petty senselessness of a bickering family that haggles over trivial concretes, while betraying all its major values, selling out its future for some spurious advantage of the moment.

To make it more grotesque, that haggling is accompanied by an aura of hysterical self-righteousness, in the form of belligerent assertions that one must compromise with anybody on anything (except on the tenet that one must compromise) and by panicky appeals to "practicality."

But there is nothing as impractical as a so-called "practical" man. His view of practicality can best be illustrated as follows: if you want to drive from New York to Los Angeles, it is "impractical" and "idealistic" to consult a map and to select the best way to get there; you will get there much faster if you just start out driving at random, turning (or cutting) any corner, taking any road in any direction, following nothing but the mood and the weather of the moment.

The fact is, of course, that by this method you will never get there at all. But while most people do recognize this fact in regard to the course of a journey, they are not so perceptive in regard to the course of their life and of their country.

There is only one science that could produce blindness on so large a scale, the science whose job it was to provide men with sight: philosophy. Since modern philosophy, in essence, is a concerted attack against the conceptual level of man's consciousness—a sustained attempt to invalidate reason, abstractions, generalizations, and any integration of knowledge—men have been emerging from universities, for many decades past, with the helplessness of epistemological savages, with no inkling of the nature, function, or practical application of principles. These men have been groping blindly for some direction through the bewildering mass of (to them) incomprehensible concretes in the daily life of a complex industrial civilization—groping, struggling, failing, giving up, and perishing, unable to know in what manner they had acted as their own destroyers.

It is, therefore, important—for those who do not care to continue that suicidal process—to consider a few rules about the working of principles in practice and about the relationship of principles to goals.

The three rules listed below are by no means exhaustive; they are merely the first leads to the understanding of a vast subject.

1. In any *conflict* between two men (or two groups) who hold the *same* basic principles, it is the more consistent one who wins.
2. In any *collaboration* between two men (or two groups) who hold *different* basic principles, it is the more evil or irrational one who wins.
3. When opposite basic principles are clearly and openly defined, it works to the advantage of the rational side; when they are *not* clearly defined, but are hidden or evaded, it works to the advantage of the irrational side.

1. When two men (or groups) hold the same basic principles, yet oppose each other on a given issue, it means that at least one of them is inconsistent. Since basic principles determine the ultimate goal of any long-range process of action, the person who holds a clearer, more consistent view of the end to be achieved, will be more consistently right in his choice of means; and the contradictions of his opponent will work to his advantage, psychologically and existentially.

Psychologically, the inconsistent person will endorse and propagate the same ideas as his adversary, but in a weaker, diluted form—and thus will sanction, assist, and hasten his adversary's victory, creating in the minds of their disputed following the impression of his adversary's greater honesty and courage, while discrediting himself by an aura of evasion and cowardice.

Existentially, every step or measure taken to achieve their common goal will necessitate further and more crucial steps or measures in the same direction (unless the goal is rejected and the basic principles reversed)—thus strengthening the leadership of the consistent person and reducing the inconsistent one to impotence.

The conflict will follow that course regardless of whether the basic principles shared by the two adversaries are right or wrong, true or false, rational or irrational.

For instance, consider the conflict between the Republicans and the Democrats (and, within each party, the same conflict between the "conservatives" and the "liberals"). Since both parties hold altruism as their basic moral principle, both advocate a welfare state or mixed economy as their ultimate goal. Every government control imposed on the economy (regardless in whose favor) necessitates the imposition of further controls, to alleviate—momentarily—the disasters caused by the first control. Since the Democrats are more consistently committed to the growth of government power, the Republicans are reduced to helpless "me-too'ing," to inept plagiarism of any program initiated by the Democrats, and to the disgraceful confession implied in their claim that they seek to achieve "the same ends" as the Democrats, but by different means.

It is precisely those ends (altruism-collectivism-statism) that ought to be rejected. But if neither party chooses to do it, the logic of the events created by their common basic principles will keep dragging them both further and further to the left. If and when the "conservatives" are kicked out of the game altogether, the same conflict will continue between the "liberals" and the avowed socialists; when the socialists win, the conflict will continue between the socialists and the communists; when the communists win, the ultimate goal of altruism will be achieved: universal immolation.

There is no way to stop or change that process except at the root: by a change of basic principles.

The evidence of that process is mounting in every country on earth. And, observing it, the unthinking begin to whisper about some mysterious occult power called a "historical necessity" which, in some unspecified way, by some unknowable means, has preordained mankind to collapse into the abyss of communism. But there are no fatalistic "historical necessities": the "mysterious" power moving the events of the world is the awesome power of men's principles—which is mysterious only to the "practical" modern savages who were taught to discard it as "impotent."

But—it might be argued—since the advocates of a mixed economy are also advocating freedom, at least in part, why does the irrational part of their mixture have to win? This leads us to the fact that—

2. In any collaboration between two men (or groups) who hold different basic principles, it is the more evil or irrational one who wins.

The rational (principle, premise, idea, policy, or action) is that which is consonant with the facts of reality; the irrational is that which contradicts the facts and attempts to get away with it. A collaboration is a joint undertaking, a common course of action. The rational (the good) has nothing to gain from the irrational (the evil), except a share of its failures and crimes; the irrational has everything to gain from the rational: a share of its achievements and values. An industrialist does not need the help of a burglar in order to succeed; a burglar needs the industrialist's achievement in order to exist at all. What collaboration is possible between them and to what end?

If an individual holds mixed premises, his vices undercut, hamper, defeat, and ultimately destroy his virtues. What is the moral status of an honest man who steals once in a while? In the same way, if a group of men pursues mixed goals, its bad principles drive out the good. What is the political status of a free country whose government violates the citizens' rights once in a while?

Consider the case of a business partnership: if one partner is honest and the other is a swindler, the latter contributes nothing to the success of the business; but the reputation of the former disarms the victims and provides the swindler with a wide-scale opportunity which he could not have obtained on his own.

Now consider the collaboration of the semi-free countries with the communist dictatorships, in the United Nations. To identify that institution is to damn it, so that any criticism is superfluous. It is an institution allegedly dedicated to peace, freedom, and human rights, which includes Soviet Russia—the most brutal aggressor, the bloodiest dictatorship, the largest-scale mass-murderer and mass-enslaver in all history—among its charter members. Nothing can be added to that fact and nothing can mitigate it. It is so grotesquely evil an affront to reason, morality, and civilization that no further discussion is necessary, except for a glance at the consequences.

Psychologically, the U.N. has contributed a great deal to the gray swamp of demoralization—of cynicism, bitterness, hopelessness, fear and nameless guilt—which is swallowing the Western world. But the communist world has gained a moral sanction, a stamp of civilized respectability from the Western world—it has gained the West's assistance in deceiving its victims—it has gained the status and prestige of an equal partner, thus establishing the notion that the difference between human rights and mass slaughter is merely a difference of political opinion.

The declared goal of the communist countries is the conquest of the world. What they stand to gain from a collaboration with the (relatively) free countries is the latter's material, financial, scientific, and intellectual resources; the free countries have nothing to gain from the communist countries. Therefore, the only form of common policy or compromise possible between two such parties is the policy of property owners who make piecemeal concessions to an armed thug in exchange for his promise not to rob them.

The U.N. has delivered a larger part of the globe's surface and population into the power of Soviet Russia than Russia could ever hope to conquer by armed force. The treatment accorded to Katanga versus the treatment accorded to Hungary, is a sufficient example of U.N. policies. An institution allegedly formed for the purpose of using the united might of the world to stop an aggressor, has become the means of using the united might of the world to force the surrender of one helpless country after another into the aggressor's power.

Who, but a concrete-bound epistemological savage, could have expected any other results from such an "experiment in collaboration"? What would you expect from a crime-fighting committee whose board of directors included the leading gangsters of the community?

Only a total evasion of basic principles could make this possible. And this illustrates the reason why—

3. When opposite basic principles are clearly and openly defined, it works to the advantage of the rational side; when they are *not* clearly defined, but are hidden or evaded, it works to the advantage of the irrational side.

In order to win, the rational side of any controversy requires that its goals be understood; it has nothing to hide, since reality is its ally. The irrational side has to deceive, to confuse, to evade, to hide its goals. Fog, murk, and blindness are not the tools of reason; they are the only tools of irrationality.

No thought, knowledge, or consistency is required in order to destroy; unremitting thought, enormous knowledge, and a ruthless consistency are required in order to achieve or create. Every error, evasion, or contradiction helps the goal of destruction; only reason and logic can advance the goal of construction. The *negative* requires an absence (ignorance, impotence, irrationality); the *positive* requires a presence, an existent (knowledge, efficacy, thought).

The spread of evil is the symptom of a vacuum. Whenever evil wins, it is only by default: by the moral failure of those who evade the fact that there can be no compromise on basic principles.

"In any compromise between food and poison, it is only death that can win. In any compromise between good and evil, it is only evil that can profit." (*Atlas Shrugged*)

Why Should One Act on Principle?

Leonard Peikoff

The following is a transcription of the talk delivered by Dr. Leonard Peikoff at the Ford Hall Forum in Boston on April 24, 1988. It has received very little editing and consequently retains the character of an informal, oral presentation. In this selection, Dr. Peikoff discusses what proper principles consist of and what role they ought to play in an individual's quest to answer life's practical, ethical and moral questions.

Why Should One Act on Principle?

Leonard Peikoff

There is no bromide more common today than the statement that we live in a "complex" world. Whatever the subject of discussion, this claim is routinely offered at the outset as a kind of magic incantation and all-purpose depressant. Its effect is not to inspire people to think, but to induce a sense of helplessness, weariness, hopelessness. It is used not to solve problems, but to assure people that there are no solutions.

The past, our cultural spokesmen often suggest, was different; once upon a time we could find answers to our questions and know what to do, but no longer. Life is just too complicated now for—here is the dread word—"simple" answers. The word "simple" itself has become the basis of a whole new condemnation, contained in the modern term "simplistic." When I argue with people, I hear all kinds of attacks from them thanks to my Objectivist views—I am selfish, impractical, too idealistic, atheistic—but the commonest attack by far is: you are being "simplistic."

"Simplistic" is not the same as "oversimplified." If you accuse someone of "oversimplifying," you imply that it is all right to simplify, but that one must do it rationally, not leaving out important factors. The modern charge "simplistic" conveys the notion that it is not merely an issue of some omitted factor; it implies that the simple, the simple as such, is naive, unrealistic, bad. The term is an anti-concept intended to smuggle into our minds this idea: you have simplified something and *by that very fact* you have erred, distorted, done wrong. This amounts to legislating simplicity out of existence. I call this attitude "complexity-worship"—and it is everywhere today.

How should we deal with all the "complex" situations we encounter, according to the conventional wisdom? The answer implicit in today's practice is: by disintegration. That is: break up the initial problem into many parts, then throw most out as too complicated to consider now, then throw some more out. Keep eliminating aspects until finally you get a narrow concrete left on the table to argue about.

Suppose, for example, that some American businessmen are upset about Japanese sales in the U.S., which they feel are cutting into their own sales, and they go to the government for relief. Of course, if they came to me, I would say: you must decide whether you advocate the principle of free trade or the

235

principle of protectionism. Then I would offer a proof of the evils of protectionism, showing why it will harm everyone in the long run, American businessmen included, and why the principle of free trade will ultimately benefit everyone. That would be the end of the dilemma, and the people demanding tariffs would be sent home packing.

But this kind of analysis would be ruled out today by any congressional committee or academic commission studying economic problems. We cannot be "simplistic," they would say; we cannot talk in generalities like "free trade" or "protectionism." How, they would ask, can we possibly make sweeping statements on this level, which involve every country, every product, every group of consumers and producers, every era of history? Life is just too complex for that. What then do we do in the face of such complexity? Basically, they answer, we have to narrow our focus profoundly. We must talk about not free trade in general, but free trade with Japan—and not Japanese industry as a whole, of course, but only Japanese cars; we'll have to leave computers and TV sets for another committee to wrestle with. And we'll have to leave trucks out, since that introduces too many tricky factors; automobiles are enough to worry about—but maybe we should include small pickup trucks, because they're pretty close to cars; let's farm that one out to a subcommittee to study separately—and of course we're not talking about forever here or even ten years. We'll confine ourselves to a year, say, or even just this season, and we'll renegotiate the issue the next go-round. In the end, the question being debated is not: should we adopt a policy of free trade with foreign countries? but rather: should we place a 30 percent import duty on certain kinds of Toyotas and Datsuns for the next six months?

Now, we are told, the question is not "simplistic." Unfortunately, now it is also not rationally answerable. How is one to decide what to do in this case, once one has thrown out the appeal to principles as naive? The answer is: you hold hearings, and all the lobbyists involved scream, bribe or make threats, and everybody offers contradictory compromises. The Toyota people say that 30 percent is unfair, but if we cut it to 20 percent they will try "voluntarily" to sell less in the U.S. The Chrysler people insist that this is not good enough, but maybe they can pay their workers more if Toyota is really squelched—so the labor unions jump in and demand a crackdown on Toyota, while the consumer groups are busy demanding more of the cheaper Japanese cars. What finally comes out of it all? Some range-of-the-moment deal—a "moderate" squeeze on the Japanese answered by a new Japanese retaliation against us, a new government subsidy to Detroit, a new agency to help consumers finance auto loans, a bigger budget deficit and another committee to review the whole situation next month or year. After all, we are told, no policy is set in stone. There are no absolutes. We have to be "flexible" and "experimental."

Philosophically, this is called *pragmatism*. In this approach, there are no principles, like "free trade" or "protectionism"; there are only concretes, like Toyotas or Chryslers, and groups of people who fight over them with opposite desires. So the only solution is to find some temporary expedient that will appease the loudest screamers for the moment—and then take a drink until the whole mess erupts again.

It is no wonder that people who employ this method believe that life is complex and that there are no answers to any problems. Yet the paradox is that they use this method because, they insist, life is too complex for us to rely on principles.

Some philosophical thought is clearly in order here. Is life complex? If so, does man have a rational (as against a pragmatic) means of dealing with its complexity? If so, do our leaders fail as badly as they do because they are rejecting man's proper means of dealing with complexity? My answer to all these questions is a resounding yes. My thesis this evening is: life *is* complicated, enormously so; but man has a conceptual faculty, a faculty of forming principles, which is specifically his weapon for coping with complexity. Yet our leaders, thanks to centuries of bad philosophy, distrust and reject this faculty, and are therefore helpless to lead or to know what to do.

Let us begin by defining "complex." "Complex" is a quantitative idea; the "complex" is that which involves *many* elements or units, all tied together or interrelated. The "simple," by contrast is that which involves one, or at most a few, units. For example: if the officials of the Ford Hall Forum want to attract a large audience, they have to grapple with many different issues: whom should they invite? does he have to be famous? what should he speak about? will he agree to come? can he condense his talk into 50 minutes? how will he fit into the rest of the year's program? This is a relatively complex problem. By contrast, if the audience is here on the night of the talk, clamoring at the doors, and someone inside asks: what do we do now?—that is a *simple* problem, the solution being to open the doors and let the people in. Here we have no complexity; there is only one element to deal with.

Now the first thing to note is that human life is inherently complex. Contrary to all the propaganda we hear, this is *not* a distinctively modern problem. It is not a result of the Industrial Revolution, the growth of population or the fact of worldwide communication. All these developments have brought certain new factors into our lives, but they have also removed problems. They have given each of us in many contexts fewer units to think about and have thus made life *simpler.* Consider, for example, the utter simplicity of feeding yourself today via a trip to the supermarket to buy some frozen food, as against the situation in the medieval days. Think how many different questions and separate tasks would have been involved in that era for you merely to reach the point of having a dinner on the table fit to eat.

Man's life is complex in every era, industrial or not. He always has countless choices to make, he has the whole world spread before him, he must continually make decisions and weigh results keeping in mind a multiplicity of factors. Even in the most primitive times, the caveman had to decide what to hunt, what risks to take, what weapons to use, how to make them, how to protect his kill, how to store, preserve, apportion it. And he had to do all this long before there was any science, long before there were any rulebooks to guide him in all these activities. In his context of knowledge, stalking his prey was an enormous complexity, no easier for him than our hardest problems in our advanced context are for us to solve.

"Simplicity," in the absolute sense, is the prerogative only of animals. Animals function automatically to sustain themselves; they are programmed to act in certain ways without the need to work, produce wealth, choose among alternatives, weigh results. They merely react to some dominant sensation in a given situation; a dog, for instance, smells his bone and runs to get it. What could be simpler? But man cannot survive by reacting mindlessly to sensations.

No human being can escape the problem of dealing with complexity and somehow making it simple and therefore manageable. This applies to the modern pragmatists, too, who make such a fetish of complexity. But they try to solve the problem by reverting to the animal level—by narrowing their focus to some isolated concrete, like the dog reacting to the smell of a bone, while evading all the other concretes to which it is connected in reality. They solve the problem of complexity by throwing out vast amounts of relevant information, thereby reducing themselves to helplessness.

The proper, human method is the exact opposite. We need to *retain* all the data we can—the more facts we can keep in mind in making any decision, the better off we are—but we need to retain all these facts in a dealable-with form. We can't be expected to read or rattle off to ourselves, before every action, a whole encyclopedia of past human experiences, or even a single volume of tips, rules and practical suggestions. Somehow we must gather and retain a wealth of information, but in a *condensed* form. This is exactly what is accomplished by the distinctively human faculty, the conceptual faculty—another name for which is *"reason."*

Concepts are man's means of condensing information. They are his means of unit-reduction. *They are his means of converting the complex into the simple, while nevertheless losing no information in the process.*

If I utter the statement "All men are mortal," for example, none of you has any trouble in understanding and applying it. You know what it means for your own life, you make up wills and buy insurance policies to cover the practical contingencies it involves, and you know that mortality applies to all men, past, present, and future. Here is a tremendous wealth of data—information about an unlimited number of units, stretching across the globe from pre-history into the endless future, wherever there were, are or will be men; and yet you have no trouble retaining this vast scale of information in the form of the few words "All men are mortal." Do you do it by elimination, by narrowing your focus to only one or two men and brushing the rest aside as too complicated? Do you merely look at yourself and a few friends, then say: "I can't deal with the others now, life is too complicated, I'll appoint a subcommittee to worry about the rest"?

On the contrary, the key is precisely that you take *all* the units involved in "man"—you retain all the countless real-life instances, including the ones you've never seen and never will, and you put them together into a single new unit, the term "man," which integrates the totality. You accomplish this feat by processing your perceptual data—by asking: what do various entities have in common? what is essential to them? what differentiates them from the other things I see? In the process, you grasp that, in contrast to other creatures, men all share a certain kind of consciousness, the faculty of reason. So you set aside all the differences among men—including height, hair color, fingerprints, intelligence—and you reach the idea of a rational being, and then designate this by a single word. The result is a vast complexity turned into a simplicity, into a single unit. Now you have the ability to focus, in one frame of awareness, on all the cases to which it applies. You can know truths about all of them, because they come under "man," they are subsumed by the concept.

Against this background, let us look specifically at *principles.* A principle is a basic generalization. It is a conceptual statement integrating a wealth of information about all kinds of concretes that we otherwise would be helpless to deal with or keep in mind. Yet we are able to do it by reducing this information to a few words or even just a few letters, like "$e = mc^2$." A principle is man's major form of using concepts—using them to reduce the complexity facing him while retaining all the information that is essential for successful action.

There are principles in every field of human endeavor, and men rely on them continually. There are principles of physics, of chemistry, of agriculture—even principles of effective public speaking, which take countless experiences of past speakers and the effects they have, positive and negative, with countless different topics on countless different audiences, and condense it all into brief, intelligible rules to guide future speakers (such as: "motivate your audience," and "give examples").

In all these fields, principles are not controversial. Reason has been allowed to perform its proper function and has been seen to be indispensable. In these fields, principles are not asked to compete with tea-leaf readings or with divine revelations.

But in the field of morality, the situation, tragically, is the opposite. In the realm of the humanities, we are still in the age of pre-reason. As a result, people do not see the need of concepts to decide *moral* questions. They do not see that the reason we need moral principles is the same reason we need principles in every realm.

A moral principle is a basic conceptual statement enabling us to choose the right course of action. A proper morality takes into account all the real-life choices men must make. It tells us the consequences to expect from the different choices facing us. It organizes all such information for us, by selecting the essentials; it integrates all the data into a handful of basic rules that we can easily keep in mind, deal with and live by—just as a single concept, "man," integrates all its instances into a single unit.

If you had no concept of "man," you could not decide whether a new entity you meet is a man or not. If he were a lot taller and blonder than anyone you had seen so far, say, you would stare in confusion—until you decided what is essential to being a man, i.e., until you conceptualized the relevant data. The same applies to evaluating an action. If you have no moral principles telling you which acts are right and which are wrong, or what is essential to judging a given situation and what is irrelevant, how are you to know what to do and what to avoid?

There are two opposite approaches to moral questions: the principled approach vs. the pragmatist approach. The one tries to integrate, the other to disintegrate. The one tries to broaden the data an individual works with, to draw on all the relevant knowledge man has accumulated, to gain a larger vision and context for the answer to the question—which can be achieved only by invoking man's means of condensing data, concepts. The other tries to narrow the data base, to shrink the subject to the animal level, to reduce the units by staring only at some isolated percepts.

Suppose, for example, I ask: should one rob a bank?

In pattern, the conceptual individual thinks: "A bank is someone's property." Here we see from the very outset the *broadening* of perspective—he is looking for the abstraction a bank falls under, the concept that names its essence in this context: property. And he grasps that in this respect a bank is just like a home or a machine or a book or a pair of shoes: it is a creation that does not grow on trees, but has to be produced by somebody. Which at once opens his mind to a flood of new data—to everything he knows about the source of books, shoes, banks and the rest: that they presuppose knowledge, inventiveness, independent judgment, focus, work. All these observations are integrated and retained in his mind through a simple principle: "Property is a product of human thought and effort." From which it becomes apparent that, if men wish to live, they must have title to their product, they need the right to keep and use the results of their effort. This—the right to property—is another principle, which condenses and subsumes all our knowledge of the destructive results of depriving men of their property, not only through bank robbery, but through a thousand other methods besides: it covers what happens when men break-and-enter private homes, or raid farms, or establish socialist states, or plagiarize manuscripts or steal hubcaps. By the device of conceptualizing the action of bank-robbing—i.e., reducing it to essentials and bringing it under principles—we know how to evaluate it. We know that if such behavior is condoned or permitted, the principle involved will lead in the long run to destruction.

The pattern is clear. We are confronted by a concrete—bank-robbing—and we deal with it by considering only a relatively few units, the few principles I mentioned. Yet these contain all the information we have ever gathered about the relevant requirements of human life. So we reach an immediate, decisive answer.

Now, by contrast, ask a pragmatist mentality: should I rob a bank?—and his first move is not to conceptualize, but to particularize. The immediate question that comes to his mind is: which bank are we talking about? Chase Manhattan? The 42nd St. branch? Let's not be "vague" and "simplistic" about this. And how much do you propose to steal? he wants to know; a big bank might not even miss $10,000. And who will you use the money for—yourself, AIDs victims, the poor? Now where are we? Having moved in this direction, having disintegrated the question and treated each bank as a unique case, how is he to decide what to do? You know how—precisely the way bank robbers *do* decide. They ask: can I get away with it? Or, more exactly: do I *feel* like trying to get away with it today? Once a man abandons principles, once he dismisses as naive generalities such abstract concepts as ownership, property rights, honesty, justice, there is no way to decide concrete cases except by arbitrary feeling—either his own feeling or that of a group with which he identifies. He ends up using the same method of decision as that of the Japanese tariff committee.

Observe the inversion being perpetrated here. The advocate of principles is the man who actually benefits from the vast data bank of life. He is the one who keeps in mind, when making a decision, the intricate network of interrelated factors, including the implications of his action for countless similar situations. He is the one who truly faces and deals with the *complexity* of life, yet he is accused of being "simplistic." On the other hand, the pragmatist, who scoffs at principles—the man who puts on blinders, eliminates most of the relevant data and ends up staring at an isolated case without context or clue, like a newborn baby—he is the one praised for appreciating the complexity of life and for not being "simple-minded."

If ever I heard a Big Lie, this is it.

The people who reject principles reject the human method of dealing with complexity. But since they don't have the animal's means of coping, either, they are left helpless. In the end, they have recourse only to raw feeling or gang warfare. This is how our politicians are now deciding the life-and-death issues of our economy and foreign policy.

If a man lives by principles, his course of action is in essence predictable; you know what to expect of him. But if a man rejects principles, who knows what he will do next?

Observe that all our leading candidates today, Democratic and Republican alike, take detailed stands on every concrete one can imagine; they issue separate position papers filled with clauses and statistics to cover every trouble spot in Washington and the world—yet no one knows what they stand for or what they will do in office. No one can retain all these disintegrated concretes or add them up into a coherent, predictable direction. The candidates offer us an abundance of plans—but there is no connection among their plans, no unifying principles, neither in domestic affairs nor in foreign. Under these conditions, elections become a crapshoot—especially when we remember that our candidates are masters of the pragmatic "flip-flop," as it is now called. After all, we are told, every concrete situation is unique; what applied yesterday is not necessarily relevant today. The candidates and office-holders themselves do not know what they are going to do or say next. They are not trying to deceive the country by cunningly concealing some devious ulterior motive; they are merely responding to the latest hole in the dike by sticking fingers in at random, i.e., without any principles to give them guidance. Thus: it is an outrage, said one candidate, to capitulate as President Carter did to the vicious Iranian kidnappers—and here is my plan, he said a while later, for shipping the Iranians arms in exchange for hostages. Or: Russia is an "evil empire" that no one should trust, he said—and here is the new arms treaty that I trust them to obey. Or: let's get rid of some government departments, let's abolish the Department of Education—and a few years later a new initiative from him, a proposal to create a Department of Veterans Affairs.

Even today's politicians feel the need to offer the electorate something more inspiring than shifting concretes. Typically, what they do to fill this need is to use abstract words without reference to reality, not as principles but as empty slogans, to be sprinkled through their oratory as garnish, committing them to nothing, yet sounding large and visionary—words like "peace" or "love" or "Americanism" or the "global environment" or the "public good." The most brazen practitioner of this policy, though certainly not the only one, was Gary Hart, with his periodic invocation of the need for "new ideas"—which no one could find in any of his detailed position papers.

If we are to save our country, what we need is not better politicians, but the only thing that can ever produce them: a code of morality. A proper morality is a set of principles derived from reality, principles reducing the vast complexity of human choices to simple, retainable units, telling us which actions support human life and which ones destroy it. Primarily, the code offers guidance to the individual; then, in the social realm, it offers guidance on political questions. A man who acts on moral principles in this sense is neither a martyr nor a zealot nor a prig. He is a man whose actions are guided by man's distinctive faculty of cognition. For man, principled action is the only successful kind of action. Moral principles are not ends in themselves; they are means to an end. They are not spiritual luxuries reserved for "higher" souls, or duties owed to God or heaven. They are a practical, earthly necessity to anyone concerned with self-preservation.

If moral principles are to function successfully in human life, however, if they are to play their vital role, they must be accepted as *absolutes*. You cannot be "flexible" about them, or bend them according to your own or your group's feelings; you cannot compromise them. This is the opposite of the pragmatist philosophy that dominates our culture; so I want to pursue the point. This will make the role of principles in man's life stand out even more clearly.

Let's go back to our bank robber and imagine trying to reach a moral compromise with him. You are the banker, say, and your first response is to tell the intruder to stop, because the property in question is yours. The robber says: no, I want your money, all of it. At this point, instead of calling in the police or standing on principle, you decide to compromise; you agree—without duress, as your idea of a moral resolution—to give the robber only part of the money he came to steal. That, after all, would show "flexibility" on your part, tolerance, compromise, the willingness to negotiate—all the things we hear everywhere are the good. Do you see what such a policy would mean and lead to? In Ayn Rand's words, it would mean a "total surrender"—the recognition of the robber's *right* to your property. Once you make this kind of concession, you leave yourself helpless: you not only give up some of your property, but also abandon the *principle* of ownership. The robber, accordingly, gains the upper hand in the relationship and the power to determine its future. He gains the inestimable advantage of being sanctioned as virtuous. What he concedes in the compromise is merely a concrete (he forgoes some of the loot)—temporarily; temporarily, because now there is no way you can stop him when he comes back with a new demand tomorrow.

The same kind of analysis applies to every case of moral compromise. Imagine, for example, a country with the means to defend itself—e.g., Britain or France in the '30s—which capitulates, in the name of being "flexible," to some of the arbitrary demands of an aggressor, such as Hitler. That kind of country thereby invites more demands—to be answered by more "flexibility." Such a country is doomed from the start (until and unless it changes its fundamental policy). By conceding the propriety of "some" aggression, it has dropped the *principle* of self-defense and of its own sovereignty, which leaves it without moral grounds to object to the next depredation.

Or suppose you accept the "moderate" idea that individual rights are not absolute and may be overridden by government controls "when the public good requires it"—when the public needs more welfare payments or more Medicare or more censorship of obscenity. In this case, you have agreed with the collectivists that individual rights are not inalienable; that the public good comes above them; that man exercises certain prerogatives not by right, but by the permission of society, as represented by the government. If so, the principle of individual rights has been entirely repudiated by you—in favor of the principle of statism. In other words, in the name of achieving a "compromise" between clashing systems, the essence of one, capitalism, has simply been thrown out, while the essence of the other, socialism, has become the ruling absolute.

Or consider a judge who tries not to be too "extremist" in regard to justice; he decides to "modify" justice by a dose of political favoritism under pressure from the bosses of the local clubhouse. He has thereby dropped the principle of justice. Justice cannot countenance a single act of injustice. What sets the terms of this judge's compromise, therefore, and decides his verdicts is the principle of favoritism, which permits whatever whims the bosses authorize, including even many verdicts that are not tainted, when this is politically palatable to the bosses. In such a court, a fair verdict is possible, but only by accident. The essence of the system, and its ultimate result, is the elimination of fairness in favor of pull.

Either you accept a proper principle—whether individual rights, self-defense, justice or any other—as an absolute, or not at all.

There is no "no-man's land" between opposite principles, no "middle of the road" which is untouched by either or shaped equally by both. The fact is that man cannot escape the rule of some kind of principles; as a conceptual being, he cannot act without the guidance of some fundamental integrations. And just as, in economics, bad money drives out good, so, in morality, bad principles drive out good. To try to combine a rational principle with its antithesis is to eliminate the rational as your guide and establish the irrational. If, like Faust, you try to make a deal with the devil, then you lose to him completely. "In any compromise between food and poison," Ayn Rand observes, "it is only death that can win. In any compromise between good and evil, it is only evil that can profit."

The reason for this is not that evil is more powerful than good. On the contrary, the reason is that evil is powerless and, therefore, can exist only as a parasite on the good.

The good is the rational; it is that which conforms to the demands of reality and thereby fosters man's life, along with all the values life requires. Such a policy acquires no advantages whatever from its antithesis. To continue our examples: a banker does not need the help of a robber who is trying to loot him. Nor does a free country need the attacks of an aggressor. Nor does an individual seeking to sustain himself need the jails of a dictator. Nor does the administration of justice benefit from subversion by corrupt bosses. By its very nature, the good can only lose by trafficking with the evil.

The evil is in exactly the opposite position. The evil is the irrational; it is that which contradicts the facts of reality and thereby threatens man's life. Such a policy cannot be upheld as an absolute or practiced consistently—not if one wishes to avoid immediate destruction. Evil has to count on some element of good; it can exist only as a parasite, only as an exception to the virtues on which it is relying. "The irrational," in Ayn Rand's words, "has everything to gain from the rational: a share of its achievements and values." A producer does not need a robber, but a robber does need the producer on whom he preys. And so do robber-nations need freer countries—which they seek not to annihilate, but to rule and loot. And no collectivists, not even the Nazis or the Communists, want to throttle every act of individual self-assertion; they need men to think and act as individuals to some extent, or their own regimes would collapse. And no political boss seeks to reverse every proper verdict; the boss mentality counts on the appearance of justice, so that men will respect and obey the courts, so that then, when he wishes it, the boss can intervene behind the scenes and cash in on that respect.

Evil is not consistent and does not want to be consistent. What it wants is to get away with injecting itself into the life-sustaining process sometimes—short-range, out-of-context, by arbitrary whim. To achieve this goal, all that it needs is a single concession by the good: a concession of the *principle* involved, a concession that evil is proper "sometimes." Such a compromise is evil's charter of liberty. Thereafter, the irrational is free to set the terms and to spread by further whim, until the good—and man—is destroyed.

The power of the good is enormous, but depends on its consistency. That is why the good has to be an issue of "all or nothing," "black or white," and why evil has to be partial, occasional, "grey." Observe that a "liar" in common parlance is not a man who always, conscientiously, tells falsehoods; there is no such creature; for the term to apply to you, a few venal whoppers on your part are enough. Just as a "hypocrite" is not a man who scrupulously betrays every one of his own ideas. Just as a "burglar" is not a man who steals from everybody he meets. Just as a person is a "killer" if he respects human life 99.9 percent of the time and hires himself out to the Mafia as an executioner only now and then. The same applies to every kind of corruption. To be evil "only sometimes" *is* to be evil. To be good is to be good *all* of the time, i.e., as a matter of consistent, rational principle.

This is why Objectivism is absolutist and why we condemn today's cult of compromise. These cultists would achieve the same end-result more honestly by telling men without equivocation to eschew the good and practice the evil. Evil is delighted to "compromise"—for it, such a deal is total victory, the only kind of victory it can ever achieve: the victory of plundering, subverting and ultimately destroying the good.

Why should one act on principle? My answer is: in the end, men cannot avoid it—some principle always wins. If the right principles, the rational ones, are not conscious, explicit absolutes in men's minds, then their evil opposites take over by default and ultimately win out. That is why, in our pragmatist, unprincipled age, all the wrong principles *are* winning. That is why every form of irrationality, cowardice, injustice and tyranny is sweeping the world.

It is not enough, therefore, merely to act "on principle." Man needs to act consciously on *rational* principles, principles based on the facts of reality, principles that promote and sustain human life. If you accept irrational principles, such as religious dogmas or mystical commandments, you will find that you can't live by them consistently, precisely because they *are* irrational and clash with reality, and you will be driven to pragmatism in despair as your only alternative.

For example, if your moral principle is self-sacrifice, you can't expect to follow it consistently, as an absolute—not if you want to stay alive. Remember that a principle integrates countless concretes. If you tried to practice *as a principle* the injunction to give up—to give up your values for the sake of God or of others—think what such a course would demand. Give up your property—others need it. Give up your pursuit of happiness—you are not on earth to gratify selfish desires. Give up your convictions—who are you to think you know the truth when God or society, who is your master, thinks otherwise? Give up your choice of personal friends—you are supposed to love everybody, above all your enemies; that, after all, is an act of real sacrifice. Give up your self-defense—you are supposed to turn the other cheek when Russia takes over Nicaragua—or Florida. Even if you decide to renounce everything—to become like the medieval saints, mortify the flesh, drink laundry water, sleep on a rock for a pillow—so long as you are motivated by any personal quest, even if it is only for joy in heaven, you are still condemned as selfish. Who could obey such a code? Who could follow, day after day, in all the concrete situations of life, such a rule? No one could, and no one ever did. Yet that is what would be meant by accepting self-sacrifice as virtue, i.e., as a moral *principle*.

What then have men done in the face of such an inverted moral code? Instead of running from it in horror and proclaiming an ethics of rational self-interest, they accept the creed of self-sacrifice—but quickly add that, of course, there are no absolutes and one has to compromise and be "moderate" in order to survive. In other words, they preach *irrational* principles, then half-practice, half-evade them. No wonder they are filled with terror at the prospect of acting on principle.

If you hold irrational principles, your principles become a threat to your life, and then compromise and pragmatism become unavoidable. But that too is no answer; it is merely another threat to your life.

The only solution is a code of rational principles—a logical, scientific approach to morality—an ethics based on *reality*, not on supernatural fantasy or on social convention.

This leads us to the base of philosophy, metaphysics, on which ethics itself depends—and to the principle that underlies all other principles. I mean the principle that there *is* a reality, that it is what it is, that it exists independent of man, and therefore that we must recognize the facts of reality, like them or not, and live accordingly. This is the fundamental which any rational approach to ethics presupposes. Morality consists of absolutes only because it is based on facts which are absolute.

On the other hand, if a man says that there is no reality—or that reality is anything he or society wants it to be—then there are no moral principles, either, and no need of any. In this kind of setup, all he has to do is assert his arbitrary wishes—no matter how bizarre or contradictory—and the world will fall into line. This is the actual foundation of the pragmatist viewpoint. Pragmatism as a philosophy does not start by attacking moral principles; it starts by denying reality; it rejects the very idea of an external world to which man must adhere. Then it concludes: anything goes—there are no absolutes—there's nothing to stand in our way anymore.

Am I exaggerating here? Last month, I was speaking at a convention of philosophers in Oregon. The man who spoke before me on the program was a philosopher who had moved a few years before to Washington, D.C., to work for the National Endowment for the Humanities. At one point in his talk, he explained to the audience what he called, ironically, the "metaphysical lesson" he had learned from dealing with Congress. The people he met in the halls of Congress, he began, often wore buttons announcing this lesson explicitly. The buttons read: "Reality is negotiable."

When he first went to Washington, he said, he had thought that people began the legislative process by studying the facts of a given problem, the data which were an indisputable given and *had* to be accepted. He had thought that politicians debated which policy was appropriate on the basis of these facts. What he observed, however, was that Congressmen would come to the bargaining table with their policy decisions long since made, and then rewrite any unpleasant facts to make them fit in with these decisions. For example, if a Republican objected that a new social program would increase the budget deficit, the Democratic aides would be sent off to redo the projections for next year's tax revenues; they would jack up the expected GNP or project a new rate of interest or come up with some other prediction which would ensure that, in their new calculations, everything would come out as they wanted and no budget deficit would result. The Republicans accepted this approach and operated by the same method.

But what about the real numbers, you ask—the real predictions, the real facts? Who knows and who cares? you would be answered. "Reality is negotiable."

These buttons are supposed to be an "in" joke. But the joke is that they are no joke: the wearers learned the message they are flaunting in all their Ivy League schools, and they believe it—a fact proved by their actions, which are not merely concrete-bound, but militantly so. Their actions, as we may put it, are not merely unprincipled, but unprincipled on principle.

How do you fight a mentality like this and prevent it from leading you to disaster? You need to begin on the deepest level; you need more than a code of ethics. You need a philosophy that recognizes and upholds reason, a philosophy built on the fact that facts are *not* negotiable—that what is, *is*.

In one sense, "What is, is" is the most complicated statement you can utter; it pertains not just to every man, dog or star, but to everything, everything that is, was or ever will be. It gives us, in effect, the results of a tour of the entire universe—in the form of three brief words, which, if you understand and accept them, fix in your mind and make available to you for the rest of your life the essential nature of existence. *That* is the most eloquent example there is of our conceptual faculty at work, expanding incalculably the range and power of our minds, reducing complexity to simplicity by the power of principle—in this case, metaphysical principle. Nothing less can give men the means to live in the world successfully or the foundation to act on moral principle.

Why should one act on principle? The deepest and final answer is: for the same reason one should jump out of the path of a speeding truck—because if one doesn't, one will be squashed by an unforgiving nemesis: an absolute reality.

Part 4

A Defense for Businessmen

"A battle of this kind requires special weapons. It has to be fought with the full understanding of your cause, a full confidence in yourself, and the fullest certainty of the moral rightness of both. Only philosophy can provide you with these weapons."

—Ayn Rand, "Philosophy: Who Needs It," 1974

Atlas Shrugged:
America's Second Declaration of Independence

Onkar Ghate

Why is it that, in spite of the Founding Fathers' tremendous achievement, America has spiraled away from freedom? Dr. Onkar Ghate argues that in *Atlas Shrugged*, Ayn Rand presents America's second Declaration of Independence—a declaration that upholds the individual's moral right to exist—his right to moral independence. Based on a talk originally delivered by Dr. Ghate on March 1, 2007, this essay retains the flavor of an oral presentation.

Atlas Shrugged:
America's Second Declaration of Independence

Onkar Ghate

Ayn Rand's novel *Atlas Shrugged* is selling far more today, over 500,000 copies in 2009, than in its first year of sales after publication in 1957. In the midst of the current massive growth in the government's power over the economy—financial bailouts, "emergency powers" exerted over the banking system, trillions in spending, soaring deficits, more state-run health care added to existing programs like Social Security and Medicare that already have trillions of dollars in unfunded liabilities—in the midst of all this, Americans are right to turn to Rand's epic novel.

For far more than just a story containing an eerily similar situation (the novel depicts the economic breakdown of the United States), *Atlas Shrugged* offers us an explanation for why, decade after decade, the government's power continues to expand and, even more important, a way out. It presents the ideas we must implement to reverse course. Indeed, in my estimation, *Atlas Shrugged* is nothing short of America's second Declaration of Independence.

To understand this radical claim, we need to begin by rewinding some 230 years, to the birth of the nation, to consider both what the American Revolution accomplished and what it failed to accomplish.

It is easy to forget how new an idea America is. The Founding Fathers invented a new type of government.

All previous forms of government had, to some degree or other, placed power in the hands of the state at the expense of the individual.

Theocracy placed power in the hands of priests and popes, who, as spokesmen for the supernatural, were to be obeyed without question. Monarchy placed power in the hands of a king or queen, whose subjects lived and died by the ruler's edicts. Aristocracy placed power in the hands of a hereditary elite, who trampled on the members of the lower classes. Democracy placed power in the hands of the majority, who could do what they wished to any minority.

In all these systems, recalcitrant individuals were dealt with in the same way. They were greeted with the instruments of physical compulsion: with imprisonment, torture, and death.

The priests placed Galileo under house arrest and burned Bruno at the stake. The king beheaded Thomas More. The aristocrats butchered individual peasants en masse. The Athenian democracy forced Socrates to drink hemlock.

To all such outrages, the Founding Fathers said: No more.

They devised a system that placed power into the hands of the individual at the expense of the state. The individual, they declared, possesses the inalienable rights to life, liberty, property, and the pursuit of happiness. The government does not stand above the individual, as his master, but below him, as his servant.

"To secure these rights," Jefferson wrote in the Declaration of Independence, "governments are instituted among men, deriving their just powers from the consent of the governed." If a government trespasses on the rights of the individual, "it is the right of the people to alter or to abolish it, and to institute new government."

In the Declaration, the Founding Fathers were of course declaring political independence from Britain. More deeply, however, they were declaring independence from priests and from kings, from aristocrats and from the will of the majority.

They were creating a sanctuary for *individuals* with unbowed minds—for the Galileos and Socrateses of the world, who were henceforth to meet with a different fate.

What motivated the Founding Fathers to take the enormously dangerous action of creating a new country? Why did they risk their lives, their fortunes, and their sacred honor?

The key to understanding their motivation is that they were this-worldly, fact-based idealists.

As students of the Enlightenment, of Europe's Age of Reason, the Founding Fathers believed in the perfectibility of man. If man unfailingly uses his rational mind, and if he carefully studies and formulates the methods by which in fact human values and prosperity are achieved, then perfection, they held, here on earth, is within man's grasp.

This, precisely, is what the Founding Fathers did with regard to the subject of government. They painstakingly studied the forms and history of governments, in order to define a perfect method of governance. The result was the Constitution of the United States, with its innovative set of checks and balances, designed to prevent any emergence of absolute power.

To most British subjects, British rule was good (which, comparatively speaking, it was) and good enough. But to the Founding Fathers, good was not good enough. As idealists, they sought perfection. When they saw the possibility for action, therefore, they rebelled—when few other men would have done so.

To burn with this type of idealism requires a profound self-esteem. It requires a spirit that wants to see perfection made real, for itself and in its own life. Genuine self-esteem—not the "we're all okay" variety—is an earned esteem of your own soul. It is the conviction that you are deserving of success and happiness, because you are continuously working to achieve these.

If you wonder about the imposing stature of the Founding Fathers, of men like Washington, Franklin, and Jefferson, this is the key. They were men of genuine self-esteem; men who took the perfection of their own lives, mind, character, and happiness with the utmost seriousness. They were abstract thinkers and also doers: men of wide and constantly expanding erudition, who were also lawyers, farmers, printers, business owners, architects, and inventors.

This kind of individual will jealously guard his freedom—his freedom to follow his own judgment, to make his own choices, and to enjoy the values and wealth he creates. To such an individual, the issue of his own perfectibility is a daily reality, which he will allow no one to usurp. To such an individual, the idea that he is a sinful or irrational or wretched creature, desperately in need of a superior to tell him what to do, has no reality. This kind of an individual will allow no king or government to dictate his convictions or dispose of his fortune and life—not for any reason or to any degree.

For the Founding Fathers, the motto "live free or die" had real meaning. Without freedom, they would be dead—their mode of existence would be dead—their unrelenting, unbowed pursuit of their own perfection would be dead. And so they fought.

The Declaration of Independence was a declaration of self-esteem. It was signed by men proud to fight for their *full* freedom.

But their achievement is eroding.

The Founding Fathers would be shocked by the power that is now concentrated in the hands of the American government at the expense of the individual.

Can you imagine Thomas Jefferson submitting to building inspectors, who would decide if Monticello is up to government code? Pleading with FDA officials to be allowed to take an experimental drug that, according to his own scientific judgment, would be beneficial for him to take? Allowing Social Security administrators to dictate how much he has to save for retirement and where he can invest it? Patiently watching the tax collector take his money and pour it down the aid drains of the Middle East and Africa? Prostrating himself before the FCC, which would determine whether or not his broadcast content is obscene? Can you imagine Thomas Jefferson seeking the government's permission to eat irradiated spinach, screw in an incandescent light bulb, or buy a trans-fatty French fry? Would he allow the government to thus dictate to him what he ought and ought not to do? The answer is obvious.

Today, however, Americans do not have the self-esteem to protest these usurpations of their judgment, their choice, their freedom.

America's declaration of self-esteem has not taken full root.

Why not?

Although the core of self-esteem is an earned confidence in one's power to think and to produce—which Americans have earned in abundance—full self-esteem requires that one self-consciously value one's self. Full self-esteem requires that one know in explicit, moral terms that one is good—and why.

This moral conviction neither the Declaration of Independence nor any other writing of the Founding Fathers provides Americans.

Consider why this is so. The European Enlightenment had promised to put morality on a rational, mathematically precise foundation, but it could never deliver on its promise. And far too many of its intellectual leaders assumed that the content of morality would be essentially Christian morality, stripped of its mystical trappings, and, somehow, defended by rational argument. The Founding Fathers agreed with the European intellectuals.

Jefferson, for instance, made his own compilation of Jesus' teachings. Jefferson's compilation, which omits the miraculous from the New Testament, includes the Sermon on the Mount. Indeed, Jefferson in a letter refers to Jesus as "the sublime preacher of the sermon on the mount."

But ask yourself this: Does the Sermon on the Mount not indict Jefferson and the other Founding Fathers?

When the British struck America's right cheek, did Jefferson in the Declaration tell America to turn to offer them the left? Did Jefferson love his enemy—or did he go to war with him? Did Jefferson, who had a gallery of worthies in his home, portraits of men like Isaac Newton and John Locke, think that the blessed are the poor in spirit—or that the only people worthy of admiration are those who choose to make something of their spirit? Did Jefferson and the other Founding Fathers think that the meek shall inherit the earth—or that, in Locke's words, the rational and the industrious shall? Did Jefferson give up riches—or did he seek them?

On every essential, the Founding Fathers did the opposite of what the Sermon commands.

And that's because the Sermon on the Mount is a declaration of war on man's self-esteem.

Anyone who has achieved anything and taken pride and joy in his accomplishments, is condemned by Jesus. "Woe unto you that are rich! for ye have received your consolation. Woe unto you that are full! for ye shall hunger. Woe unto you that laugh now! for ye shall mourn and weep."

Who then has a right to feel good about themselves, according to the Sermon? The meek and the poor in spirit—which means: those who have no cause to esteem themselves.

This is the key to understanding the direction of America's political history.

The Founding Fathers created a new form of government and thereby opened up a continent to their kind of individuals—individuals of self-esteem, individuals who were ready to drop their old, backward cultures and work for a better future, individuals who valued themselves so highly that they sought the best for themselves and in themselves by coming to America.

But the Founding Fathers left these individuals unable fully to understand or appreciate their own greatness, open to every form of abuse, and vulnerable to every sort of moral denunciation from a moral code that had dominated the Old World for centuries.

And the denunciations soon came. The new country had exploded with breathtaking feats of productivity. Most responsible for this prosperity were individuals who had never had a chance to exist before: capitalists and industrialists. Oil, steel, railroads, new financial instruments—these and other innovations the Rockefellers, the Carnegies, the Vanderbilts, and the J. P. Morgans brought into the New World and taught men how to value. For this, they were denounced as robber barons.

In essence, it was Jesus' voice rising against them: "Woe unto you that are rich! For ye shall suffer; woe unto you that build railroads and oil derricks! For ye shall mourn and weep."

But more than just moral denunciations came. If America was to be the land of the ideal, as the Founding Fathers had promised, and if the ideal is in fact that the meek and poor in spirit shall inherit the earth, then America's government needed drastic overhaul.

All the new governmental powers, the alphabet soup of regulatory agencies that Jefferson would have rebelled against, were justified by attacking the men of self-esteem in the name of the meek and the poor in spirit.

What is the moral justification, for instance, for the FDA's existence? Rich, greedy drug companies—i.e., those who discover and manufacture life-saving pharmaceuticals—will exploit and experiment on hapless patients, so the government must oversee the companies' every move. Besides, how can the meek be served, unless the government, through its approvals and rejections, favors the kinds of drugs the meek need? And how can the poor in spirit achieve blessedness, if in their mindlessness they ingest a pill that they could have known might kill them? So to protect the blessed from their own ignorance or irrationality, we need wise government officials to approve drugs and dictate to everyone what pills he may and may not swallow.

Or what is the moral justification for the creation of Social Security? To quote from the Administration's website, in an article about the history of social security, it is "the government's duty to provide for the welfare of the poor." If a person is too meek to provide for his own old age, then those who are richer should be forced to provide for his retirement. If a person is too ignorant or irresponsible to save for his own retirement—if he is that poor in spirit—then the government must step in and, in his name, strip everyone of control over his retirement plans.

Or what was the moral justification for the income tax, ratified in 1913? "Soak the rich."

Now to all of this—to whatever form the sacrifice of men of achievement and self-esteem to men without achievement and self-esteem takes—Ayn Rand in *Atlas Shrugged* says: No more.

In one of the world's great acts of independence, Rand declares, in effect, that the essence of the Sermon on the Mount, along with everything it presupposes and everything it implies, is evil.

The idea that the good consists in achieving the good of others—of your neighbors, of your country, or even of your enemies—of anyone or anything, real or imagined, that is not you—the idea that you must sacrifice your personal values without even an expectation of return—the idea that nobility means being selfless, and wickedness means being concerned with self—the idea that morality is synonymous with altruism, and immorality synonymous with egoism—all of this is challenged in *Atlas Shrugged*.

Of this whole approach to good and evil, Rand asks questions no one dared to ask.

What, she asks in *Atlas Shrugged*, is the good according to this morality? Supposedly, it's that you achieve the good of others. But what then is their good? Presumably, that they in turn achieve the good of still other people. But then we are again faced with the same unanswered question: what is the good of these other people?

To the question "What is the good?" this approach to morality actually provides you with no answer. It gives you only a chain of arrows, leading to nowhere; a string of zeroes, adding up to nothing. The code upholds no ultimate value or positive ideal. It is unconcerned with the main task of the science of ethics: namely, of defining the good that you must achieve and live up to.

So what does this do to people in actual practice? It means that it is impossible to know whether you have ever achieved the good—or failed in the attempt.

Consider first what this does to a man of self-esteem. To anyone striving to be good, this code declares that you have never done enough. No matter how much you've sacrificed, you can never achieve your own moral perfection. You can never reach the ideal.

Have you ever wondered why the demands for sacrifice just continue to grow and grow? The income tax, for instance, started off as something that of course would apply only to the very rich and that of course would be capped at 7% of income. But then it grew to 15%, 20% and 25% of income, and included in its clutches more and more productive citizens. Can we, as productive individuals, at any stage protest that we've sacrificed enough, that we've already achieved the good of others? Don't be so naïve—we're answered—who said the good was achievable?

Or why is it that decade after decade, as the United States pours money into Asia, Africa and the Middle East, still more handouts are demanded from us? Can we ever protest that we've sacrificed enough, that we've achieved the good of others? Again the same answer: Surely you're not so naïve as to think the good is achievable?

The result, therefore, to any rational person striving to be good, is a state of moral anxiety, self-doubt, and guilt. No matter how much he has sacrificed, the thought haunts him that to be good he should have sacrificed still more. Many decent people therefore stop striving to be one hundred percent moral—"Not everyone can be a saint," they conclude—and they thereby abandon the quest for self-esteem.

Now what of the scoundrels who are actually unconcerned with achieving happiness and moral perfection within their own souls? No matter the nature of their concrete actions or how dreadful the outcomes of those actions so far, so long as their motive is not self-interest, anything is permitted to them. Whatever they do, they retain the halo of morality.

Have you ever wondered why, when the so-called humanitarians at the U.N. produce debacle after debacle and corruption after corruption, their power and prestige only increase? Have you ever wondered why, when government program after government program leads to disaster—when Social Security jeopardizes your financial future, public education turns out barely literate children, and Medicare causes skyrocketing costs—the scope and funding of these programs only increase? Have you ever wondered why, as individuals were murdered in the thousands and tens of thousands in Communist Russia and China, many onlookers in the East and West alike said: Give them more time, they may eventually achieve the good of others?

Atlas Shrugged gives us the answer. Nothing can count as *failure* to achieve the good of others, because nothing counts as *success*.

"'The good of others' is a magic formula that transforms anything into gold, a formula to be recited as a guarantee of moral glory and as a fumigator for any action, even the slaughter of a continent. . . . You need no proof, no reasons, no success . . . —all you need to know is that your motive was the good of others, not your own. Your only definition of the good is a negation: the good is the 'non-good for me.'" (*Atlas Shrugged*)

What we have here is a negative morality. This code is unable to specify the nature of the good. But it does define, in precise detail, the nature of evil. To be concerned with advancing your own interests, is evil; to escape evil, therefore, you must sacrifice your values.

The only concrete advice the code offers you is: sacrifice, sacrifice, and then sacrifice some more. This is the real focus of the code and why Rand names it the morality of sacrifice.

Sacrifice your money to strangers who have not earned it, proclaims the Sermon on the Mount, and sacrifice your love to enemies who hate you. Sacrifice the values of both matter and spirit. Sacrifice, sacrifice, sacrifice.

But does this morality of sacrifice not contain some enormous, hidden double standard?

As Rand asks in *Atlas Shrugged*: "Why is it moral to serve the happiness of others, but not your own? . . . Why is it immoral to produce a value and keep it, but moral to give it away? And if it is not moral for you to keep a value, why is it moral for others to accept it? If you are selfless and virtuous when you give it, are they not selfish and vicious when they take it? Does virtue consist of serving vice? Is the . . . purpose of those who are good, self-immolation for the sake of those who are evil?"

Now what, in effect, is the Sermon on the Mount's answer to these questions?

"The . . . monstrous answer is: No, the takers are not evil, provided they did not earn the value you gave them. It is not immoral for them to accept it, provided they are unable to produce it, unable to deserve it, unable to give you any value in return." (*Atlas Shrugged*)

Why, for instance, do drug companies not have the right to sell their inventions to anyone and everyone eager to buy them? Because the companies invented the drugs. Why do we, the public, through the FDA, have the right to dictate what drugs these companies can and cannot sell, how they must research, test, manufacture, and label them, what uses they can and cannot be prescribed for, and who can purchase them? What gives us this incredible power? The fact that we didn't invent the drugs.

Or why does an employee not have the right to keep and invest all his income as he judges best for his old-age? Because he earned the money. Why do we, the public, through the Social Security Administration, have the right to take part of his income and dole it out to whomever we think needs it? Precisely because we, and the recipients, didn't earn the money.

"Such is the secret core of your creed, the other half of your double standard: it is immoral to live by your own effort, but moral to live by the effort of others—it is immoral to consume your own product, but moral to consume the products of others . . . —it is the parasites who are the moral justification for the existence of the producers, but the existence of the parasites is an end in itself." (*Atlas Shrugged*)

If you want just one example to fix in your mind the gruesome essence of the morality of sacrifice, and what it does to self-esteem, consider America's response to 9/11.

When the Twin Towers were attacked and thousands of individuals killed, many people in the Middle East danced in the streets. But others there, although sympathetic to the revelers, sought to hide the revelry from view. They worried that the attacks had gone too far this time, and that Americans would refuse to suffer such an outrage. They worried that our self-esteem was not completely extinguished, and that their gloating would revive it. They worried about our indignation and our wrath.

And in the immediate aftermath there were some signs of these on the part of Americans. There was anger and desire for revenge. People wanted the President to do something. Responding to the country's mood, the Bush Administration promised a campaign of shock and awe, and the extraction of "Infinite Justice."

But then—there is little doubt—Bush asked himself: "What would Jesus do?" Tragically, it was a question to which Bush knew the answer.

Even as we pursued some of the killers, a more fundamental injunction emerged: we had to love our enemy. Operation Infinite Justice was renamed so as not to offend the Islamic world. Gone was the extraction of justice, replaced by the goal of bringing democracy to the Middle East, so that its inhabitants could elect whomever they wished, killers like Hamas emphatically not excluded. A campaign of shock and awe did still materialize—but not in the way originally meant.

Imagine the utter shock of the Islamic warriors and their numerous supporters, when they realized that it was not U.S. bombs dropping on their heads, but packets of lentils, barley stew, biscuits, peanut butter, and strawberry jam, along with the message: "This is a food gift from the people of the United States of America." Imagine the awe they must have felt at their own power.

They had attacked the Pentagon and toppled the Twin Towers, and this had brought them not what it brought the Japanese after Pearl Harbor, namely U.S. soldiers bent on their complete destruction or unconditional surrender, but U.S. soldiers bent on rebuilding their hospitals and mosques and bringing them the vote—the young American soldiers all the while dying in the attempt.

We are proving to these people that the meek shall inherit the earth and that blessed indeed are the poor in spirit. As they regroup in Afghanistan, Pakistan, Iran, and elsewhere, the confidence and power these killers and their numerous supporters feel is real: it is granted to them by the morality of sacrifice.

The Sermon on the Mount and all its variations through the centuries— *Atlas Shrugged* reveals—is a morality of evil and for evil.

But it has a fatal flaw. It requires that its victims accept it.

"I saw that the enemy was an inverted morality—and that my sanction was its only power . . . . I saw that there comes a point, in the defeat of any man of virtue, when his own consent is needed for evil to win . . . . I saw that I could put an end to your outrages by pronouncing a single word in my mind. I pronounced it. The word was '*No*.'" (*Atlas Shrugged*)

This is the beginning of Ayn Rand's declaration of moral independence.

To win your moral independence, she declares, you must first say "No" to the corrupt ideal of sacrifice. You must reject as unspeakably evil any morality that demands sacrifices, whether the sacrifice of your values to the misfortune or irrationality of others, or the sacrifice of their values to your misfortune or irrationality.

Whether it be a relative demanding an attention he has not earned, or the latest health-care scheme from Washington promising to give us something for nothing by soaking the rich, we must say "No." The moment the good requires victims—it ceases to be good.

To win your moral independence, you must uphold every individual's moral right to exist—beginning with your own. You have the right to exist, a moral right to your own life and to trying to achieve happiness within its days and years.

No one has a moral right to demand that you gain his permission to exist by slavishly ministering to his needs and protecting him from his own shortcomings. No one has a claim on your life. The moment someone waves his pain or need or failures or misfortune around, proclaiming that these entitle him to your values, he removes himself from any moral consideration.

The Founding Fathers grasped, politically, that no one gains a right to your life by virtue of his real or alleged superiority. Neither priest nor king nor aristocrat nor the majority gains a right to your life by virtue of superior social position, mystic visions, ancestors, wealth, or numbers.

What must now be grasped, morally, is that no one gains a claim to your life by virtue of his real or alleged inferiority. No one gains a moral claim to your life by virtue of his inferior wealth, power, happiness, intelligence, health, ability, knowledge, or judgment.

What this means is that your moral stature is not at the mercy of whether someone else has failed, or perhaps could not even be bothered, to provide for his own health care or retirement.

Politically, the Declaration of Independence taught us to reject the notion of undeserved serfdom. Morally, *Atlas Shrugged* teaches us to reject the notion of unearned guilt.

In place of unearned guilt, one should embrace the nature of one's existence as an individual human being—a being that must seek and create values in order to remain vibrantly alive.

This is the precondition of self-esteem: to seek in all things the best for one's self.

To embrace life is to recognize that the whole act of valuing arises in the context of one's own life and the need to make it go well. From a child choosing a toy to a teenager choosing a friend to an adult choosing a career or a lover or a form of government—the need to do so arises from the same question: What will advance my life?

The precondition of self-esteem is to refuse, as the Founding Fathers refused, to settle for anything less than the ideal in one's life.

And to this quest for the ideal, the science of morality, properly conceived, is an indispensable aid. Its task is to teach you fully what to value and how to value. Its task is to teach you how to attain life and happiness.

Atlas Shrugged accordingly offers a new conception of the moral ideal—a new conception of the sacred and the exalted, far different from that of the Sermon on the Mount. Fundamental to its new moral code are the actual requirements of life and happiness. Central to its new ideal, therefore, are the virtues of thought, production, and trade.

Atlas Shrugged is a hymn to man's mind. Every value that man has achieved had to first be discovered by some individual mind or minds. From picking fruits to hunting with spears to planting crops in order to harvest them months later—from the invention of theater, as a source of enjoyment and emotional fuel, to the discovery of perspective in painting to the creation of music—from the identification of the laws of motion to the formulation of the laws of logic—from the discovery of germs and antibiotics to the invention of the transistor and the computer—for each of these steps, some mind had to figure it out. This is the source of human life and happiness. To worship life, therefore, means to worship man's intelligence.

And if it is your own life that you seek, then the development of your intelligence becomes the most fundamental of goals. To learn to think, to make connections, and to see farther than you have so far seen—to learn to think carefully, systematically, logically, and objectively—to learn to see the full implications of your ideas—all this becomes the most important of tasks.

The scope of your knowledge and the power of your thinking will dictate the success or failure of all your value pursuits, from earning a university degree to succeeding as a doctor or computer programmer or CEO, to raising kids who are competent and independent.

For Ayn Rand as for the Founding Fathers, abstract thought is not a game in which one cynically marvels at the alleged paradoxes of the universe. Thought—abstract thought—is purposeful. It demands a serious dedication to your life.

It demands the honesty of a mind seeking all the facts, because these and only these will dictate its conclusions about how to act. It demands the independence of a mind reaching its own verdict, no matter how many people say otherwise. It demands the integrity of a mind committed to acting on its own considered judgments. Thought is purposeful. Thought is selfish. Thought is for the sake of production.

The virtue of production, *Atlas Shrugged* shows, means a dedication to making the ideal real. It means far more than holding a job. It is a dedication to the work of "remaking the earth in the image of one's values." (*Atlas*

Shrugged) It represents the proper union of the spiritual and the material. What the novel shows is that the souls of an artist and of an industrialist are the same.

The artist has a new vision of beauty, of what could be, and he strives to give it material form—to erect a sculpture of a woman, to paint a beautiful landscape, or to write *Cyrano de Bergerac*. The industrialist has a new vision of prosperity, of what could be, whether it be railroads crisscrossing the continent, a metal superior to steel, or a computer on every desk, and he works endlessly to bring it into existence. All production is born of a dedication to one's life in reality. It is the earthly form of idealism. Without it, there is no self-esteem.

A producer, in his dealings with other men, demands a non-sacrificial mode of existence. In issues of both matter and spirit, in money and in love, he is a trader.

"A trader does not ask to be paid for his failures, nor does he ask to be loved for his flaws. . . . Just as he does not give his work except in trade for material values, so he does not give the values of his spirit—his love, his friendship, his esteem—except in payment and in trade for human virtues, in payment for his own selfish pleasure, which he receives from men he can respect." (*Atlas Shrugged*)

Notice how different this is from the Sermon on the Mount. And notice that on this approach trade is moral not because it achieves the welfare of the meek or the wealth of the nation. Trade's justification is not that it somehow commutes selfishness into selflessness. Adam Smith's invisible hand, taken as a justification, is corrupt.

Trade needs no *outside* justification. The justification of trade is precisely that it is a trade: it is an interaction in which each person is able to pursue his self-interest and happiness. It is the only form of interaction in which individuals meet one another as equals, not as exploiter and exploited. When you trade your paycheck for a new computer, both you and the seller are better off. You both obtain something more valuable to you than that which you gave up. Trade is the only form of human interaction that at once demands self-esteem—it demands that each trader be seeking the best for his own life—and, in turn, allows each person to preserve his self-esteem, because he has neither sacrificed his self to others, nor tried to cheat reality through the double standard of demanding the sacrifice of others to self.

Trade, production, and thought—these form the core of *Atlas Shrugged*'s new, life-based morality.

Notice how starkly this ideal contrasts to the Sermon on the Mount's religious conception of morality. Faith, hope, and charity are its virtues.

Faith means belief in the absence of logic. It is the opposite of thought.

Hope means that you are unable to reach the ideal, that perfection is beyond your reach, but that by God's grace you might obtain it, usually in some alleged afterlife. Hope is the opposite of working to create the ideal in this life. It is the opposite of production.

Charity means giving yourself over body and soul to your neighbor and even your enemy, with the expectation of no return. It is the opposite of trade.

Jesus on the cross exhibited these virtues. He had the faith that there was an other-worldly father. He had the hope that he would gain the grace of this other-worldly being. He had the charity to sacrifice his own soul for the redemption of sinners. The result was his death.

For a morality of life, this cannot be the image of the moral ideal. What then is? The great thinkers and producers. The scientists, philosophers, artists, inventors, and industrialists who make a human mode of existence possible— individuals like Aristotle, Newton, Edison and Rockefeller. Men such as these are the heroes of *Atlas Shrugged*.

Remember Jefferson's gallery of worthies? Who were some of the individuals included in it, other than himself? Philosophers like Francis Bacon and John Locke; scientists like Isaac Newton and Benjamin Franklin; political thinkers and men of action like Voltaire, Turgot, and Thomas Paine. In *Atlas Shrugged*'s terms, these are men of the mind.

And this gallery of worthies itself captures the greatness of America's founding: it was the possibility of such men and such achievements that served as the Revolution's deepest motive power. But the tragedy of the Revolution is that Jefferson and the other Founding Fathers still thought of Jesus as the sublime preacher of the Sermon on the Mount.

What *Atlas Shrugged* shows us is that the choice is *either-or*. And more: it shows us that Jefferson's gallery of worthies are worthy of that which they had never been granted before: moral respect, moral admiration, and moral esteem.

In *Atlas Shrugged*, the character of Hank Rearden is the representative of the man of self-esteem, of the true American. Rearden is an industrialist of tremendous intellect, drive, and productivity, who is denounced for his achievements. And although he possesses the core of self-esteem, he's hobbled by the thought that, morally, he's unworthy. *Atlas Shrugged* is the story of his liberation. To all such men of real self-esteem, the novel throws a lifeline from the morality of sacrifice. "They had known that theirs was the power. I taught them that theirs was the glory." (*Atlas Shrugged*)

Now you might be wondering, if *Atlas Shrugged* is chock full of new ideas, if it is America's second Declaration of Independence, why did Rand choose to first present her ideas in the form of a novel? Precisely because her concern was the moral ideal.

She wanted to give material expression to her new vision of the ideal. The form in which one does this is art. The goal of her writing, she said after *Atlas Shrugged*'s publication, "*is the projection of an ideal man.*" Art allows one to experience the ideal made real. It allows one to inhabit that world for a time. As anyone who has read *Atlas Shrugged* knows, the contemplation of a great work of art is an unforgettable and indispensable experience.

Rand of course knew that one can learn a lot from *Atlas Shrugged*. But she regarded this as a secondary benefit. The book's primary, essential value is that within its pages one experiences her new ideal made perceptible and real.

Any great, Romantic work of art is, to quote from one of her latter essays, "an entity complete in itself, an achieved, realized, immovable fact of reality—like a beacon raised over the dark crossroads of the world, saying: '*This* is possible.'"

This is what *Atlas Shrugged* does for us.

But to now make real in our own lives the ideal presented in *Atlas Shrugged*, and to restore America to her greatness as the country dedicated to the individual and his happiness, we must be willing to challenge moral ideas inculcated since childhood. We must realize that one of the most difficult feats is to question our existing moral views and embrace a radically new moral code; nothing less will do. To reverse the trend toward Big Government, to halt the transfer of power from the hands of the individual to the hands of the state, we must become uncompromising champions of the individual. And we must do so not because the world might go to hell in thirty or forty years if we don't. Although it might, that's not the issue. The Founding Fathers did not create a new nation because their world was about to go to hell; they created a new nation to achieve the ideal.

But to champion the individual's moral right to his life, to his liberty of thought and action, to his selfish pursuit of property and happiness, we must be willing to challenge the Sermon on the Mount. In the name of our own self-esteem, we must proudly say "No" to a moral doctrine that chains the individual to other people, that demands that one feel guilty for success, and that divides mankind into servants and masters. We must instead embrace a code that extols the virtues of thought, production, and trade and declares that the purpose of morality is to teach you how to achieve your own life and happiness. We must recognize that a moral code of individualism is the only code compatible with America's uniqueness.

Rand's *Atlas Shrugged is* America's second Declaration of Independence.

What remains for us to do is to pledge our lives, our fortunes, and our sacred honor to understanding and realizing its vision of the moral and political ideal.

The Dollar and the Gun

Harry Binswanger

Dr. Harry Binswanger, in this essay first published in *The Objectivist Forum* in 1983, revisits the equivocation that anti-business advocates commonly employ between economic power (symbolized by the dollar) and political power (symbolized by the gun). To properly defend business and advance capitalism, this equivocation must be identified and argued against at every opportunity. Dr. Binswanger provides the businessman with the philosophical tools to engage in this analysis.

The Dollar and the Gun

Harry Binswanger

To advocates of capitalism, the following scenario is all too familiar.

You are in a conversation with an acquaintance. The conversation turns to politics. You make it clear you are for capitalism, laissez-faire capitalism. Eloquently, you explain the case for capitalism in terms of man's rights, the banning of physical force and the limitation of government to the function of protecting individual freedom. It seems clear, simple, unanswerable.

But instead of seeing the "light-bulb look" on the face of your acquaintance, you see shock, bewilderment, antagonism. At the first opportunity, he rushes to object:

"But government has to protect helpless consumers from the power wielded by huge multinational corporations."

Or: "Freedom is impossible under strict capitalism: people must have jobs in order to live, and they are therefore forced to accept the employer's terms."

Or: "In a complex industrial society such as ours, government planning must replace the anarchy of the marketplace."

These apparently diverse objections all commit the same logical fallacy, a fallacy grounded in the deepest philosophical premises of those who commit it. To defend capitalism effectively, one must be able to recognize and combat this fallacy in whatever form it may appear. The fallacy is equivocation—the equivocation between economic power and political power.

"Political power" refers to the power of government. The special nature of that power is what differentiates government from all other social institutions. That which makes government government, its essential attribute, is its monopoly on the use of physical force. Only a government can make *laws*—i.e., rules of social conduct backed up by physical force. A "government" lacking the power to use force is not a government at all, but some sort of ugly pretense, like the United Nations.

A non-governmental organization can make rules, pass resolutions, etc., but these are not laws precisely because they cannot be enforced on those who choose not to deal with that organization. The penalty for breaking the rules of, e.g., a fraternal organization is expulsion from the association. The penalty for breaking the law is fines, imprisonment, and ultimately, death. The symbol of political power is a gun.

A proper government points that gun only at those who violate individual rights, to answer the physical force they have initiated, but it is a gun nonetheless.

Economic power, on the other hand, is the ability to produce material values and offer them for sale. E.g., the power of Big Oil is the power to discover, drill and bring to market a large amount of oil. Economic power lies in assets—i.e., the factors of production, the inventory and the cash possessed by businesses. The symbol of economic power is the dollar.

A business can only make you an offer, thereby expanding the possibilities open to you. The alternative a business presents you with in a free market is: "Increase your well-being by trading with us, or go your own way." The alternative a government, or any force-user, presents you with is: "Do as we order, or forfeit your liberty, property or life."

As Ayn Rand wrote, "economic power is exercised by means of a *positive*, by offering men a reward, an incentive, a payment, a value; political power is exercised by means of a *negative*, by the threat of punishment, injury, imprisonment, destruction. The businessman's tool is *values*; the bureaucrat's tool is *fear.*" (*Capitalism: The Unknown Ideal,* p. 48)

Economic power stems from and depends upon the voluntary choices of the buying public. *We* are the ones who make big businesses big. One grants economic power to a company whenever one buys its products. And the reason one buys is to profit by the purchase: one values the product more than the money it costs—otherwise, one would not buy it. (The savage polemics against the profits of business are demands that the entire gain should go to one side—that "the little guy" should get all of the gain and businesses none, rather than both profiting from the transaction.)

To the extent a business fails at producing things people choose to buy, it is powerless. The mightiest Big Multinational Conglomerate which devoted its power to producing items of no value would achieve no effect other than its own bankruptcy.

Economic power, then, is purely benevolent. It does not include the power to harm people, enslave them, exploit them or "rip them off." Marx to the contrary notwithstanding, the only means of *exploiting* someone is by using physical force—i.e., by employing the principle of political power.

The equivocation between economic and political power attacks capitalism from both sides. On the one hand, it blackens the legitimate, peaceful, self-interested activities of traders on a free market by equating these activities with the predatory actions of criminals and tyrannical governments. For example, the "power of huge multinational corporations" is thought of as the power to rob the public and to coerce employees. Accepting the equivocation leads one to conclude that government intervention in the economy is necessary to the protection of our freedom against economic power.

On the other hand, the equivocation whitewashes the interventionist actions of government by equating them with the benevolent, productive actions of businesses and private individuals. For example, when the government attempts to substitute arbitrary bureaucratic edicts for the intricately coordinated plans of individuals and businesses, this is referred to as "planning." The systematic destruction of your savings through legalized counterfeiting is styled "managing" the money supply. Antitrust laws, which make it illegal to become too effective a competitor, are held necessary to preserve "free competition." Socialist dictatorship is spoken of as "economic democracy."

Americans have always held individual rights and freedom to be sacred and have looked with proper suspicion upon the power of government. The opponents of freedom have flopped grandly whenever their true colors have been perceived by the American public (e.g., the McGovern campaign). The victories of the statists have required camouflage. The equivocation between economic and political power, by reversing the meaning of all the crucial political concepts, has been essential to the spread of anti-capitalism in this country.

The demagogic, rabble-rousing attacks on "Big Business" are the most direct example of the equivocation in practice. Whether it is multinational corporations or conglomerates or monopolies or "oligopolies," the fear of "concentrations of economic power" is the theme played upon in endless variations by the left. The anti-bigness theme often appeals to the "conservatives" as well; the first serious breach of American capitalism, the Sherman Antitrust Act of 1890, was and is supported by conservatives. Senator Sherman's rationale for the Act is a classic case of the equivocation: "If the concerted powers of [a business] combination are intrusted to a single man, *it is a kingly prerogative* inconsistent with our form of government." (emphasis added)

In today's depressed economy where "obscene profits" have turned into (lovely?) losses, the anti-business theme is being played in a new key: the target has shifted to foreign businesses. The equation of the dollar and the gun remains however. To wit: "Senator Paul Tsongas (D-Massachusetts) believes that the high-technology challenge from Japan is as serious to the United States' long-term security as the defense threat posed by the Soviet Union." (*Infoworld*, May 30, 1983)

The Soviet Union threatens us with nuclear annihilation. The Japanese "threaten" us with the opportunity to buy cheap, reliable computer parts.

One could point out that the law of comparative advantage, a cornerstone of economic science, dictates that one country's superior productive ability can only benefit all those with whom it trades, that if Japanese firms can produce computer parts at lower cost than U.S. firms can, then our firms will necessarily have a comparative advantage in some other area of production, that any government intervention to protect some U.S. firms from foreign competition sacrifices other U.S. firms and the public at large to inefficiency, lowering our standard of living. But all this would be lost on the kind of mentality that equates imports with bombs.

Anticapitalists go through the most elaborate intellectual contortions to obscure the difference between economic power and political power. For example, George Will, a popular columnist often mistaken for a pro-capitalist, announces that we must abandon the distinction because "any economic arrangement is, by definition, a political arrangement." He attacks the idea that "only people produce wealth; government does not" on the grounds that "Government produces the infrastructure of society—legal, physical, educational— . . . that is a precondition for the production of wealth." (*The New Republic*, May 9, 1983)

It is true that laws protecting rights are a precondition for the production of wealth, but a precondition of production is not production. In enforcing proper laws, the government does not produce anything—it merely *protects* the productive activities performed by private individuals. Guns cannot create wealth. When a policeman prevents a mugger from stealing your wallet, no value is created; you are left intact, but no better off.

The absence of a loss is not a gain. Ignoring that simple fact is involved in the attempt to portray the government's gun as a positive, creative factor. For instance, tax relief is viewed as if it were government encouragement. In reality, tax breaks for schools, churches, homeowners, etc., are reduced penalties, not support. But socialist Michael Harrington writes:

> The Internal Revenue Code is a perverse welfare system that hands out $77 billion a year, primarily to the rich. The special treatment accorded to capital gains results in an annual government benefit of $14 billion for high rollers on the stock exchange. *(Saturday Review*, November 1972)

Harrington equates being forced to surrender to the IRS one-quarter of your earnings (the tax rate for capital gains), with being given a positive benefit by the government. After all, the IRS could have taken it all.

Just as the absence of a loss is not a gain, so the absence of a gain is not a loss. When government handouts are reduced, that is not "balancing the budget on the backs of the poor"—it is a reduction in the extent to which the poor are balanced on the backs of the rest of us.

The distinction between economic power and political power—seemingly self-evident—is in fact premised upon an entire philosophic framework. It requires, above all, two principles: (1) that wealth is produced by individual thought and effort, and (2) that man is an end in himself.

From the standpoint of today's philosophy, which denies both premises, the equation of economic power and political power is not a fallacy but a logically necessary conclusion.

In regard to the first premise, the dominant view today is that "the goods are here." This attitude comes in several variants, and most people switch freely among them, but in every case the result is the idea that economic power is not earned.

In one variant, the production of wealth is evaded altogether; wealth is viewed as a static quantity, which can only change hands. On this view, one man's enrichment is inevitably at the price of another's impoverishment, and economic power is necessarily obtained at others' expense.

For example: in a full-page advertisement run last year in the *New York Times*, a pornographic magazine promoted its series of articles on "Big Oil: The Rape of Free Enterprise." The ad charged "the oil companies have a vise-like grip on the production and distribution of oil and natural gas—and set the market prices. These giants also own vast holdings of coal and uranium. . . . we're over a barrel— and it's an oil barrel." (January 25, 1982)

Despite the ad's use of the word "production," the language conveys the impression that barrels of oil, stockpiles of gas, coal and uranium are not produced, that they were just lying around until—somehow—those demonic giants seized them in their "vise-like grip." The truth is that finding, extracting, refining, delivering and storing oil and other energy sources is such an enormous undertaking that companies too small to be known to the general public spend more than $100 million *each* on these tasks annually.

The notion that wealth is a static quantity overlooks one telling detail: the whole of human history. If wealth only shifted hands, if one man's gain were always at the price of another's loss, then man could never have risen from the cave.

In other moods, people acknowledge that wealth is produced, but, following Marx, view production as exclusively a matter of using physical labor to transform natural resources into finished products. In the midst of the "computer revolution," when technological discoveries are shrinking yesterday's multi-million-dollar room-sized computer down to the size of a briefcase and making it available for the cost of a used car, people cling to the notion that the mind is irrelevant to production.

On the premise that muscles are the source of wealth, the accumulation of wealth by corporations is a sign of the exploitation of the workers: the economic power of those who do not sweat and toil can have been gained only by preying upon those who do.

In a final variant, people do not deny entirely the role of intelligence in production, but view wealth as an anonymous social product unrelated to individual choice, effort, ambition and ability. If today's standard of living is due equally to the work of Thomas Edison, any random factory worker, and the corner panhandler, then everyone has a right to an equal "share of the pie." Again, the conclusion is that any man's possession of above-average wealth means that he has exercised some magical power of diverting the "fair share" of others into his own pocket.

In any variant, the immortal refutation of "the goods are here" approach to wealth is provided by *Atlas Shrugged*. As Galt says in explaining the meaning of the strike he leads, "We've heard it shouted that the industrialist is a parasite, that his workers support him, create his wealth, make his luxury possible—and what would happen to him if they walked out? Very well. I propose to show to the world who depends on whom, who supports whom, who is the source of wealth, who makes whose livelihood possible and what happens to whom when who walks out."

Once it is admitted that wealth is the product of individual thought and effort, the question arises: Who should own that product? On an ethics of rational egoism, the answer is: he who created it. On the moral premise of altruism, however, the answer is: anyone who needs it. Altruism specializes in the separation of creator and his creation, of agent and beneficiary, of action and consequences.

According to altruism, if you create a good and I do not, that very fact deprives you of the right to that good and makes me its rightful owner, on the principle, "from each according to his ability; to each according to his need."

On that premise, anyone who possesses a good needed by another must surrender it or be guilty of theft. Thus altruism turns businessmen into extortionists, since they charge money for relinquishing possession of the goods rightfully belonging to others. A government whose political power is directed to protecting businesses' control over their product is, from the altruist standpoint, initiating physical force against the rightful owners of those goods. By this moral code, the economic power of business *is* political power, since the wealth of businesses is protected by government, instead of being turned over to the needy.

Altruism engenders an inverted, death-dealing version of property rights: ownership by right of non-production.

Is this an exaggeration? Look at the statements of those who take altruism seriously—for example, George Will, who lauds the "willingness to sacrifice private desires for public ends."

Urging "conservatives" to embrace the welfare state, Will quotes approvingly from the 1877 Supreme Court case of *Munn v. Illinois*, in which the court ruled that a State could regulate the prices of private businesses: "When, therefore, one devotes his property to a use in which the public has an interest, he, in effect, grants to the public an interest in that use, and must submit to be controlled by the public for the common good, to the extent of the interest *he has thus created*." (emphasis added)

One must submit to be controlled—why? Because he created a value. Controlled—by whom? By "the public"—i.e., by all those who have not created that value. Philosophically, the equivocation between economic power and political power rests on the metaphysics of causeless wealth and the ethics of parasitism. Psychologically, it appeals to a fear of self-reliance, the fear that is the dominant emotion of the kind of dependent mentality Ayn Rand called the "second-hander."

The second-hander feels that the distinction between the dollar and the gun is "purely theoretical." He has long ago granted the smiles and frowns of others the power to dictate his values and control his behavior. Feeling himself to be metaphysically incompetent and society to be omnipotent, he believes that having to rely on himself would mean putting his life in jeopardy. A society of freedom, he feels, is a society in which he could be deprived of the support on which his life depends.

When you talk to him in your terms, telling him that we are all separate, independent equals who can deal with each other either by reason or by force, he literally doesn't know what you are talking about. Having abandoned his critical faculty, any idea, any offer, any deal is compulsory to him if it is accompanied by social pressure. You may tell him that in order to survive, man must be free to think. But he lacks the concepts of independent survival, independent thought, and even of objective reality; his credo is Erich Fromm's: "Love is the only sane and satisfactory answer to the problem of human existence." (*Man for Himself*, p. 133)

I will conclude with another scenario. Imagine that you survive a shipwreck and have to steer your lifeboat to one of two desert islands where you will have to remain for several years. On each island there is one inhabitant. The western island is the property of a retired multi-millionaire, who lives there in high luxury, with a mansion, two swimming pools and all the accoutrements of great wealth. The eastern island is inhabited by a propertyless beachcomber who lives in rags and eats whatever fruit and fish he can scrounge up. Let's add that the millionaire is an egoist and strict capitalist, while the beachcomber is a saint of altruism who will gladly share his mud hut with you. Would you, or anyone, head east to escape being "exploited" by the millionaire's economic power?

So much for the idea that one is threatened by the economic power of others.

But one doesn't have to resort to desert-island fables. The same practical demonstration of the life-giving nature of economic power and the fatal nature of unbounded political power is provided by the hundreds of thousands of people—Boat People they are called—who cling to their pathetic, overloaded vessels, fleeing the lands of the gun and heading toward whatever islands of even semi-capitalism they can find left in the world.

If for every hundred refugees seeking to flee collectivist dictatorships we could exchange one intellectual who urges us to fear the dollar and revere the gun, America might once again become a land of liberty and justice for all.

An Answer for Businessmen

Ayn Rand

This short article by Ayn Rand was first published on May 15, 1962, in an unidentified news magazine found among her papers. In her inspiring message to businessmen, she encourages them not to cede the realm of ideas to their ideological enemies but to instead apply to that realm the same clear thinking that they engage in when forming evaluations and judgments in the course of their business activities.

An Answer for Businessmen

Ayn Rand

If you want to save capitalism there is only one type of argument that you should adopt, the only one that has ever won in any moral issue: the argument from self-esteem. Check your premises, convince yourself of the rightness of your cause, then fight for capitalism with full, moral certainty.

The world crisis of today is a moral crisis—and nothing less than a moral revolution can resolve it: a moral revolution to sanction and complete the political achievement of the American Revolution. We must fight for capitalism, not as a practical issue, not as an economic issue, but, with the most righteous pride, as a moral issue. That is what capitalism deserves, and nothing less will save it.

I should like to suggest that you begin by applying to the realm of ideas the same objective, logical, rational criteria of judgment that you apply to the realm of business. You do not judge business issues by emotional standards—do not do it in regard to ideological issues. You do not build factories by the guidance of your feelings—do not let your feelings guide your political convictions.

Don't Try to Cheat People in Business

You do not count on men's stupidity in business, you do not put out an inferior product "because people are too dumb to appreciate the best"—do not do it in political philosophy; do not endorse or propagate ideas which you know to be false, in the hope of appealing to people's fears, prejudices or ignorance. You do not cheat people in business—do not try to do it in philosophy: the so-called common man is uncommonly perceptive.

You do not doubt your own judgment in business—do not doubt it in the realm of ideology; do not let the unintelligible gibberish of the "liberal" intellectuals intimidate you or discourage you; do not conclude: "It must be deep, because I don't understand it" or "If this is what intellectual stuff is like, then all ideas are impractical nonsense." Ideas are the greatest and most crucially practical power on earth.

You do not hire men as heads of your business departments, without firsthand

279

knowledge of the nature of their jobs and of how to judge their performance—do not do it in regard to your public relations department; learn to judge whether the stuff they are selling you is poison or not. You do not hire witch-doctors as mechanics or engineers—do not hire them as P.R.'s.

Know Your Friends and Your Enemies

Know how to tell your friends from your enemies. Know whom to support in philosophical and political issues. If you are unable to speak freely, if you are bound and gagged by the disgraceful injustice of such evils as the antitrust laws—at least, do not praise, spread or support the philosophy of your own destroyers; do not grant them the sanction of the victim. Give some thought to the possibility of establishing a civil liberties union—for businessmen.

And if you still wish to have a "social" mission or purpose—there is no greater service that you can render mankind than by fighting for your own rights and property.

"You're guilty of a great sin, Mr. Rearden."

Ayn Rand

This excerpt from Ayn Rand's 1957 novel, *Atlas Shrugged*, captures a stirring discussion between the industrialist-hero, Hank Rearden, and the apparently fallen-from-grace heir to d'Anconia Copper, Francisco. In this exchange, Rearden begins to understand that he has consistently followed one moral code in the pursuit of his business but has compromised his values when dealing with other men. Rearden learns that he has unknowingly been strengthening his enemies.

"You're guilty of a great sin, Mr. Rearden."

Ayn Rand

He sat down on the edge of his desk, crossed his arms, looked at Francisco, who remained standing respectfully before him, and asked with the cold hint of a smile, "Why did you come here?"

"You don't want me to answer, Mr. Rearden. You wouldn't admit to me or to yourself how desperately lonely you are tonight. If you don't question me, you won't feel obliged to deny it. Just accept what you do know, anyway: that I know it."

Taut like a string pulled by anger against the impertinence at one end and by admiration for the frankness at the other, Rearden answered, "I'll admit it, if you wish. What should it matter to me, that you know it?"

"That I know and care, Mr. Rearden. I'm the only man around you who does."

"Why should you care? And why should I need your help tonight?"

"Because it's not easy to have to damn the man who meant most to you."

"I wouldn't damn you if you'd only stay away from me."

Francisco's eyes widened a little, then he grinned and said, "I was speaking of Mr. Danagger."

For an instant, Rearden looked as if he wanted to slap his own face, then he laughed softly and said, "All right. Sit down."

He waited to see what advantage Francisco would take of it now, but Francisco obeyed him in silence, with a smile that had an oddly boyish quality: a look of triumph and gratitude, together.

"I don't damn Ken Danagger," said Rearden.

"You don't?" The two words seemed to fall with a singular emphasis; they were pronounced very quietly, almost cautiously, with no remnant of a smile on Francisco's face.

"No. I don't try to prescribe how much a man should have to bear. If he broke, it's not for me to judge him."

"If he broke . . . ?"

"Well, didn't he?"

Francisco leaned back; his smile returned, but it was not a happy smile. "What will his disappearance do to you?"

"I will just have to work a little harder."

Francisco looked at a steel bridge traced in black strokes against red steam beyond the window, and said, pointing, "Every one of those girders has a limit to the load it can carry. What's yours?"

Rearden laughed. "Is *that* what you're afraid of? Is that why you came here? Were you afraid I'd break? Did you want to save me, as Dagny Taggart wanted to save Ken Danagger? She tried to reach him in time, but couldn't."

"She did? I didn't know it. Miss Taggart and I disagree about many things."

"Don't worry. I'm not going to vanish. Let them all give up and stop working. I won't. I don't know my limit and don't care. All I have to know is that I can't be stopped."

"Any man can be stopped, Mr. Rearden."

"How?"

"It's only a matter of knowing man's motive power."

"What is it?"

"You ought to know, Mr. Rearden. You're one of the last moral men left to the world."

Rearden chuckled in bitter amusement. "I've been called just about everything but that. And you're wrong. You have no idea how wrong."

"Are you sure?"

"I ought to know. Moral? What on earth made you say it?"

Francisco pointed to the mills beyond the window. "This."

For a long moment, Rearden looked at him without moving, then asked only, "What do you mean?"

"If you want to see an abstract principle, such as moral action, in material form—there it is. Look at it, Mr. Rearden. Every girder of it, every pipe, wire and valve was put there by a choice in answer to the question: right or wrong? You had to choose right and you had to choose the best within your knowledge—the best for your purpose, which was to make steel—and then move on and extend the knowledge, and do better, and still better, with your purpose as your standard of value. You had to act on your own judgment, you had to have the capacity to judge, the courage to stand on the verdict of your mind, and the purest, the most ruthless consecration to the rule of doing right, of doing the best, the utmost best possible to you. Nothing could have made you act against your judgment, and you would have rejected as wrong—as evil—any man who attempted to tell you that the best way to heat a furnace was to fill it with ice. Millions of men, an entire nation, were not able to deter you from producing Rearden Metal—because you had the knowledge of its superlative value and the power which such knowledge gives. But what I wonder about, Mr. Rearden, is why you live by one code of principles when you deal with nature and by another when you deal with men?"

Rearden's eyes were fixed on him so intently that the question came slowly, as if the effort to pronounce it were a distraction: "What do you mean?"

"Why don't you hold to the purpose of your life as clearly and rigidly as you hold to the purpose of your mills?"

"What do you mean?"

"You have judged every brick within this place by its value to the goal of making steel. Have you been as strict about the goal which your work and your steel are serving? What do you wish to achieve by giving your life to the making of steel? By what standard of value do you judge your days? For instance, why did you spend ten years of exacting effort to produce Rearden Metal?"

Rearden looked away, the slight, slumping movement of his shoulders like a sigh of release and disappointment. "If you have to ask that, then you wouldn't understand."

"If I told you that I understand it, but you don't—would you throw me out of here?"

"I should have thrown you out of here anyway—so go ahead, tell me what you mean."

"Are you proud of the rail of the John Galt Line?"

"Yes."

"Why?"

"Because it's the best rail ever made."

"Why did you make it?"

"In order to make money."

"There were many easier ways to make money. Why did you choose the hardest?"

"You said it in your speech at Taggart's wedding: in order to exchange my best effort for the best effort of others."

"If that was your purpose, have you achieved it?"

A beat of time vanished in a heavy drop of silence. "No," said Rearden.

"Have you made any money?"

"No."

"When you strain your energy to its utmost in order to produce the best, do you expect to be rewarded for it or punished?" Rearden did not answer. "By every standard of decency, of honor, of justice known to you—are you convinced that you should have been rewarded for it?"

"Yes," said Rearden, his voice low.

"Then if you were punished, instead—what sort of code have you accepted?"

Rearden did not answer.

"It is generally assumed," said Francisco, "that living in a human society makes one's life much easier and safer than if one were left alone to struggle against nature on a desert island. Now wherever there is a man who needs or uses metal in any way—Rearden Metal has made his life easier for him. Has it made yours easier for you?"

"No," said Rearden, his voice low.

"Has it left your life as it was before you produced the Metal?"

"No—" said Rearden, the word breaking off as if he had cut short the thought that followed.

Francisco's voice lashed at him suddenly, as a command: "Say it!"

"It has made it harder," said Rearden tonelessly.

"When you felt proud of the rail of the John Galt Line," said Francisco, the measured rhythm of his voice giving a ruthless clarity to his words, "what sort of men did you think of? Did you want to see that Line used by your equals— by giants of productive energy, such as Ellis Wyatt, whom it would help to reach higher and still higher achievements of their own?"

"Yes," said Rearden eagerly.

"Did you want to see it used by men who could not equal the power of your mind, but who would equal your moral integrity—men such as Eddie Willers— who could never invent your Metal, but who would do their best, work as hard as you did, live by their own effort, and—riding on your rail—give a moment's silent thanks to the man who gave them more than they could give him?"

"Yes," said Rearden gently.

"Did you want to see it used by whining rotters who never rouse themselves to any effort, who do not possess the ability of a filing clerk, but demand the income of a company president, who drift from failure to failure and expect you to pay their bills, who hold their wishing as an equivalent of your work and their need as a higher claim to reward than your effort, who demand that you serve them, who demand that it be the aim of your life to serve them, who demand that your strength be the voiceless, rightless, unpaid, unrewarded slave of their impotence, who proclaim that you are born to serfdom by reason of your genius, while they are born to rule by the grace of incompetence, that yours is only to give, but theirs only to take, that yours is to produce, but theirs to consume, that you are not to be paid, neither in matter nor in spirit, neither by wealth nor by recognition nor by respect nor by gratitude—so that they would ride on your rail and sneer at you and curse you, since they owe you nothing, not even the effort of taking off their hats which you paid for? Would this be what you wanted? Would you feel proud of it?"

"I'd blast that rail first," said Rearden, his lips white.

"Then why don't you do it, Mr. Rearden? Of the three kinds of men I described—which men are being destroyed and which are using your Line today?"

They heard the distant metal heartbeats of the mills through the long thread of silence.

"What I described last," said Francisco, "is any man who proclaims his right to a single penny of another man's effort."

Rearden did not answer; he was looking at the reflection of a neon sign on dark windows in the distance.

"You take pride in setting no limit to your endurance, Mr. Rearden, because you think that you are doing right. What if you aren't? What if you're placing your virtue in the service of evil and letting it become a tool for the destruction of everything you love, respect and admire? Why don't you uphold your own code of values among men as you do among iron smelters? You who won't allow one per cent of impurity into an alloy of metal—what have you allowed into your moral code?"

Rearden sat very still; the words in his mind were like the beat of steps down the trail he had been seeking; the words were: the sanction of the victim.

"You, who would not submit to the hardships of nature, but set out to conquer it and placed it in the service of your joy and your comfort—to what have you submitted at the hands of men? You, who know from your work that one bears punishment only for being wrong—what have you been willing to bear and for what reason? All your life, you have heard yourself denounced, not for your faults, but for your greatest virtues. You have been hated, not for your mistakes, but for your achievements. You have been scorned for all those qualities of character which are your highest pride. You have been called selfish for the courage of acting on your own judgment and bearing sole responsibility for your own life. You have been called arrogant for your independent mind. You have been called cruel for your unyielding integrity. You have been called anti-social for the vision that made you venture upon undiscovered roads. You have been called ruthless for the strength and self-discipline of your drive to your purpose. You have been called greedy for the magnificence of your power to create wealth. You, who've expended an inconceivable flow of energy, have been called a parasite. You, who've created abundance where there had been nothing but wastelands and helpless, starving men before you, have been called a robber. You, who've kept them all alive, have been called an exploiter. You, the purest and most moral man among them, have been sneered at as a 'vulgar materialist.' Have you stopped to ask them: by what right?—by what code?—by what standard? No, you have borne it all and kept silent. You bowed to their code and you never upheld your own. You knew what exacting morality was needed to produce a single metal nail, but you let them brand you as immoral. You knew that man needs the strictest code of values to deal with nature, but you thought that you needed no such code to deal with men. You left the deadliest weapon in the hands of your enemies, a weapon you never suspected or understood. Their moral code is their weapon. Ask yourself how deeply and in how many terrible ways you have accepted it. Ask yourself what it is that a code of moral values does to a man's life, and why he can't exist without it, and what happens to him if he accepts the wrong standard, by which the evil is the good. Shall I tell you why you're drawn to me, even though you think you ought to damn me? It's because I'm the first man who has given you what the whole world owes you and what you should have demanded of all men before you dealt with them: a moral sanction."

Rearden whirled to him, then remained still, with a stillness like a gasp. Francisco leaned forward, as if he were reaching the landing of a dangerous flight, and his eyes were steady, but their glance seemed to tremble with intensity.

"You're guilty of a great sin, Mr. Rearden, much guiltier than they tell you, but not in the way they preach. The worst guilt is to accept an undeserved guilt—and that is what you have been doing all your life. You have been paying blackmail, not for your vices, but for your virtues. You have been willing to carry the load of an unearned punishment—and to let it grow the heavier the greater the virtues you practiced. But your virtues were those which keep men alive. Your own moral code—the one you lived by, but never stated, acknowledged or defended—was the code that preserves man's existence. If you were punished for it, what was the nature of those who punished you? Yours was the code of life. What, then, is theirs? What standard of value lies at its root? What is its ultimate purpose? Do you think that what you're facing is merely a conspiracy to seize your wealth? You, who know the source of wealth, should know it's much more and much worse than that. Did you ask me to name man's motive power? Man's motive power is his moral code. Ask yourself where their code is leading you and what it offers you as your final goal. A viler evil than to murder a man, is to sell him suicide as an act of virtue. A viler evil than to throw a man into a sacrificial furnace, is to demand that he leap in, of his own will, and that he build the furnace, besides. By their own statement, it is *they* who need you and have nothing to offer you in return. By their own statement, you must support them because they cannot survive without you. Consider the obscenity of offering their impotence and their need—their need of *you*—as a justification for your torture. Are you willing to accept it? Do you care to purchase—at the price of your great endurance, at the price of your agony—the satisfaction of the needs of your own destroyers?"

"No!"

"Mr. Rearden," said Francisco, his voice solemnly calm, "if you saw Atlas, the giant who holds the world on his shoulders, if you saw that he stood, blood running down his chest, his knees buckling, his arms trembling but still trying to hold the world aloft with the last of his strength, and the greater his effort the heavier the world bore down upon his shoulders—what would you tell him to do?"

"I . . . don't know. What . . . could he do? What would *you* tell him?"

"To shrug."

The Sanction of the Victims

Ayn Rand

This is Ayn Rand's last piece of writing. She delivered the lecture in New Orleans on November 21, 1981, before an audience of businessmen, and it was later published in *The Objectivist Forum* in April 1982. In this article, Miss Rand illustrates the businessmen's own role in their victimization and provides them with guidance regarding how not to aid their enemies and instead fight for the world they desire and deserve.

The Sanction of the Victims

Ayn Rand

Since the subject of these seminars is investment, I must start by stating that I am not an economist and have no purely economic advice to give you. But what I am anxious to discuss with you are the preconditions that make it possible for you to gain and to *keep* the money which you can then invest.

I shall start by asking a question on a borrowed premise: *What human occupation is the most useful socially?*

The borrowed premise is the concept of social usefulness. It is not part of my philosophy to evaluate things by a *social* standard. But this is the predominant standard of value today. And sometimes it can be very enlightening to adopt the enemy's standard. So let us borrow the notion of "social" concern for just a little while—just long enough to answer the question: What human occupation is the most useful socially?

Since man's basic tool of survival is his mind, the most crucially important occupation is the discovery of knowledge—i.e., the occupation of *scientists*. But scientists are not concerned with society, with social issues or with other men. Scientists are, essentially, loners; they pursue knowledge for the sake of knowledge. A great many scientific—and technological—facts were known before the Industrial Revolution, and did not affect human existence. The steam engine, for instance, was known in ancient Greece. But knowledge of that sort remained an exclusive concern that lived and died with scientists—and, for century after century, had no connection to the lives of the rest of mankind.

Now, suppose that a group of men decided to make it their job to bring the *results* of the achievements of science within the reach of men—to apply scientific knowledge to the improvement of man's life on earth. Wouldn't such men be the greatest social benefactors (as they have been since the Industrial Revolution)? Shouldn't the socially concerned humanitarians, those who hold social usefulness as their highest value, regard such men as heroes?

If I say: No, such men are not regarded as heroes today—they are the most hated, blamed, denounced men in the humanitarians' society—would you believe me? Or would you think that I'm inventing some sort of irrational fiction? And would you say that something is wrong—terribly wrong—in such a society?

But this isn't all; there is something much worse. It isn't merely the fact that these heroic men are the victims of an unspeakable injustice: it is the fact that they are first to perpetrate that injustice against themselves—that they adopt a public "stance" of perpetual apology and universal appeasement, proclaiming themselves guilty of an unspecified evil, begging the forgiveness of every two-bit intellectual, every unskilled laborer, every unemployed politician. No, this is not fiction. That country is the United States of America today. That self-destroying group of men is *you,* the American businessmen.

When I say "you," I mean the group as a whole—I accept the tenet that present company is excepted. However, if any of you find a shoe that fits, wear it with my compliments.

Karl Marx predicted that capitalism would commit suicide. The American businessmen are carrying out that prediction. In destroying themselves, they are destroying capitalism, of which they are the symbol and product—and America, which is the greatest and freest example of capitalism mankind has ever reached. There is no outside power that can destroy such men and such a country. Only an inner power can do it: the power of morality. More specifically: the power of a contemptibly evil idea accepted as a moral principle—altruism.

Remember that "altruism" does not mean kindness or consideration for other men. Altruism is a moral theory which preaches that man must sacrifice himself for others, that he must place the interest of others *above* his own, that he must live for the sake of others.

Altruism is a monstrous notion. It is the morality of cannibals devouring one another. It is a theory of profound hatred for man, for reason, for achievement, for any form of human success or happiness on earth.

Altruism is incompatible with capitalism—and with businessmen. Businessmen are a cheerful, benevolent, optimistic, predominantly American phenomenon. The essence of their job is the constant struggle to *improve* human life, to satisfy human needs and desires—*not* to practice resignation, surrender, and worship of suffering. And *here* is the profound gulf between businessmen and altruism: businessmen do not sacrifice themselves to others—if they did, they would be out of business in a few months or days—they *profit*, they grow *rich*, they are rewarded, as they should be. *This* is what the altruists, the collectivists and other sundry "humanitarians" hate the businessmen for: that they pursue a personal goal and succeed at it. Do not fool yourself by thinking that altruists are motivated by compassion for the suffering: they are motivated by hatred for the successful.

The evidence is all around us, but one small example sticks in my mind as extremely eloquent. In the early 1930s an assistant of Jane Addams, the famous social worker, went on a visit to Soviet Russia and wrote a book about her experience. The sentence I remember is: "How wonderful it was to see everybody equally shabby!" If you think you should try to appease the altruists, *this* is what you are appeasing.

The great tragedy of capitalism and of America is the fact that most businessmen *have* accepted the morality of altruism and are trying to live up to it—which means that they are doomed before they start.

Another, contributory evil is the philosophical root of altruism, which is: mysticism—the belief in the supernatural, which preaches contempt for matter, for wealth, well-being, or happiness on earth. The mystics are constantly crying appeals for your pity, your compassion, your help to the less fortunate—yet they are condemning you for all the qualities of character that make you able to help them.

Evil theories have to rely on evil means in order to hold their victims. Altruism and collectivism cannot appeal to human virtues—they have to appeal to human weaknesses. And where there are not enough weaknesses, they have to manufacture them. It is in the nature of altruists and collectivists that the more they need a person or a group, the more they denounce their victims, induce guilt, and struggle never to let the victims discover their own importance and acquire self-esteem. The businessmen are needed most by the so-called "humanitarians" —because the businessmen produce the sustenance the "humanitarians" are unable to produce. Doctors come next in the hierarchy of being needed—and observe the hostility, the denunciations, and the attempts to enslave the doctors in today's society.

Most businessmen today have accepted the feeling of guilt induced in them by the altruists. They are accused of anything and everything; for instance, the ecologists denounce businessmen's refusal to sacrifice themselves to the snail darter and the furbish lousewort.

But *the businessmen's actual guilt* is their treason against themselves, which is also their treason against their country. The statement that aroused such fury among the collectivists—"What's good for General Motors is good for the country"—was true. And the reverse is also true: What's bad for industry is bad for the country.

I am here to ask you a question on my own—not on *borrowed*—premises: What are you doing to the advocates of capitalism, particularly the young?

Appeasement is a betrayal not only of one's own values, but of all those who share one's values. If—for whatever misguided reason—businessmen are indifferent to and ignorant of philosophy, particularly moral and political philosophy, it would be better if they kept silent rather than spread the horrible advertisements that make us cringe with embarrassment. By "us" I mean advocates of capitalism. Mobil Oil ran ads in the *New York Times* which stated the following (I quote from memory): "Of the expression free, private, responsible enterprise, we strike out 'free' and 'private' as nonessential." One of the big industries advertises on television that they are full of "people working for people," and some other big company announces on television that its goal is "ideas that help people." (I do not know what the ghastly P.R. men who come up with these slogans wanted us to think: that the companies worked "for free," or that they traded with people rather than with animals?)

The worst of the bunch is some new group in Washington, D.C., called something like "Committee for the American Way," which puts out a television commercial showing some ugly, commonplace people of all kinds, each proclaiming that he likes a different type of music ("I like rock 'n roll." "And I like jazz." "And I like Beethoven," etc.)—ending on a voice declaring: "*This* is the American way—with every man entitled to have and express his own opinion."

I, who come from Soviet Russia, can assure you that debates and differences of *that* kind were and are permitted in Soviet Russia. What about political or philosophical issues? Why didn't those upholders of the American Way show people disagreeing about nuclear weapons? Or about abortion? Or about "affirmative action"? If that committee stands for the American Way—there is no such Way any longer.

Observe also that in today's proliferation of pressure groups, the lowest sort of unskilled laborer is regarded as "the public," and presents claims to society in the name of "the public interest," and is encouraged to assert his "right" to a livelihood—but the businessmen, the intelligent, the creative, the successful men who make the laborer's livelihood possible, have no rights, and no (legitimate) interests, are not entitled to *their* livelihood (their profits), and are not part of "the public."

Every kind of ethnic group is enormously sensitive to any slight. If one made a derogatory remark about the Kurds of Iran, dozens of voices would leap to their defense. But no one speaks out for businessmen, when they are attacked and insulted by everyone as a matter of routine.

What causes this overwhelming injustice? The businessmen's own policies: their betrayal of their own values, their appeasement of enemies, their compromises—all of which add up to an air of moral cowardice. Add to it the fact that businessmen are creating and supporting their own destroyers.

The sources and centers of today's philosophical corruption are the universities. Businessmen are both contemptuous of and superstitiously frightened by the subject of philosophy. There is a vicious circle involved here: businessmen have good ground to despise philosophy as it is taught today, but it is taught that way because businessmen abandoned the intellect to the lowest rungs of the unemployables. All the conditions and ideas necessary to turn men into abjectly helpless serfs of dictatorship, rule the institutes of today's higher education as a tight monopoly, with very few and rare exceptions. Hatred of reason and worship of blind emotions, hatred of the individual and worship of the collective, hatred of success and worship of self-sacrifice—these are the fundamental notions that dominate today's universities. These notions condition (and paralyze) the minds of the young.

If you want to discover how a country's philosophy determines its history, I urge you to read *The Ominous Parallels* by Leonard Peikoff [Mentor, 1983].

This brilliant book presents the philosophical similarities between the state of America's culture today and the state of Germany's culture in the Weimar Republic in the years preceding the rise of Nazism.

It is the businessmen's money that supports American universities—not merely in the form of taxes and government handouts, but much worse: in the form of voluntary, private contributions, donations, endowments, etc. In preparation for this lecture, I tried to do some research on the nature and amounts of such contributions. I had to give it up: it is too complex and *too vast* a field for the efforts of one person. To untangle it now would require a major research project and, probably, years of work. All I can say is that millions and millions and millions of dollars are being donated to universities by big business enterprises every year, and that the donors have no idea of what their money is being spent on or whom it is supporting. What is certain is only the fact that some of the worst anti-business, anti-capitalism propaganda has been financed by businessmen in such projects.

Money is a great power—because in a free or even a semi-free society, it is a frozen form of productive energy. And, therefore, the spending of money is a grave responsibility. Contrary to the altruists and the advocates of the so-called "academic freedom," it is a moral crime to give money to support ideas with which you disagree; it means: ideas which you consider wrong, false, evil. It is a moral crime to give money to support your own destroyers. Yet that is what businessmen are doing with such reckless irresponsibility.

On the faculties of most colleges and universities, the advocates of reason, individualism and capitalism are a very small minority, often represented by a feeble specimen of window dressing. But the valiant minority of authentic fighters is struggling against overwhelming odds and growing, very slowly. The hardships, the injustices, and the persecutions suffered by these young advocates of reason and capitalism are too terrible a story to be told briefly. These are the young people whom businessmen should support. Or, if businessmen are too ignorant of academic issues, they should leave academic matters alone. But to support irrationalists, nihilists, socialists, and communists—who form an impenetrable barrier against the young advocates of capitalism, denying them jobs, recognition, or a mere hearing—is an unforgivable outrage on the part of irresponsible businessmen who imagine that it is morally safe to give money to institutions of higher learning.

The lasting influence of the universities is caused by the fact that most people question the truth or falsehood of philosophical ideas only in their youth, and whatever they learn in college marks them for life. If they are given intellectual poison, as they are today, they carry it into their professions, particularly in the humanities. Observe the lifeless grayness, the boring mediocrity of today's culture—the empty pretentiousness and mawkish sentimentality of today's stage, screen, and television writing. There are no serious dramas any longer—and such few as attempt to be serious are of a leftist-collectivist persuasion.

On this subject, I can speak from personal experience. For several years, a distinguished producer in Hollywood has been attempting to make a television mini-series or a movie of my novel *Atlas Shrugged*. He was stopped on two counts: (1) he could not find a writer able to write a Romantic drama, even though there are many good writers in Hollywood; and (2) he could not raise the money for his project.

Allow me to say, even though I do not like to say it, that if there existed a novel of the same value and popularity as *Atlas Shrugged*, but written to glorify collectivism (which would be a contradiction in terms), it would have been produced on the screen long ago.

But I do not believe in giving up—and so, in answer to many questions, I chose this occasion to make a very special announcement:

I am writing a nine-hour teleplay for *Atlas Shrugged*.

I intend to produce the mini-series myself.

There is a strong possibility I will be looking for outside financing to produce the *Atlas Shrugged* series. [Miss Rand died a few months later, before completing the teleplay.]

In conclusion, let me touch briefly on another question often asked me: What do I think of President Reagan? The best answer to give would be: But I don't think of him—and the more I see, the less I think. I did not vote for him (or for anyone else) and events seem to justify me. The appalling disgrace of his administration is his connection with the so-called "Moral Majority" and sundry other TV religionists, who are struggling—apparently with his approval—to take us back to the Middle Ages, via the unconstitutional union of religion and politics.

The threat to the future of capitalism is the fact that Reagan might fail so badly that he will become another ghost, like Herbert Hoover, to be invoked as an example of capitalism's failure for another fifty years.

Observe Reagan's futile attempts to arouse the country by some sort of inspirational appeal. He is right in thinking that the country needs an inspirational element. But he will not find it in the God-Family-Tradition swamp.

The greatest inspirational leadership this country could ever find rests in the hands of the most typically American group: the businessmen. But they could provide it only if they acquired philosophical self-defense and self-esteem.

Here is what young Americans have to say about it.

I quote from the May 15, 1980, issue of *The Intellectual Activist*, a newsletter published by Peter Schwartz:

> Feminists threaten to publicize the names of psychologists who hold their convention in a state which has not yet endorsed the Equal Rights Amendment. Unionists protest political functions that serve lettuce not approved by Cesar Chavez. Yet businessmen are willing not simply to tolerate denunciations of free enterprise, but to financially sponsor them.

And: I quote from an article by M. Northrup Buechner, "The Root of Terrorism," in the October 1981 issue of *The Objectivist Forum*, published by Harry Binswanger:

> Imagine the effect if [some] prominent businessmen . . . were to defend publicly their right to their own lives. Imagine the earthshaking social reverberations if they were to assert their moral right to their own profits, not because those profits are necessary for economic progress or the elimination of poverty (which are purely collectivist justifications), but because a living being has the right to live and progress and do the best he can for his life for the time he has on this earth.

I recommend both these publications highly.

As for me, I will close with a quotation which is probably familiar to you—and I will say that the battle for capitalism will be won when we find a president capable of saying it:

> The world you desired can be won, it exists, it is real, it is possible, it's yours.
>
> But to win it requires your total dedication and a total break with the world of your past, with the doctrine that man is a sacrificial animal who exists for the pleasure of others. Fight for the value of your person. Fight for the virtue of your pride. Fight for the essence of that which is man: for his sovereign rational mind. Fight with the radiant certainty and the absolute rectitude of knowing that yours is the Morality of Life and that yours is the battle for any achievement, any value, any grandeur, any goodness, any joy that has ever existed on this earth.

"I work for nothing but my own profit."

Ayn Rand

Hank Rearden, Ayn Rand's industrialist-hero from *Atlas Shrugged*, stands trial for "the greedy crime of withholding from the public a load of the Metal which it had been his greedy crime to offer in the public market." Rearden, after refusing to enter a defense—to contribute to the appearance that the proceedings are intended to serve the cause of justice—makes a statement that, if made by today's businessmen, would allow them to engage in their noble and productive livelihoods without hindrance.

"I work for nothing but my own profit."

Ayn Rand

I work for nothing but my own profit—which I make by selling a product they need to men who are willing and able to buy it. I do not produce it for their benefit at the expense of mine, and they do not buy it for my benefit at the expense of theirs; I do not sacrifice my interests to them nor do they sacrifice theirs to me; we deal as equals by mutual consent to mutual advantage—and I am proud of every penny that I have earned in this manner. I am rich and I am proud of every penny I own. I have made my money by my own effort, in free exchange and through the voluntary consent of every man I dealt with—the voluntary consent of those who employed me when I started, the voluntary consent of those who work for me now, the voluntary consent of those who buy my product. I shall answer all the questions you are afraid to ask me openly. Do I wish to pay my workers more than their services are worth to me? I do not. Do I wish to sell my product for less than my customers are willing to pay me? I do not. Do I wish to sell it at a loss or give it away? I do not. If this is evil, do whatever you please about me, according to whatever standards you hold. These are mine. I am earning my own living, as every honest man must. I refuse to accept as guilt the fact of my own existence and the fact that I must work in order to support it. I refuse to accept as guilt the fact that I am able to do it and to do it well. I refuse to accept as guilt the fact that I am able to do it better than most people—the fact that my work is of greater value than the work of my neighbors and that more men are willing to pay me. I refuse to apologize for my ability—I refuse to apologize for my success—I refuse to apologize for my money. If this is evil, make the most of it. If this is what the public finds harmful to its interests, let the public destroy me. This is my code—and I will accept no other. I could say to you that I have done more good for my fellow men than you can ever hope to accomplish—but I will not say it, because I do not seek the good of others as a sanction for my right to exist, nor do I recognize the good of others as a justification for their seizure of my property or their destruction of my life. I will not say that the good of others was the purpose of my work—my own good was my purpose, and I despise the man who surrenders his. I could say to you that you do not serve the public good—that nobody's good can be achieved at the price of human sacrifices—that when you violate the rights of one man, you have violated the rights of all, and a public of rightless creatures is doomed to destruction. I could say to you that you will and can achieve nothing but universal devastation—as any looter must, when he runs out of victims. I could say it, but I won't. It is not your particular policy that I challenge, but your moral premise. If it were true that men could achieve their good by means of turning some men into sacrificial animals, and I were asked to immolate myself for the sake of creatures who wanted to survive at the price of my blood, if I were asked to serve the interests of society apart from, above and against my own—I would refuse, I would reject it as the most contemptible evil, I would fight it with every power I possess, I would fight the whole of mankind, if one minute were all I could last before I were murdered, I would fight in the full confidence of the justice of my battle and of a living being's right to exist. Let there be no misunderstanding about me. If it is now the belief of my fellow men, who call themselves the public, that their good requires victims, then I say: The public good be damned, I will have no part of it!"

Afterword

Modern Management

Ayn Rand

What follows is Ayn Rand's response to the question "What is or should be the nature of the 'faith' subscribed to by modern management?" It was first published in *The Atlantic Economic Review* in September 1958.

Modern Management

Ayn Rand

The modern businessman needs a new philosophy of life and a new code of morality—a morality based on reason and self-interest.

The "Protestant Ethic," as described in *The Organization Man*, was not a philosophical code of morality. It was a popular make-shift, a bootleg set of rules for "practical" action—and, from the start, it was fighting a losing war against the official morality of the Judaic-Christian tradition: the morality of altruism, mysticism, and self-immolation to the welfare of others. Capitalism is incompatible with the morality of altruism—and what we are seeing now is the last stage of their conflict.

The world crisis of our age is the result, the climax and the dead-end of the altruist code. Businessmen—and wider: all men of ability—are its first victims. When *need*, rather than achievement, is regarded as a primary moral claim, it is not the "meek" but the *mediocre* who inherit the earth.

The source of the disaster lies in our modern philosophy. The essence of pragmatism, Positivism, Scientism and all the rest of the neo-mystic, Platonic schools of non-thought, is a single basic theory: that man's mind is impotent, that reason is an illusion and that objective reality does not exist, or, if it does, man has no power ever to perceive it. If you regard this as harmless, academic speculation, take a look at the pages of *The Organization Man* and you will see that the miserable little socialized, self-abnegating mediocrities described by Mr. Whyte are the exact, practical realization of those philosophical theories. After years of being battered, in school and college, with the question: "Who are you to know?" the average young man will regard himself as a helpless zombie and will seek obedience to the group as his only road to safety. The next and final step is for communist Russia—or any other consistent exponent of an anti-mind, anti-self philosophy—to take him over.

If the American businessman has had a tendency to be anti-intellectual, it is the above kind of philosophers who have made him so. He knew that one cannot live by such philosophies and he committed the tragic error of attempting to live without any philosophy. This is his greatest mistake: that he regards as intellectuals men whose sole claim to the title is their denial of the intellect.

What we need now is a union of the intellectual and the businessman. We need a *new type of intellectuals*, men who are thinkers, men not of some super-reality, but of this earth—in short, Aristotelians. Platonism, in one version or another, was the philosophy of all the dark ages and of all the collectivist dictatorships in history. Aristotelianism was the father of the Renaissance, of the Industrial Revolution, of science, of individualism, of capitalism and of the United States.

If the real businessmen—the first-raters—will give one hour of their eighteen-hour work-day to consider the nature and the power of philosophy, they will see that the base is being cut from under their feet, that the rest of their time—as well as most of their public speeches—is given to the support, the financing and the glorification of their own destroyers. Then let them challenge the reign of entrenched mediocrity. Let them stop preaching their enemy's creed. Let them stop apologizing for their ability and their success. Let them stop seeking the collectivist sanction of "public service." Let them proclaim their *moral* right to exist and to earn a profit.

In short, let them check their philosophical premises—and their Public Relations Departments.

Part 5

Additional Resources

To learn more about Ayn Rand, her ideas, how they apply to business and what intellectual ammunition is available for businessmen to defend themselves, please read or visit the resources on the following pages.

Additional Resources

ABOUT AYN RAND

- www.aynrand.org/aynrand
- *Ayn Rand*, Jeff Britting (New York: Overlook Duckworth, 2004).
- *Facets of Ayn Rand*, Mary Ann Sures and Charles Sures (Irvine, CA: Ayn Rand Institute Press, 2001).
- *100 Voices: An Oral History of Ayn Rand*, ed. Scott McConnell (New York: Penguin, 2010).
- *Ayn Rand: A Sense of Life* (DVD; director's cut), produced and directed by Michael Paxton (Strand Releasing, 2004).
- *Letters of Ayn Rand*, ed. Michael S. Berliner (New York: Dutton, 1995).
- *Journals of Ayn Rand*, Ayn Rand, eds. David Harriman and Leonard Peikoff (New York: Dutton, 1997).

ABOUT *ATLAS SHRUGGED*

- *Atlas Shrugged*, Ayn Rand (New York: Random House, 1957).
- www.atlasshrugged.com
- *Essays on "Atlas Shrugged,"* ed. Robert Mayhew (Lanham, MD: Lexington Books, 2009).

AYN RAND'S PHILOSOPHY: OBJECTIVISM

- www.aynrand.org/objectivism
- *Objectivism: The Philosophy of Ayn Rand*, Leonard Peikoff (New York: Meridian, 1993).
- *The Ayn Rand Lexicon*, Harry Binswanger (New York: Meridian, 1988).
- *Objectively Speaking*, eds. Marlene Podritske and Peter Schwartz (Lanham,

MD: Lexington Books, 2009).

- *Ayn Rand Answers*, Ayn Rand, ed. Robert Mayhew (New York: New American Library, 2005).

THE MORALITY OF CAPITALISM

- *Capitalism: The Unknown Ideal*, Ayn Rand (New York: New American Library, 1966).
- www.principlesofafreesociety.org
- www.aynrand.org/capitalism

AYN RAND'S FICTION

- *Anthem*, Ayn Rand (New York: Penguin, 1995).
- *Atlas Shrugged*, Ayn Rand (New York: Random House, 1957).
- *The Early Ayn Rand*, ed. Leonard Peikoff (New York: New American Library, 1984).
- *The Fountainhead*, Ayn Rand (Indianapolis: Bobbs-Merrill, 1968).
- *Three Plays*, Ayn Rand (New York: Signet, 2005).
- *We the Living*, Ayn Rand (New York: Random House, 1959).

AYN RAND'S NONFICTION

- *The Art of Fiction*, ed. Tore Boeckmann (New York: Penguin, 2000).
- *The Art of Nonfiction*, ed. Robert Mayhew (New York: Penguin, 2001).
- *The Ayn Rand Column*, ed. Peter Schwartz (New Milford, CT: Second Renaissance Books, 1998).
- *The Ayn Rand Letter*, ed. Ayn Rand (Gaylordsville, CT: Second Renaissance, Inc., n.d.).
- *Capitalism: The Unknown Ideal*, Ayn Rand (New York: New American Library, 1966 and 1967).

- *Introduction to Objectivist Epistemology*, Ayn Rand (New York: Penguin, 1990).
- *The Objectivist Newsletter*, ed. Ayn Rand (Gaylordsville, CT: Second Renaissance, Inc., n.d.).
- *Philosophy: Who Needs It*, Ayn Rand (New York: Bobbs-Merrill, 1982).
- *Return of the Primitive: The Anti-Industrial Revolution*, Ayn Rand, ed. Peter Schwartz (New York: Meridian, 1999).
- *The Romantic Manifesto*, Ayn Rand (New York: New American Library, 1971).
- *Russian Writings on Hollywood*, ed. Michael S. Berliner (Irvine, CA: Ayn Rand Institute Press, 1999).
- *The Virtue of Selfishness*, Ayn Rand (New York: New American Library, 1964).
- *The Voice of Reason*, ed. Leonard Peikoff (New York: New American Library, 1989).

Part 6

About the Contributors

ABOUT THE CONTRIBUTORS

John Allison
Mr. Allison is former chairman of BB&T Corporation, a $152 billion financial-holding company. Mr. Allison began his service with BB&T in 1971 and has managed a wide variety of responsibilities throughout the bank. He became president of BB&T in 1987 and was elected chairman and CEO in July 1989. During Mr. Allison's tenure as CEO from 1989 to 2008, BB&T grew from $4.5 billion to $152 billion in assets. In March 2009 he joined the faculty of Wake Forest University Schools of Business as Distinguished Professor of Practice.

Harry Binswanger
Dr. Binswanger, instructor at the Objectivist Academic Center, is the author of *The Biological Basis of Teleological Concepts*, the editor of *The Ayn Rand Lexicon* and co-editor of the second edition of Ayn Rand's *Introduction to Objectivist Epistemology*. He is currently completing a book on the theory of knowledge.

Yaron Brook
Dr. Brook is president and executive director of the Ayn Rand Institute. A former finance professor, he has published in academic as well as popular publications and is frequently interviewed in the media. He has appeared on CNN, Fox Business Network, Fox News Channel, CNBC and PBS, among others. He lectures on Objectivism, business ethics and foreign policy at college campuses and for corporations across America and throughout the world.

Alex Epstein
Mr. Epstein is a fellow specializing in business issues at the Ayn Rand Center for Individual Rights (a division of the Ayn Rand Institute). Mr. Epstein is a widely published writer, whose work has appeared in numerous publications around the world, including *Investor's Business Daily*, *San Francisco Chronicle*, *Houston Chronicle*, and the *Washington Times*. Mr. Epstein is also a frequent guest speaker at universities around the country—including Duke, Berkeley, and UCLA—and a frequent guest on nationally syndicated radio programs.

Debi Ghate
Ms. Ghate is vice president of Academic Programs at the Ayn Rand Institute, where she oversees educational programs for students, educators and others on Ayn Rand's philosophy, Objectivism. Her writing has appeared in newspapers such as the *Christian Science Monitor*, *Philadelphia Inquirer*, the *Providence Journal*, and *Education Update*. She is also the senior director for the Anthem Foundation for Objectivist Scholarship, an organization separate from ARI that supports scholarly work based on Ayn Rand's corpus.

Onkar Ghate

Dr. Ghate holds a Ph.D. in philosophy from the University of Calgary. He is senior fellow at the Ayn Rand Institute, where he specializes in Ayn Rand's philosophy of Objectivism and teaches philosophy in the Institute's Objectivist Academic Center. Recent publications include "Objectivism: The Proper Alternative to Postmodernism" (in *Postmodernism and Management: Pros, Cons and the Alternative*), among other scholarly articles on Ayn Rand's fiction and philosophy. He has also appeared as a guest on BBC radio, CNBC, CBS Evening News and Fox News Channel.

Keith Lockitch

Dr. Lockitch holds a Ph.D. in physics and is a fellow at the Ayn Rand Institute. He writes and edits for the Institute and teaches courses on writing for the Institute's Objectivist Academic Center. His writings have appeared in such publications as the *Washington Times*, *Orange County Register*, *San Francisco Chronicle*, *The Objective Standard* and the science policy journal *Energy and Environment*.

Leonard Peikoff

Dr. Peikoff worked closely with Ayn Rand for many years and was designated by her as heir to her estate. He has taught philosophy at Hunter College, Long Island University and New York University. He is the author of *The Ominous Parallels* and of *Objectivism: The Philosophy of Ayn Rand*, the definitive presentation of Ayn Rand's philosophy. He is currently at work on his third book, *The DIM Hypothesis* (forthcoming).

Ayn Rand (1905–1982)

Novelist and philosopher Ayn Rand, author of *The Fountainhead*, *Atlas Shrugged* and many other fiction and nonfiction works, is the originator of the philosophy of Objectivism. More than 27 million copies of her books have been sold.

John B. Ridpath

Dr. Ridpath holds a Ph.D. in economics and is a retired associate professor of economics and social science at York University in Toronto. Specializing in intellectual history, he is a frequent lecturer on college campuses on the morality of capitalism. Dr. Ridpath is a member of the board of directors of the Ayn Rand Institute.

Peter Schwartz

Mr. Schwartz is the author of *The Foreign Policy of Self-Interest: A Moral Ideal for America*, editor/contributing author of Ayn Rand's *Return of the Primitive: The Anti-Industrial Revolution*, and co-editor of *Objectively Speaking*—a collection of interviews with Ayn Rand. He is the founding editor and publisher of *The Intellectual Activist* and a former chairman of the board of directors of the Ayn Rand Institute.

ABOUT THE AYN RAND INSTITUTE

The Ayn Rand Institute, a nonprofit educational organization, was established in 1985 to serve as the center for the advancement of Ayn Rand's philosophy of Objectivism.

Objectivism, which Ayn Rand called "a philosophy for living on earth," provides a comprehensive, integrated view of existence and the nature of man. It advocates objective reality, reason, self-interest and laissez-faire capitalism.

The Institute brings Ayn Rand's ideas to the attention of students, scholars, businessmen, professionals and the general public. Its Objectivist Academic Center and Ayn Rand Campus offer courses in Ayn Rand's ideas, and it provides intellectual and financial support to professors and scholars. Other programs include free classroom sets of Ayn Rand's novels to teachers, essay contests for high school and college students, a network of campus Objectivist clubs and a campus speakers bureau. The Ayn Rand Center for Individual Rights, located in Washington, D.C., advances the principle of individual rights as the cornerstone for a fully free, laissez-faire capitalist society through its public policy and outreach efforts.

For more information about the activities of the Institute, please contact:

THE AYN RAND INSTITUTE
P.O. Box 51808
Irvine, CA 92619-9930

www.aynrand.org

Read the most influential novel in America.

Ayn Rand's prophetic novel parallels the events of our times with astonishing insight.

It is the story of John Galt, a man who said that he would stop the motor of the world—and did. Tremendous in scope, breathtaking in its suspense, it is a mystery about the murder—and rebirth—of man's spirit.

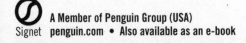